Whatever Happened to Gorgeous George?

The Blood and Ballyhoo of Professional Wrestling

Other publications from Crowbar Press

Inside Out
by Ole Anderson, with Scott Teal

Wrestlers Are Like Seagulls
by James J. Dillon, with Scott Teal & Philip Varriale

Assassin: The Man Behind the Mask
by Joe Hamilton, with Scott Teal

"Is That Wrestling Fake?"
by Ivan Koloff, with Scott Teal

Bruiser Brody
by Emerson Murray, edited by Scott Teal

Wrestling with the Truth
by Bruno Lauer, edited by Scott Teal

The Solie Chronicles
by Bob Allyn, with Pamela S Allyn & Scott Teal

Wrestling in the Canadian West
by Vance Nevada

Long Days and Short Pays
by Hal West, edited by Scott Teal

Drawing Heat
by Jim Freedman

ATLAS: Too Much, Too Soon
by Tony Atlas, with Scott Teal

The Last Laugh
by Bill De Mott, with Scott Teal

HOOKER
by Lou Thesz, with Kit Bauman

The Last Outlaw
by Stan Hansen, with Scott Teal

NIKITA
by Nikita Koloff, as told to Bill Murdock

The Strap
by Roger Deem

BRISCO
by Jack Brisco, as told to Bill Murdock

The Mighty Milo
by Phillips Rogers

"I Ain't No Pig Farmer!"
by Dean Silverstone, with Scott Teal

The Hard Way
by Don Fargo, with Scott Teal

Whatever Happened to Gorgeous George?
by Joe Jares

"It's Wrestling, Not Rasslin'!"
by Mark Fleming, edited by Scott Teal

BRUISER
The World's Most Dangerous Wrestler
by Richard Vicek, edited by Scott Teal

The Mat, the Mob & Music
by Tom Hankins, edited by Scott Teal

BREAKING KAYFABE
THEY CALL ME BOOKER
by Jeff Bowdren, edited by Scott Teal

BATTLEGROUND VALHALA
by Michael Majalahti, edited by Scott Teal

Florida Mat Wars: 1977
by Robert D. VanKavelaar, with Scott Teal

When It Was Real
by Nikita Breznikov, with Scott Teal

The Annotated Fall Guys
by Marcus Griffin,
annotated by Steve Yohe & Scott Teal

Pain Torture Agony
by Ron Hutchison, with Scott Teal

Raising Cain: From Jimmy Ault to Kid McCoy
by Frankie Cain & Scott Teal

Master of the Ring
by Tim Hornbaker

Tonight! Tonight! Tonight!
by Bert Prentice & Scott Teal

— Wrestling Archive Project —
by Scott Teal
Volume #1 • Volume #2

– Through the Lens ... Through the Ropes –
Compiled by Scott Teal
— Volume #1 —
Southeastern Championship Wrestling
— Volume #2 —
Championship Wrestling from Florida
— Volume #3 —
All South Wrestling Alliance

— The Great Pro Wrestling Venues —
Volume #1 — Madison Square Garden
by Scott Teal & J Michael Kenyon
Volume #2 — Nashville, volume 1
by Scott Teal & Don Luce
Volume #3 — Alabama: 1931-1935
by Jason Presley
Volume #4 — Japan
by Haruo Yamaguchi,
with Koji Miyamoto & Scott Teal
Volume #5 — Knoxville: 1905-1960
Volume #6 — Knoxville: 1961-1991
by Tim Dills & Scott Teal
Volume #7 — Amarillo: 1911-1960
Volume #8 — Amarillo: 1961-1997
by Kriss Knights & Scott Teal

— Classic Arena Programs —
Volumes #1-2 — SLAM-O-GRAM
Volumes #3-4 — Florida
Volume #5 — Knoxville
Volumes #6-9 — St. Louis

Whatever Happened to Gorgeous George?

The Blood and Ballyhoo of Professional Wrestling

by Joe Jares

Editing & Layout by Scott Teal

CROWBAR PRESS

Gallatin, Tennessee

Whatever Happened to Gorgeous George?
The Blood and Ballyhoo of Professional Wrestling

Published by Crowbar Press
106 Tattnal Court
Gallatin, Tennessee 37066

http://www.crowbarpress.com

Book layout and cover design by Scott Teal

Library of Congress Cataloging-in-Publication Data

Jares, Joe
    Whatever Happened to Gorgeous George? / by Joe Jares

1. Jares, Joe.   2. Sports—United States—Biography.   3. Wrestling—United States—Biography.   I. Title.

Printed in the United States of America
ISBN 978-1-940391-05-2

Second edition / October 2015
Second edition, 2nd printing / March 2022

Table of Contents

Introduction 6

Acknowledgements 8

1. My Father the Thing 9

2. Whatever Happened to Gorgeous George? 18

3. Indian Chiefs, Lords, and Masked Marvels 30

4. The Lady with the Cauliflower Head 45

5. Annals of Villainy 60

6. Carnival Impresarios 77

7. The Fans: "Killer Kowalski Believes in Sauerkraut" 97

8. Backstage with the Boys 107

ADDENDUM

1. Thumbnail Biographies of the Greatest Pro Wrestlers 117

2. Holds You Probably Never Saw in the Olympics 125

3. Wrestlers versus Boxers 128

4. Wrestling Football Players (Or Vice Versa) 130

5. Ring Aliases 134

6. Masked Marauders of the Mat, A Collection of Devils, Demons, Phantoms, Xs, and One Pussycat 137

7. A Chronology of Pro Wrestling in America 140

8. Heavyweight Title Succession at a Glance 146

9. Big Gates and Crowds 148

An Interview with the Author 150

On the Road with Frank Jares 157

NOTE: This is a reissue of the book first published in 1974. New material (newspaper clippings, photos, and an interview with the author), all of which enhances the narrative, has been added to this edition. Some details in the original text, like deaths and current whereabouts, have changed.

Introduction

When various people found out that I, an otherwise sane journalist, sports fan, and father of two, was writing a book on professional wrestling, the reaction often went something like this:

"My ninety-year-old grandmother used to love it. When the matches were on, you couldn't drag her away from the set. We tried to tell her it was fake, but she refused to believe us. Do they still have wrestling?"

Indeed they do. St. Louis Promoter Sam Muchnick grossed $427,000 in 1971. In 1972, Cleveland took in $447,071.50 and promoters in the state of Illinois grossed $1,003,651. Promoter Abe Ford staged thirteen shows at the Boston Garden that year and the Garden's share alone was $148,000. The monthly exhibitions in New York City's Madison Square Garden regularly drew more than 20,000 people and grossed more than $100,000.

Reliable figures for the whole country are difficult to find and verify, but there is no doubt that wrestling is alive and well and thriving in the U.S.A. Triangle Publications (*TV Guide, Daily Racing Form*), in its annual sports-attendance booklet, estimated that wrestling drew 5,421,637 spectators in 1972, up more than 1,500,000 from the previous year, outgaining pro football, baseball, basketball and ice hockey. Promoter Muchnick estimates the annual attendance at 20 million at least.

While there are no matches televised nationwide, wrestling is still prospering from TV and vice versa. There are about 245 wrestling shows on U.S. channels — KCOP in Los Angeles, WXON in Detroit, WCIX in Miami, KTVW in Seattle, KOA in Denver, etc. — and about 50 more in Canada. Wrestler-promoter Verne Gagne of Minneapolis claims that the combined ratings of all the little local wrestling shows are greater than the ratings for the Super Bowl. There must be a new generation of enthralled grandmas out there.

Wrestling is bigger than ever — "ever" in this case covering a lot of time because the sport could very well be the oldest known to man. Hunting and fishing were matters of survival rather than recreation, and the cavemen probably pushed and tugged each other for amusement around their fires before they swam, threw punches, or ran races.

The Greeks, Egyptians, Tartars, Japanese, and practically every other civilization enjoyed wrestling as a sport, but it is from Great Britain that we get most of our American "catch-as-catch-can" style. In England, it was also known as "catch that catch may," or, going back to 1393, "cacche who that cacche might," all meaning to lay hold of the opponent any way possible. San Francisco etymologist Peter Tamony claims that the word "hippie" comes from British countryside grappling, in which an opponent "on the hip" was to be at an advantage or in command and often led to throwing him for a "fall." The word "wrestling" itself comes from Old and Middle English.

U.S. Presidents George Washington, Zachary Taylor, Abraham Lincoln, William Howard Taft and Calvin Coolidge all wrestled at one time or another. Coolidge's home state, Vermont, was in the early 1700s America's first hotbed of wrestling. Most popular was the Irish "collar and elbow style," in which each wrestler would start by placing one hand on his opponent's shoulder on or near the collar line and the other hand on the arm just above the elbow. *"Jest step down and finger my collar, I doubledang dare ye,"* was a typical challenge, and long red underwear, with the flap sewn shut, of course, was a typical indoor costume until the late 1870s.

Somewhere along the line, wrestling got transferred to the backrooms of sporting men's taverns and to traveling carnivals, where show biz, blarney and ballyhoo — and some would say fakery — were mixed in. William Muldoon, an ex-cop who became known as "The Solid Man of Sport" after a popular song of the day, made his reputation in booze joints, theaters and, in one spectacular match, under a big tent at McAllister and Jones streets in San Francisco. Farmer Burns took on all comers while touring with the Conners & Green specialty show and Turner's English Gaiety Show. His protégé, Frank Gotch, traveled with the Sells-Floto circus in 1916, wrestling Bob Managoff twice a day.

From the carnivals and opera-house stages, it moved to arenas — smoky places reeking of beer and workingmen's sweat. Splintery stands for general-admission ticketholders, Stage Door Sallies waiting to feel a wrestler's muscles, stentorian ring announcers in bow ties and, after most of the crowd had cleared out and gone home, a few small boys turning over empty beer cups and stomping on them, filling the hall with echoing *pops*. I grew up on the fringes of that world, as the reader will shortly learn, with a father who so wanted my neck to be thick and strong that, when I was an infant and on my stomach in the crib, he would force my head down with one finger, then slightly relieve the pressure so I could push my head back up again — and again and again until my mother caught him at it. But I'm getting ahead of myself, encroaching on chapter one.

As Hotspur said in Shakespeare's *Henry IV, Part 1*,

"Let them grapple."

Joe Jares
Riverdale, N.Y.

Suzy and Joe Jares

Acknowledgements

The author wishes to thank *Sports Illustrated* for the copyrights to *My Father the Thing* and *George Was Villainous, Gutsy and Gorgeous*, which, in slightly different form, make up chapters one and two of this book. Thanks also to Goodwin Goldfaden of Adco Sports Book Exchange in West Hollywood, Calif., for various loans and trades of hard-to-find books, photos, periodicals and programs; to Bill Schroeder and Braven Dyer Jr. for use of the library at the Citizens Savings Athletic Foundation [now the L.A. '84 Athletic Foundation] in Los Angeles; to Tim Salinger for finally prying some material out of the Olympic Auditorium staff; to Roy Blount Jr. and Larry Keith of *Sports Illustrated* for numerous clippings and personal memories, and to Nick D'Incecco of Prentice-Hall for having nerve, patience and a sense of humor.

Sports publicists at many universities were quick to send information on wrestling alumni, even if those alumni were villains. Cheers for Tommy Bryant, West Texas State; Bob Condron, Southern Methodist; Jack DeGrange, Dartmouth; Tom Greenhoe, Minnesota; Heywood Harris, Tennessee; John Keith, Oklahoma; Bob Kinney, West Point; David Leonard, Colgate; Tom Miller, Indiana; Ted Nance, Houston; Will Perry, Michigan; Pat Quinn, Oklahoma State; Al Shrier, Temple; Tom Simons, Nebraska; Fred Stabley, Michigan State; Bob Steiner, California; Charley Thornton, Alabama; Roger Valdiserri, Notre Dame; and Mike Wilson, Washington State.

Journalists Bud Collins, Ron DePaolo, Ronald Green, Jeff Prugh and Earl Gustkey, and photographer Rich Clarkson dug into their files and memories to help. My mother let me prowl through her stacks of diaries. National Wrestling Alliance president Sam Muchnick was always ready with helpful, courteous answers and explanations, and most of all, Houston promoter Paul Boesch proved himself to be the strongest and most entertaining booster of pro wrestling in the country.

(added July 2015)

Thanks to my publisher, Scott Teal, whose love of the grappling business and patience with authors entitle him to a championship belt.

And most of all, to my wife, Suzy, who cheerfully donated her editing/copy-reading skills. (with an antipathy toward cauliflower ears, she is glad I became a writer, not a wrestler.)

Not that it helped me much in childhood frays, but I was the only kid on my block who could boast, with absolutely no fear of contradiction, "*My father can lick your father.*" Frank August Jares, Sr., was a professional wrestler, the nastiest, meanest, basest, most arrogant, cheatingest, bloodthirstiest, eye-gouger around. No rule, referee or sense of fair play ever hampered his style. In short, the sort of man a boy could look up to.

Chapter 1
My Father the Thing

In his prime, Pop was just a shade under six feet tall and weighed 230 pounds, with short brown hair, a neck like a steel pillar, big biceps and ears much more like cauliflowers than rose petals. Most people can fold their ears in half, but Pop's seem to be made of solid gristle and will not bend more than half an inch. He had, and still has, rather full lips and prominent cheekbones, a Slavic countenance that would fit perfectly in a Warsaw union meeting or the Notre Dame line. His wrestling stage name was Brother Frank, the Mormon Mauler from Provo, Utah, but really he was just Frankie Jares from northside Pittsburgh, the son of a Bohemian butcher from Czechoslovakia and a U.S.-born mother, also Bohemian. He never heard English spoken until he went out on the streets to play with the other kids. At age 12, he had both upper arms decorated with tattoos, and at 14, he was out of school and driving a truck. Naturally, he grew up to be a tough guy, but sometimes a gentle, tough guy. He spanked me only twice in my life. Even though he traveled a lot, I thought I knew him, but I actually did not know him well at all until I spent one summer with him in Tennessee and Alabama — the summer of 1956.

Pop was Southern junior heavyweight wrestling champion, operating out of Nashville (the senior champ, I figured, had to be King Kong, but I never met him). I finished my freshman year at USC in June and flew from Los Angeles to Nashville to join Pop, Mom and Frankie, Jr., who were living in a nice trailer park alongside some *Grand Ole Opry* stars and other assorted footloose folk. It was my job to accompany the old man on the southern wrestling circuit — usually Birmingham on Monday, Nashville on Tuesday, Kingsport on Wednesday, Thursday to Bristol, Friday to Knoxville, and Saturday in Chattanooga. After the matches in Chattanooga, we would drive all night back to Nashville, stopping once on the way at a mountain cafe for sausage sandwiches and ice-cold milk. Sunday was rest time at the trailer-park swimming pool. Back on the road Monday. "*I don't know a single damn highway number,*" Pop said, "*but I can take you to the back door of any arena in the United States by the shortest route.*"

He told me I was a bodyguard, a ridiculous idea (the only thing I guarded was his

Brother Frank & Joe Jares, circa 1941

Joe at age 15 with his dad at Kuhio Beach in Honolulu in summer 1953.

precious 1956 Studebaker Golden Hawk, a favorite target of his enemies after the matches). On his brawny arms, he had that faded green artwork — a flag, an anchor, a star, a sailor girl, an Indian maiden, a Kewpie doll, and so on. The only tattoo that would have fitted on one of my arms was a skinny snake, and not even that if the snake were coiled. Pop often said I had arms like garden hoses and a neck like a stack of dimes. He could see better out of his one good eye than I could with my glasses. But we entertained each other, I by listening and he by telling tales of his travels, his brawls, his riots, and his bloody third-fall finishes.

For instance, somewhere between Nashville and Blytheville, Ark., he told me about Hawaii. There he had not been Brother Frank, but The Golden Terror — mysterious scourge of the mat: yellow mask, black sleeveless shirt and, according to irate fans, yellow streak down back. By pulling hair, illegally using the ropes, and just generally ignoring the Boy Scout Code, he prevented any good-guy opponent, or "babyface" in the lingo of the trade, from ripping off his cover. Actually, he had such an intricate way of fastening the hood that it would have taken the Pacific Fleet to unmask him. And if it had happened, nobody would have known him anyway. Well, hardly anybody. In his free time, Pop wore his own face as he lifted weights and wrestled at the YMCA with various islanders, including one Harold Sakata (later to become Tosh Togo, the evil Jap ring villain, and, still later, Oddjob in the movie *Goldfinger*). *"You know,"* said one of his friends after a workout, *"you're such a good wrestler, you should go down and challenge The Golden Terror."* Pop felt a little like Clark Kent, and somehow, no one connected the giveaway tattoos.

Of course, there had been other aliases. Pro wrestling is a world of unrelated brothers and Italian noblemen from the Bronx. Every Indian is a chief, every Englishman a lord, every German a Nazi. Pop was once Furious Frank Jaris. And Frank Dusek of the roughhouse Nebraska Dusek clan. And Frank Schnabel, brother of that despicable duo, Hans and Fritz. One of his finest guises was The Thing. He used a horrible orange-red dye on the hair on his head and on a new crop of whiskers. He fixed up a wooden suitcase with THE THING printed on it in spangles and a hidden button that could be pressed to bring forth a sound similar to an aroused rattlesnake. He flew to Chicago to make his fortune and was granted an athletic commission license in the name of M.T. Bochs. He strolled the sidewalks of such towns as Gary, Ind., and Racine, Wis., in top hat, elegant topcoat, vest, striped pants and spats — and that fluorescent hair. Decent citizens who had seen his matches would curse him. *"That's just what you are,"* said one little old lady, *"a dirty, dirty thing."*

Pop smiled politely and said, *"Why, thank you."* As long as little old ladies had no hatpins he was polite to them. But he made no fortune and eventually went back to being the plain old Mormon Mauler. A Midwestern fan magazine later recalled:

> "Chicago wrestling fans were once treated to a novel experience when a wrestler named The Thing came into their midst. The Thing was a product of the West Coast and his face was blanketed with whiskers.

> "Although he was a good wrestler, he got nowhere in the race for heavyweight honors and we wonder just where he is wrestling now."

Between southern whistle stops that summer of 1956, as the souped-up Studebaker cruised along at 60 mph and we tried to hit rural mailboxes with empty Dr. Pepper bottles, Pop often talked about wrestling fans, as testy a group as you can find this side of a Brazilian soccer stadium.

Fan Knifes Mat Performer

Redding, Calif., March 15 (Æ) —A knife-weilding spectator got into the act at a team wrestling match last night.

Frank Jares was lying with his head on the mat just outside the ropes. An irate customer rushed up and hit the wrestler between the eyes with his knife.

Jares' partner, Hard Boiled Haggerty, leaped from the ring and chased the knifer over customers and seats.

Haggerty lost the chase.

Redding, California • March 14, 1951

One time in Pico Rivera, Calif., Pop told me, he was walking to the dressing room between bleachers, and a man twelve feet above him reached down to hit him, slipped, fell to the concrete floor, and broke his own neck. At various times in the ring, Pop had been hit by whiskey bottles, lighted cigarettes and paper clips shot from rubber bands. During a match against Vincent Lopez in Redding, Calif., Pop pulled himself under the ropes while flat on his back, a sneaky trick to get the referee to make the babyface let go of his ankle. A ringsider stood up and slashed Pop's forehead with a beer-can opener. The wound took seventeen stitches to repair. He also had been stabbed with a knife, cut with a broken mirror, and punctured with fingernail files.

In Bremerton, Wash., Pop treated kindly, fair-dealing giant Primo Camera with something less than minimal courtesy. As he ran the gantlet on his perilous journey to the dressing room, an indignant woman threw a lighted book of matches that hit his sweaty body with a painful sizzle. He stopped to analyze the woman's ancestry (even Pop could not hit a lady), but between them stepped a belligerent man who said, *"That's my wife."*

Pop slugged him and yelled, *"Then teach her better manners."*

The arena erupted into a riot, and dear old Dad had to stay under police guard in the dressing room half the night.

The fans were really stirred up one night in Bridgeport, Conn., he said. They completely misunderstood Pop's gentle nature and were intent on dismembering him. *"I know my crowds,"* he said. *"If you don't have the experience, you get killed. You have to jump right into the middle of the milling mob, never go in the opposite direction. A silent crowd is even more vicious. That silent 'heat,' that's the vicious crowd. The punchers and scratchers are much less dangerous. They wind up hitting each other most of the time."*

Well, this night in Bridgeport, Pop was in the middle, all right, and not enjoying it, but he happily sighted a policeman battling his way through the mob. The cop finally made it to Pop's side, and then, unhesitatingly, bashed him over the head with a Billy club.

At the Wilmington (Calif.) Bowl in the mid-'40s, Pop and his original partner, Brother Jonathan (who was really from Utah), won a tag-team match and were chased around the building by an angry pack of sailors intent on seeing justice done. The Brothers finally made it into the dressing room, but one sailor slipped inside before they got the door locked. Another wrestler held the sailor and said, *"Here he is, Frank."* Pop walked toward him with fist cocked, and the poor man collapsed in a faint.

Then there was South Gate, Calif. For thirty-two straight weeks, Pop recalled, he and Wee Willie Davis took on and defeated all comers, each week with some nefarious tactic. Their favorite ploy was to have Willie, a huge man, slowly back up into his own corner so Pop, standing outside the ropes, could reach through his legs and yank the opponent's legs out from under him. There were twenty-seven sellouts in those wild thirty-two weeks. After a while, the South Gate police refused to respond to any more riot calls, so promoter Frank Pasquale had to hire his own guards.

One night after the South Gate chaos, Pop was driving through East Los Angeles when he was forced off the road by four men in a jalopy. They were going to teach Brother Frank some manners! They got him as he was halfway out the driver-side door and beat and stomped him until he got away by rolling under the car. Pop was so furious; he went out and bought a pistol, stashing it in his glove compartment for the right moment. Nothing happened the next week, although he and Wee Willie were as wicked in victory as ever. But two weeks later, the quartet forced his car over at almost exactly the same spot. Pop leaped out of the car brandishing the pistol like Jesse James (not the Houston wrestler Jesse James, but the outlaw). Three of the attackers jumped back into their car and sped away, with Pop emptying the pistol into their trunk. The fourth was so scared he fled across a field, leaving one of his shoes in the middle of the street. Pop twisted the shoe into a useless hunk of leather and ended his gun-slinging career the next day by tossing the weapon into the sea.

At Long Beach Civic Auditorium, he told me, a drunken fan once climbed up on the ring apron and hit him behind the neck. Pop shoved him off the way a man would shoo a fly. A woman sitting at ringside claimed the man landed on her, and she sued the arena, Pop, and everybody else in sight. She lost the suit (because, luckily, the match had been kinescoped and the jury could see for itself what happened), but it still cost Pop more than $500 in legal fees. After the trial, a man in the courtroom — the very same one who had climbed onto the apron — walked up and apologized. He did not offer to pay Pop's lawyer.

Of course, antagonizing the customers was the whole idea, Pop explained, so you had to expect a little jab from a fingernail file once in a while. On those long rides between little towns, he told me about "finishes," building up the "heat" to just the right temperature until the arena seemed ready to explode, then ending the match in some super-duper, slam-bang manner guaranteed to bring all the people back the following week for a sequel.

There was this time down in Panama, where he was known as Hermano Frank, a holy man from Utah with seven wives. He wanted to be a heel, as usual, but the Panamanians loved everything he did and he gradually became, much to his chagrin, a babyface (just imagine The Joker helping Batman catch crooks). Because he had no opponent who knew how to wrestle, he taught a husky sailor, Strangler Olson, how to "work" (throw fake punches, apply harmless step-over toeholds, etc.) and play the villain's role.

For the big finish, Strangler was to throw Pop out of the ring and be disqualified, thereby setting up a juicy return match. To make it look better, Pop had a razor blade carefully secreted in the waistband of his trunks. During the inevitable confusion at ringside, he was supposed to cut himself just slightly on the forehead. It would not hurt any more than running a fingernail over the skin, but it would look as bad as a battle wound. However, Pop could not find the blade and used the next handiest thing; a bottle cap lying nearby. He stood up with a face full of gore, and the fans went berserk, attacking poor Olson like maniacs.

"The crowd was beating the poor guy to death," said Pop. "I figured I had to save his life. So I started screaming, 'Let me at him! I'll kill him! Let me at him!' The mob parted and allowed me to get to him. I pretended to beat him right through the dressing room doorway and the door slammed safely behind us."

Some finishes were more goofy than bloody. In San Bernardino, Calif., Pop and a cohort were wrestling the Dirty Duseks in an all-heel main event. A moth landed in the center of the ring, so he put up his hand and stopped the match with silent-movie pantomime. Very slowly, he leaned over and tried to pick up the delicate little moth and, naturally, it fluttered up and away. In awe, he looked up and watched its flight. Then, boom! That dirty

Duseks Capture Tag Team Bout

Ernie and Emil Dusek won the tag team rematch last night at the San Bernardino arena from Wee Willie Davis and Brother Frank Jares, but again the decision was another puzzle and it caused a near riot.

It appeared that Davis had Emil on the mat and Referee Joe Varga had to all appearances finished the three count which would have ended the match.

A bitter dispute started and as Jares attempted to attack Emil the pair slugged with elbow smashes and Emil got Frank on the mat. Varga started the three count and here Dusek was declared a winner.

Previously Brother Frank had tossed Ernie in seven minutes with an arm stretch and body press. Emil then used elbow smashes and body blocks to put Davis down for the count to even the match.

Wee Willie, announced in all earnestness that he and Jares would put up $1,000 to get the Duseks back in the ring at an early date, but the brother from Nebraska got a big guffaw out of the remark. Officers had to escort Davis to the dressing room.

In the opening tussle on the card Chief War Cloud used two flying tackles to flatten Don Lee in 16 minutes to win and in the next match, a two out of three falls affair, Tony Martinez finished in a draw.

Adkins, a husky Australian champion, used a step-over toe hold to win in 20 minutes. Martinez took the next fall with a body press in six minutes and in the remaining period neither secured a fall.

San Bernardino CA • July 24, 1948

Some kids grew up watching their fathers fit shoes, or go off on sales trips, or deliver mail. I grew up seeing my old man, Brother Frank, get mauled by various good guys of the ring, in this case Vic Holbrook, a handsome Californian.

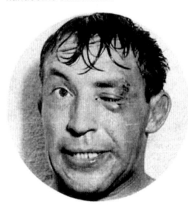

He has not been able to see out of his left eye for years, and it didn't help when Baron Michele Leone stomped him in the face and produced this lovely shiner.

Pop was never averse to twisting wrists, legs, noses, torsos, or the rules.

A tag-team match lends a little variety to a card. Here Brother Frank is getting punished for previous misdeeds as Hero Number Two awaits his turn.

(left) One of the rent-a-cops who are on hand at arenas to protect fans *and* wrestlers—and public order—tries out his headlock technique on my old man in San Bernardino, California. Just a gag shot for a photographer; but it wasn't funny one night in Connecticut when a policeman hit Pop over the head with a billy.

Emil Dusek sprang from his corner, socked Pop on his inviting chin, knocked him cold, and won the bout.

That summer in the South had its share of crazy adventures, too. Pop had been on his way to Charlotte, N.C., and was supposed to stop off in Tennessee, just to help out the local bookers for a couple of weeks. The couple of weeks stretched into nearly two years. He quickly won the Southern junior heavyweight belt from Sonny Myers in Birmingham in 1955 and from several other guys in several other cities. It was such a big territory that nice little "bits" could be re-used in practically every town. Pop kept the big fancy belt in the trunk of his car and wore it into the ring for big matches. Babyfaces loved to grab it away and chase Pop around the ring, bludgeoning him with it. He won a big trophy in Memphis, and then promptly broke it over The Mighty Atlas' head. The belt stood up under the punishment, though, and made a dazzling prop.

At least twice, he kept the title by pure luck. Sonny Myers, the handsome ex-champ from St. Joseph, Mo., had him beaten in an outdoor match in Knoxville, where threatening weather had caused the main event to go on second. Pop was left unconscious from two atomic drops administered by Myers, but Sonny hurt his knee on the second one and had to be carried from the ring. Pop was allowed to keep the title provided he gave Myers a Knoxville rematch within thirty days. Tex Riley had Pop suffering, but blew his chance when he accidentally drop-kicked the referee out of the ring and was disqualified.

```
┌────────────────────────────────────────────┐
│  WRESTLING   SATURDAY, 8:30 P.M.            │
│              MEMORIAL AUDITORIUM            │
│     Main Event! Six-Man Tag Team Match      │
│   "BRO." FRANK JARES, BABE ZEHARIAS         │
│           & "SPIDER" GALENTO                 │
│                 VERSUS                       │
│    FARMER JONES & PIG, JOE ZBYSZKO           │
│          & HOMBRE MONTANA                    │
│  ─────────────────────────────────────────  │
│   FARMER JONES & PIG VS. "SPIDER" GALENTO   │
│  ─────────────────────────────────────────  │
│          ZBYSZKO VS. ZEHARIAS               │
│  ─────────────────────────────────────────  │
│    TICKETS ON SALE SATURDAY, AUDITORIUM     │
└────────────────────────────────────────────┘
```

Chattanooga, Tennessee • May 5, 1956

Pop was wrestling Spider Galento in Chattanooga one night, and it was sort of a contest between them to see who the crowd hated the most. In such instances, the people usually pick a favorite, and he is forced into being honorable and decent. Galento entered the ring first and, by a series of struts and poses, had the fans despising him immediately, so Pop came into the ring and showed off his ill-gotten belt. Still, the crowd obviously hated Spider more, so Dad shouted up to the black section, way up in the back, that he was tired of their being deprived and he was going to give them a close look at his belt. He did just that, delaying the start of the match fourteen minutes as he slowly wandered among them. By the time he got back in the ring, the whites hated him as much as if he had sung *The Battle Hymn of the Republic* over the loud-speaker.

New good-guy Galento proceeded to please the white portion of the crowd by punishing Brother Frank with good, honest holds. In a few minutes, even the blacks were back hating my evil father. At one point, Galento had Pop by the throat and, in the time-honored wrestler's pantomime, asked the black gallery if he should hit him. "*Yes,*" they screamed. Then he asked the lower balcony.

"*Yes,*" they screamed. Then the ringsiders. "*Yes,*" they screamed, in a frenzy of anticipation for the delicious moment. But when he asked the vendor selling Cokes at ringside, Pop came alive and did the slugging himself. "*What the hell,*" muttered Spider during the next quiet headlock. "*Can't you wait until I get my heat?*"

The riots in Knoxville, Pop's most lucrative payoff town, sometimes started as he *entered* the ring, depending, of course, on how vile he had been to the hero last week. He usually needed a riot-squad escort to make it back to the dressing room after the matches. I remember once, we had to sit there until one a.m. as the mob milled around outside, Pop all the while worrying about his Studebaker. We finally walked out a side exit and encountered a large, hostile crowd. Pop just picked out the guy with the loudest mouth and challenged him to step forward or shut up. Then we calmly climbed in the car and drove off. At least, he was calm.

We always hated to go to Gadsden, Ala. The people were nasty, the arena was a junk pile, and there were no showers. The wrestlers had to take spit baths in the men's room, treatment even Class D baseball players do not get. Pop was champion and thus had a $50 guarantee, but the other boys usually had to settle for the $15 to $20 minimum. I was kept pretty busy. First, I counted the house (you could do that in the weed-patch towns) to make sure the promoter did not pull anything on the old man at payoff time. I had to guard the men's-room door while he was cleaning up and then run out and guard the Studebaker.

Woman Fan Keeps Terrible Mr. Moto In Dressing Room

WASHINGTON, March 10.—Hell hath no fury like a woman spectator at a wrestling match.

It happened last night at Turner's arena where Mr. Moto and Brother Frank Jares met Freddie Blassie and Jack Witzig in a team match.

As the four grappled during the d e c i d i n g third fall, Eleanor Clements, 20, lunged from her ringside seat and scratched Mr. Moto on the leg with a piece of broken mirror, police said.

Mr. Moto was treated in the dressing room for a minor cut. He refused to continue the match and his outmanned p a r t n e r was defeated.

Police booked Miss Clements on a charge of assault with a deadly weapon.

Washington, DC • March 9, 1955

After an unruly main event in Gadsden near summer's end, he was leaving the ring amid flying insults and flying chairs. Two or three teen-agers were giving him a particularly bad time, and he looked over at the dressing-room door and saw me peeking out, enjoying the rhubarb from a safe distance. He beckoned me out. He, a former weight-lifter who had pressed 270 pounds, snatched 260, clean and jerked 330, was calling out his arms-like-garden-hoses son to protect the family honor. Reluctantly I went, wondering why the hell I had not been born to a hod carrier. I challenged the leading heckler to come down from the stands and fight me — which should have been an easy assignment for him, but a peace officer burst out of the crowd just then and grabbed my arm, apparently thinking I was causing the hassle. Pop grabbed my other garden hose and dragged both me and the sputtering officer into the dressing room. It took an hour's argument, a phone call from the head booker in Nashville, and some phony flattery to keep the Jareses out of the Gadsden jailhouse. And when we got to the car, the aerial had been bent in half (it was not as tough as my father's ears). We never went back to Gadsden, but I'll always remember that night as the most exciting since Gorgeous George gave me a gold-plated "Georgie" bobby pin and swore me into his fan club.

The best melee of all was in lovely Kingsport, jewel of northeast Tennessee. I was in the heels' dressing room (heels always seemed to be the funniest storytellers) when someone stuck his head in the door and said, "*Riot!*" The dressing rooms were on either side of an unused stage, and when we ran to the curtains, we saw Pop fighting his way to the far doors with the aid of a couple of cops. The crowd was in a nasty mood — which was typical. Three or four of us sprinted the long way around the side hallway to the front doors, but by the time we got there, Pop had realized he was going in the wrong direction and had started back through the howling mob to the stage.

We raced back down the side hallway, bounding up the steps and saw that the policemen were busy knocking fire-breathing fans off the stage. Brother Frank was lying face down on the floor of the stage, not moving a muscle, while what seemed like the entire population of northeast Tennessee tried to reach him for one last swing or kick. Finally, the cops quieted the crowd, which must have thought the old man was dead or dying. The curtains were drawn, and I waited for the wail of an ambulance, for surely Pop was in need of medical aid. But the sly possum suddenly jumped to his feet, not a mark on him, and strode into the dressing room with a sinister grin on his face, basking in the hatred of the fans and confident that next week there would be a packed house.

How many people showed up or what foul deeds Pop perpetrated I don't know, because I returned that week to college for my sophomore year, which somehow turned out to be awfully dull.

Chapter 2
Whatever Happened to Gorgeous George?

Back in the late '40s and early '50s, before the coaxial cable was laid and before Marcus Welby took up his medical practice, when television was just as bad as it is now but newer, the most popular melodrama on the tube was professional wrestling. This was especially true in southern California, where fans could stay at home and watch villains mistreat heroes on one channel or another seven days a week (the arenas were packed despite the TV saturation). One wrestler in particular dominated those crazy times and became an American byword. Pictures of him were pasted on television screens in appliance stores. No supermarket grand opening was truly grand without him. He was acclaimed as "Mr. Television" in 1949, the same year he made thirty-two appearances at the Olympic Auditorium in Los Angeles and sold it out twenty-seven times. His name, modestly enough, was Gorgeous George.

"*I do not think I'm gorgeous,*" he would say, "*but what's my opinion against millions of others?*"

Gorgeous had a great gimmick, an extravagant routine that put him ahead of all

the monocled lords, kamikaze Japs, Indian chiefs, and masked Terrors as the biggest draw in the history of pro wrestling. First, his valet, the personification of dignity in striped pants, vest and tails, walked stiffly down the aisle and entered the ring carrying a silver-plated tray. On the tray, he had a mirror, a little carpet, and a fancified Flit gun full of perfume-scented disinfectant (*"It's Chanel No. 10,"* said Gorgeous. *"Why be half safe?"*). The valet, never smiling, set the tray down in one corner and carefully sprayed the mat.

When the time came for George's own entrance, the arena was darkened and a spotlight followed him down the aisle. A recording of *Pomp and Circumstance* was played over the loudspeaker, competing against the hisses. The valet held the ropes apart so he [George] would not have to bend too far to come into the ring, where he wiped his dainty white shoes on the carpet. The valet removed his spun-gold hairnet so everyone could admire his long blond hair done up in the latest style created by Frank and Joseph of Hollywood. They also could admire his lace or fur-trimmed robe, part of

Jefferies takes the bobby pins out of George's hair.

his priceless collection. He haughtily made an inspection and ordered his obedient servant to give the spray gun a few more squirts here and there. At the traditional meeting in the center of the ring, when the referee is supposed to run his hands down each wrestler's body, feeling for grease (artificial slipperiness is illegal), Gorgeous refused to be touched (*"Take your filthy hands off me!"* he would roar) until his valet sprayed the referee's hands. The announcer introduced him as "*The Human Orchid, The Toast of the Coast — Goooorrrrrrgeous George!"*

After the robe was doffed, he was pretty much a routine heel. He maneuvered his opponents around so the ref could not see him deliver kidney punches with his fist. He gouged eyes and bit ears. He pulled hair, but screamed foul if foes messed up his elaborate marcel (they always did). The tray made a perfect weapon for a babyface's revenge; one ex-valet still has a tray with several big dents in it from when various heroes banged it over his and G.G.'s heads. Between falls, Gorgeous gazed fondly at himself in the mirror and primped. His favorite legitimate tactic was to get his opponent in a firm headlock, leap up in the air, and flail his legs until his shoesies were just a white blur and, as he fell back to the mat, flip the poor victim over on his back — WHAM! TV announcer Dick Lane nicknamed it the "flying side headlock." But the holds and unsportsmanlike conduct were secondary to the hoopla.

"*I'll never forget my first walk down the aisle at the Olympic when my hair was blond and I was trailed by the haunting scent of perfume,"* said George. "*My purple robe was a $150 creation designed for me by Kay Cantonwine. I've got as many as 100 different robes now, one of them costing $1,900.*

"*When I flitted down that aisle, I got the biggest ovation of my life. They couldn't announce the match. The announcer burst out laughing, but I didn't mind. I was a sensation."*

Indeed he was. The matches at the Olympic were kinescoped and shown later in fifty-seven markets all over the country. Gorgeous George became a celebrity in each area, and when the Olympic promoter, John J. Doyle, sent him out on tour, he raked in as much as thirty percent of the gate. G.G. made $160,000 in 1951 and probably earned close to $2 million in his career.

The fans despised George, but the folks in show business adored him, perhaps because he was so much more ridiculously flamboyant than even the most ambitious of starlets. A top gag writer was paid $250 a week to think up jokes about Gorgeous, which soon turned up in scripts for Bob Hope, Eddie Cantor, Red Skelton, and others. G.G. made an in-person and most appropriate appearance on *Queen for a Day*. To help raise money for charity, he took part in a celebrity circus, held in a tent pitched on the Pan-Pacific Auditorium parking lot.

Bob Hope, elegantly dressed for the part, was his valet and Burt Lancaster was his wrestling opponent under the big top. Just before the match, the lights suddenly went out. A few moments later a spotlight was turned on and, in it, George and Lancaster were dancing to the "Viennese Waltz."

At least seven songs were written about Gorgeous, some with lyrics and some mercifully without. A former valet, Jack Hunter, still remembers the words to one version after twenty years: *"You would, too, if you heard them six times a week for a year and a half."*

He has an armful of muscle and a head full of curls,
he wrestles with the fellows and thrills all the girls;
a two-ton truck with a velvet sheen,
Gorgeous George is the man I mean;
He has a chest like a mountain and a face like a dream
he starts women swoonin' and makes men scream.

He was featured in possibly the worst motion picture of all time, *Alias the Champ*, made by Republic [Pictures] in 1949. It was filmed in less than two weeks and George's best lines were, "*Come, little one, it's time for my marcel*" and "*Keep your dirty hands off my hair!*" He was not nominated for an Academy Award.

On camera, in the ring or wherever, he usually stayed in character, with a little put-on routine for every occasion. Performing the Gorgeous George kiss, he would gallantly take a lady's hand and bend down to touch his lips to it, but he would turn his wrist and kiss the back of his own hand instead. He would sit in the lobby of a hotel and shriek until the manager had brand-new sheets and pillow cases put on his bed, then he'd have his room sprayed by his valet. He would pull the same sort of act in restaurants, even to the point of having other customers sprayed.

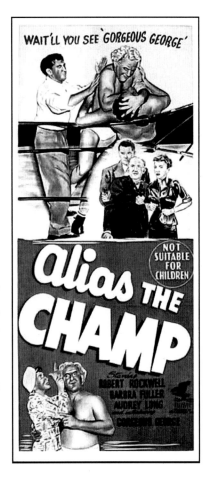

WAIT'LL YOU SEE 'GORGEOUS GEORGE'

NOT SUITABLE FOR CHILDREN

Alias THE *CHAMP*

Starring
ROBERT ROCKWELL
BARBRA FULLER
AUDREY LONG

"I was alone at the arena — alone! — and he comes up in this purple Cadillac, with his stooge," remembered ex-wrestler Dave Levin, who once promoted matches in Santa Maria, Calif. *"'Hi, Dave. How you doing?' he says and he steps back and the god-damned valet comes in and sprays my office there. Then, and only then, George steps in. It's only us three, but he had enough brains to know I'm going to tell this story a thousand times around, you see?"*

His hair was kept in place by gold-plated bobby pins which he insisted on calling Georgie pins. His first batch cost $85 a half pound, but when he found out how fast he was handing them out, he found a way to get them cheaper. He once appeared on a radio show being taped for overseas armed forces and the beribboned, high-ranking officers present decided they had better get some souvenir Georgie pins or their wives would never forgive them. Gorgeous refused to shake hands with them until his valet first sprayed their hands. Then he lined them up, had them raise their right hands, and repeat after him the customary oath:

"I solemnly swear and promise I will never confuse this gold Georgie pin with a common, ordinary bobby pin, so help me Gorgeous George."

To escape from the madding crowd, G.G. owned a large turkey ranch near Beaumont, Calif., east of Los Angeles. Naturally, his products were *"the most gorgeous turkeys in the world, the only turkeys that go to market in a limousine."*

"Wrestling helps my turkey business," he said in 1952. *"In fact, if I put that 'Gorgeous George' label on dented andirons or retired radio tubes, they would sell. I call my birds Gorgeous George turkeys and this year I'll raise thirty-five thousand on my ranch, with thirty-five thousand more farmed out among four growers. I'm investing two hundred fifty thousand dollars in the place, but it's worth it.*

"Motorists see the sign 'Gorgeous George's Turkey Ranch' *and stop by out of curiosity. Last Labor Day, in response to my radio and TV invitation, twenty-five thousand people came up. So, to make things a little easier for visitors, I plan to put in a coffee bar, serve turkey sandwiches, and expand into a sort of sight-seeing mecca."*

G.G. was just as ready to publicize his turkeys as he was to promote his matches. At the 1951 National Turkey Show in Long Beach, he decorated his display with orchid drapes, an orchid cage, and two turkeys whose feathers were dyed orchid. G.G.'s valet sprayed them every two minutes with Chanel No. 10.

Kay Cantonwine, the daughter of George's manager and, later, the operator of a successful sportswear business, made all his robes in those days. She remembers one of her lavish creations was made with thousands of lavender turkey feathers. *"The robe had a little bustle effect in back like a turkey,"* she said. *"I was scared to death he wouldn't wear it, but he loved it. It only lasted two or three wearings. I guess people kept pulling the feathers out."*

She also made him a royal-purple George Washington robe, with 100 hammered silver buttons and 250 yards of horsehair lace, and a white nylon knit poodle robe with a jewel-studded dog collar. When he wore his apple-blossom robe, the promoters would send apple-blossom perfume wafting through the arena air vents.

He had his name legally changed to Gorgeous George in 1950. Appearing before Los Angeles Superior Court Judge W. Turney Fox with his first wife, Betty [nee Hanson], he wore a violet suit, a yellow shirt and hanky, and a gray silk tie on which was painted an orchid. Betty wore a lavender suit and a mink stole.

"George is the only last name our children know," she told the judge.

The Human Orchid's original name was George Raymond Wagner. He was born in 1915 in Seward, Neb., and moved with his family to Houston when he was a small boy. His father was a house painter, his mother was an invalid, and their home was in a rough section called Harrisburg, near the ship channel. He ran away to Nebraska once, was expelled several times from junior high school, and never finished Milby High. There were little indications even then that he felt an urgent need to stand out from the crowd. At age nine, he wore a black shirt with white buttons, *"just to look different, so people would notice me."*

Tough kids from his neighborhood were called Harrisburg Rats, and out of his own rat pack came pro wrestlers Chester Hayes, Sterling (Dizzy) Davis, Jesse James, and Johnny James, plus two boys who later became valets for him, Jack

Hunter and Jake Brown. The James brothers' father owned a fruit-stand and behind it, next to Buffalo Bayou, the boys would stage wrestling matches on the sawdust left over from when a sawmill stood on the spot. If somebody wanted to watch, the boys charged admission.

Later, George and Jesse James wrestled at Greek picnics in the Houston area. Once, Jesse body-slammed George and knocked him out. A well-meaning lady in the audience poured smelling salts in his nose. She revived him all right, but she also damaged the inside of his nose and put him forever beyond the reach of draft boards. From picnics, the boys went on to challenging carnival wrestlers and working small arenas around Houston (he was occasionally billed as the "Barefoot Bohemian"), and finally, to working for the biggest matchmaker in that part of Texas.

George Wagner before he made the transformation to Gorgeous George

For a long time, George Wagner was just another good guy, or babyface. His hair was short and brown and his wallet was thin. But things changed when he met Betty Hanson, a cashier in a Eugene, Ore., movie theater. They were married in the ring in Eugene in 1939, and it proved to be such a good draw that they reenacted the wedding in several arenas around the country. Soon came the transformation from babyface to heel.

"*It started one night in Eugene,*" said Don Owen, Oregon's big wrestling promoter. "*Betty had made George a robe and, when he went in the ring that night, he took special care in folding it.*

"*The fans got on him pretty good and Betty was there and got into it with the fans. She slapped one of them and George went out of the ring and belted the fan. Even when he was a clean wrestler, George had a hot temper and would fight a buzz saw.*

"*Anyway, the booing was tremendous, and the next week, there was a real big crowd and everyone booed George. So he just took more time to fold his robe. He did everything to antagonize the fans. And from that point on, he became the best drawing card we ever had around here. In wrestling, they either come to like you or to hate you. And they hated George.*"

Gorgeous himself gave a different version of the Eugene incident:

"*It was sensational,*" he said, "*a two-hundred-fifty-dollar royal-blue robe with sequins. I took off the robe, folded it carefully, and placed it in my corner. Someone snatched it up and tossed it to somebody else. They started a game of basketball, and by the time the police got it back for me, it wasn't fit for a mop. It cost two-hundred-fifty-dollars and I just stood there and offered to wrestle the whole place I was so mad.*"

The character of Gorgeous George evolved slowly through the '40s. The brown hair became auburn. He read about his old friend, Sterling Davis, throwing gardenias to the fans in Mexico and being called Gardenia Davis. He let his hair grow longer and wavier. The big step was the day he went to a beauty salon in Hollywood to inquire about a wig. It was decided a wig would be too easy to yank off, so the beautician turned him over to two Hungarian hair stylists, Frank and Joseph, who recommended he grow his hair long and dye it blond, if he had the guts.

"If guts is all it takes, I've got plenty," he said.

Guts, gall, nerve, chutzpah — whatever it was, George had it. During World War II, he worked at a shipyard during the day and wrestled at night. One evening, he broke his leg in a match, but did not go to a doctor. Instead, he gritted his teeth, went to work at the shipyard the next morning, feigned a fall off a ladder, and enjoyed a leisurely vacation while his employer paid his medical bills.

In the early '40s, he boarded a luxury liner to Honolulu with only his ticket, no money. He threw his wallet on the floor in one of the men's rooms and reported that it had been stolen during the bon-voyage parties. It was found later that day — empty, of course. The captain and the other passengers took pity on him and he got free drinks all the way to Hawaii.

"Back in the days when gas was rationed and all that stuff," said Dave Levin, *"George was driving his car along and, damn, if he doesn't see a police car way behind. He tried to outdistance them, but it didn't work. His car didn't have the power. So, at the last moment, he started careening — his car was careening from the left side to the right side. Finally, he brings it to a halt, just as the cops are right behind him. He staggers out of the car holding his heart.*

"'Did you see that? Did you see that?' he said.

"Did they see it! Of course they did. They were chasing him!

"'Oh, my God. I thought I was a goner. The gas pedal got stuck, I couldn't get it loose.'

"He's going on and on to the cops about it. And do you know, he wound up getting gas stamps from those cops!"

Levin was a great admirer of G.G.'s quick thinking.

"I wrestled George one time in Vegas," he said. *"We did it at the Silver Slipper, upstairs, and Sally Rand, the bubble dancer, was downstairs. She was old then, but she had a good body on her. She came up between falls and presented George with an orchid, and he showed it all around and took a bow, then she kissed him. Then she walked across the ring and kissed me, and, you know, a lot George gives a damn if she kisses me, but he's such a showman! He throws down the orchid, jumps all over it, blows his top, and the people are going wild. I don't know if that was prearranged. It never was with me, I'll tell you that."*

In Texas one night, Gorgeous was handing out free orchids to the ladies. A special one would go to a special ringsider, and Gorgeous chose an eighty-year-old grandmother, who happily, but slowly, walked to the ring. Then, in full view of the crowd, he dropped the orchid, crushed it under his white shoe, and sneered at the old lady. He was very nearly mobbed.

Actor-announcer Dick Lane remembers strolling through Beverly Hills with Gorgeous. G.G. wore a white gabardine suit, black tie, and a big white panama hat with a black band. They stopped in front of a fashionable men's store and immediately a crowd gathered. G.G. beat on the window with his ivory-handled black cane until a clerk came scurrying out, then demanded to see the store's selection of hankies. The clerk obediently brought out an armload and George went through them one by one, throwing them over the man's shoulder. At last he found a black one, just like the one he was wearing, discarded his old one over the man's shoulder, carefully installed the new one, gave the clerk a $20 bill, and sauntered off.

George and Betty

He took Lane around the corner to his bank and got out his safety-deposit box. It was stuffed with cash. Lane asked him why he did not keep his money in a savings account. *"I want it right here where I can take my shoes off and walk around in it if I want to,"* said Gorgeous. *"Right now I feel like flying to Buenos Aires."*

So, he took out a handful of bills, hopped in a cab, and headed for the airport. As far as Lane knows, he did fly to Buenos Aires.

A Los Angeles golf-course owner named Nick Serfas was his valet for a tour of Australia in the summer of 1956. And he will never get over it.

"The Olympics were on and, at that time, the Australian papers were conservative," said Nick. *"They usually had six pages on sports. We got more ink than the Olympics did and it was all due to his promotional ability. He would do anything.*

"The minute we got into the Melbourne airport, they had newspapermen, radio interviewers, and television, which was brand-new, all waiting to talk to G.G. He refused to get off the plane because the promoter didn't have a girl for him.

"We were sitting around our hotel in Melbourne and he said, 'Let's go outside and cause a traffic jam.' We went out with the Georgie pins and he just stood there, and people rushed to get those pins. He'd sidle up to a girl in the crowd and say, 'I'm in room 612. Come on up and have a drink with us.' He'd say that to a dozen girls and then later have his pick!

"There were riots in Sydney, Perth, Adelaide and Newcastle. In Adelaide, he wrestled Chief Little Wolf and G.G. went into the ring drunk and they had words. They had the worst match of all time. They started really duking and the people were unhappy. This was on a cricket field, more than 12,000 people there. So

Little Wolf wins the match and Gorgeous attacked him in the ring. They had only three bobbies and they came in the ring. This was a beauty.

"*A guy named Pat, the heavyweight champion of the Pacific Fleet, was in our corner. We know we've got to get through the rioting mob to get in the dressing room and catch our plane. So Pat says,* 'Let's start swinging.' *We clipped about eight or nine people and then they got out of the way. After the showers, they tried to tip the car over. They were rocking it. So Pat started the motor and put it in gear to get away.*"

Gorgeous played the role so long and so ardently that he actually came to *believe* he was what he pretended to be, but he had a good sense of humor. He loved to play jokes.

"*He called them swerves,*" said Jack Hunter, one of the valets. "*He'd do anything for a swerve and even enjoyed one on himself. Occasionally I'd put beer instead of perfume in his atomizer. He didn't mind. He used to say,* 'A swerve a day keeps the blues away.'"

"*He enjoyed playing dummy — pretending he was deaf and dumb, but able to read lips. He'd make everyone speak slowly and carefully while he stared at their mouths. I hated seafood, so for breakfast, he'd order catfish and swing the bones in front of my face.*"

Hunter was with G.G. once when he stopped somewhere in Pennsylvania to have his hair done. George settled back in the chair and, through the ceiling mirror, saw a pair of female legs, skirts raised above the knee. While the beauty operator was gone, he got up and peeked into the next booth. Instantly, he ran out to Hunter, waiting in the car, yelling, "*My heart, my heart!*"

The woman in the other booth was a corpse whose hair was being done for the local mortuary.

Gorgeous also, at different times, had female attendants who sprayed the ring. For a long time, the role was played by his second wife, Cherie [nee Dupré]. Betty divorced him in 1952 because he was "extremely jealous" and "made her life miserable." She won custody of their two adopted children, Carol and Don (sometimes known as Gorgeous George, Jr., to the delight of bullies at school) and title to the Beaumont turkey ranch.

Cherie was a dancer and model who met G.G. in Las Vegas when he was doing a nightclub act at the Silver Slipper. She vividly remembers the first night she stooged for Gorgeous, in a Texas arena.

"*I'll never forget,*" she said. "*I had half my hair pulled out. I went through the valet routine in black net hose, heels, tights, scissor-tail coat, and red hair, then I sat ringside. He was wrestling Rip Rogers and, in the third fall, he was getting the best of George. I jumped up and squirted Rip in the eyes with the spray gun.*"

Gorgeous One In Tag Bout Wednesday

Gorgeous George will appear in his first Evansville tag team bout Wednesday night at the Coliseum as he pairs with Frank Jares against Dick Beyer and the Mighty Atlas.

Atlas lost another disputed decision to Gorgeous George last week, giving the perfumed dandy two straight victories over the Mighty One.

Beyer had earlier defeated Jares on a disqualification so there is enough old scores to settle to satisfy the most demanding mat fan.

The tag bout, for best of three falls, or one hour's time limit, will be an interesting test for Gorgeous George, who has disdained team bouts in the past.

Scotty M c W i l l i a m s, who scored an upset over Freddy Blassie, will face Don Whitler, 231 pound rough neck, in the semifinal event. Whitey Whitler, Don's father, appeared here 12 years ago in several bouts, according to promoter Leon Balkin.

Dick Beyer and Frank Jares will open the card at 8:45 p.m. (CDT) in a 15-minute, one fall bout.

On June 11, 1958, Pop teamed up with George in Evansville, Indiana.

"Rip grabbed me by the hair and threw me across the ring. Then a big guy got in the ring and threw me so high my feet hit the floodlights. The rest of the crowd threw coffee and beer on me."

She was with George when he had a series of sellout matches with Whipper Watson in Toronto. G.G. bragged to everyone that he was so sure he was going to beat Watson, he would let his hair be cut off if he lost. He lost, all right, but escaped from the ring and welshed on the bet.

Naturally, a rematch was staged in March 1959 and G.G. promised that, this time, he would live up to his promise. Watson beat him again and the crowd of nearly 14,000 people watched happily as a barber cut off his "perfumed golden locks."

He had such a lucrative thing going that George later demanded another rematch and, this time, bet *Cherie's* hair, which was red and long. He lost.

"It took seven to hold me down," she said. *"I chickened out at the last minute. The audience went frantic. Some women were crying for me; others yelled that it was what I deserved. People were grabbing for pieces of my hair. I was hysterical. I had to go out and get some feather caps until I could get a hairpiece."*

G.G.'s publicity and big gates naturally led to a mincing, strutting horde of imitators, including a currently active wrestler who goes as Gorgeous George, Jr. Some others: Gorgeous George I, Gorgeous George Grant, a lady wrestler named Lovely Louise, Beautiful Bobby Duranton and his valet Firmin, Pretty Boy Pat Patterson, Pretty Boy Larry Hennig, Luscious Lars Anderson, Nature Boy Buddy Rogers, and Magnificent Maurice, who enters the ring in a red beret, pink velvet cape, and ballet slippers. Maurice has teamed up frequently with Handsome Johnny Barend and they have a series of routines they use on TV interviews.

"Mirror, mirror in my hand, am I the handsomest in the land?" they ask in unison of their purse-sized mirrors. Then they pause. *"Yes! It said yes. Yes."*

George and Cherie

The weirdest of all is Sweet Daddy Siki, a peroxide-blond Negro who sports a long cigarette holder and white-framed sunglasses.

"In Toronto one time they named a flower after me, the Irresistible African Violet," he claims. *"Note, please, that the ladies love flowers, and that I am prettier than any flower. Everything about me is beautiful. I am almost never wrong. I have five hundred twenty muscles and two hundred one bones, and they are coordinated and combined into the most gorgeous body in the world."*

But what of the original Gorgeous, the man credited with inspiring the self-loving ballyhoo thrown out by boxing champ Cassius Clay/Muhammad Ali, the man who raked in millions at the gate? By 1962, George's drinking caught up with him. He had a serious liver ailment and doctors told him he could not wrestle anymore. He kept drinking and finally was hospitalized (visitors and other patients lined up outside his door

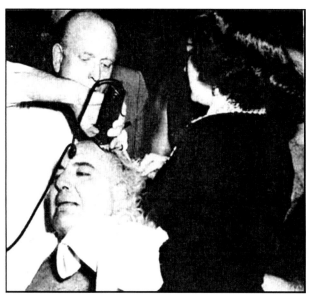

(above) When Gorgeous George vowed that he'd allow his blond marcel to be shaved off if he lost to Whipper Watson, the fans in Toronto flocked to the arena. G.G. backed out once, but lost again the following week and was trapped.

(right) The Human Orchid is now the human billiard ball, sadder, but richer, after his second straight loss to Canadian hero Whipper Watson.

(below) That's not Delilah looking pained as Gorgeous loses his hair. She is Cherie, George's second wife, who bet *her* hair on a subsequent match. Gorgeous lost again and the poor woman's head was shaved in the ring while fans cheered and cried.

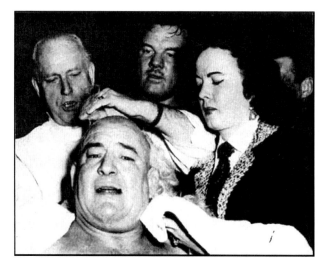

to get a glimpse of him in a lavender robe on which were painted four orchids). He stayed away from booze for a few months after he got out of the hospital, then went right back to it. He sold his San Fernando Valley tavern, Gorgeous George Ringside, and it barely paid off his debts.

Cherie divorced him in 1962 and waived alimony. She was supposed to receive $75 a week to support their son, she said, but never got a cent. George started going with a kind-hearted striptease artist and kept right on drinking.

"Sober, there wasn't a sweeter, kinder, more considerate man in the world," said Cherie. *"He didn't really have the nerve to do all those things, that's why he drank. When he was sober, he was shy.*

"I don't ever regret meeting him and marrying him. When he wasn't drinking, it was a good life."

George was so broke, at Christmas 1963, he had to make his youngest son a skateboard. Ex-valet Nick Serfas offered to loan him $2,000, but he turned it down. He had plans to start a painting business.

He was stricken with a heart attack on Christmas Eve and died two days later in County Hospital at the age of forty-eight. His stripper girlfriend had to take up a collection to bury him.

The funeral was right up to his high standards of ballyhoo. It had everything but a lavender hearse. More than 500 people showed up to sight-see, or pay their respects, or both. The coffin was covered with orchids. The wreaths and sprays sent by fans and friends all contained at least one orchid and sometimes six or eight. Fight announcer Jimmy Lennon, uncle of the Lennon sisters, sang a few hymns. The pallbearers — including the hulking Indian, Jules Strongbow, the hairy Italian, Baron Leone, and two or three other wrestlers who had known him since he was a Harrisburg Rat — wore baby orchids in their lapels. Two ex-wives (on either side of the aisle) and his stripper sweetheart were crying in the audience, and his ex-manager, Howard Cantonwine, could not bear to come in. He stayed out on the steps.

G.G. himself looked as splendid as ever, lying there in his fancy silk George Washington robe. Frank and Joseph had made three trips to the funeral parlor to make sure his coiffure was just right.

"If there had been a spark of life left in ol' Gorgeous," said longtime friend Johnny James, *"he would have stood up in that casket and taken a bow."*

Today, his grave in Valhalla Memorial Park, North Hollywood, Calif., is marked only by a plaque imbedded in the grass. It is a plaque just like hundreds, maybe thousands, of others, arranged in neat, anonymous rows and, strangely, it makes no mention of his second son. It says:

LOVE TO OUR DADDY
GORGEOUS GEORGE
1915 - 1963
CAROL AND DON

(upper left) Oh so carefully, the butler would remove the spun-gold hairnet from G.G.'s golden locks.

(upper right) Gorgeous George refused to wrestle on a mat that had not been sprayed first with Chanel scented disinfectant by his gentleman's gentleman, usually played by one of his old neighborhood buddies from the Harrisburg section of Houston or from Houston's Milby High School.

(lower left) Before the televised matches on Hollywood's KTLA, Gorgeous George sits for the finishing touches on his coiffure by Frank and Joseph, his hair stylists.

(lower right) Before climbing through the ropes for a match at Hollywood Legion Stadium, Gorgeous stops to tell a heckler that he is beneath contempt.

Chapter 3
Indian Chiefs, Lords and Masked Marvels

Pro wrestling is a form of athletics — anyone who has seen Antonino Rocca's leaps, or Bruno Sammartino's massive physique, or Verne Gagne's quick moves, would not argue that point. Just as importantly, it is also a branch of the theater, although its characterizations are so broad that it is only a distant cousin of classical drama; about as distant as a hoedown from a symphonic concert. It is most closely related to burlesque and black-hat-white-hat cowboy movies.

The Tyrone Guthrie Theatre in Minneapolis once called in local boy Gagne, who wrestled for the University of Minnesota before turning pro, to do a bit of coaching. One of the Guthrie's actors, playing the role of the deformed slave Caliban in Shakespeare's *The Tempest*, had to project his lines to the customers in the back row while wearing fangy false teeth and lying on the floor.

"It's an elocution problem," said a Guthrie official. *"We needed advice from somebody in the community who has spent time rolling on the floor in a theatrical situation while trying to speak under duress."*

Baltimore columnist Steve Gavin had the bright idea of taking a theatrical expert to the matches and getting his reaction. Harvard graduate Edward J. Golden, Jr., director of the city's Center Stage, agreed to go.

"It has the basic elements of children's theater — it is not appealing to anything sophisticated and it is keyed to an almost total naiveté," he said afterward. *"In some ways, it reminds me of a Jacobean tragedy.*

"Wrestling has all the grace and simplicity of a folk ballad, but none of the significance. It is totally physical, a physical battle of strength beautifully keyed to elicit primitive titillations. In that way, you could call it unfocused theater, since it has no point other than arousing primitive emotions spuriously.

"… Wrestling's appeal is a world beyond reason, a purely instinctive world and it succeeds beautifully. It's all done very well."

Dignified orchestra conductor Arturo Toscanini was such a fan that he would sit in his living room and scream to the hero on the television screen, *"Keel heem! Keel heem!"* Al Jolson and Will Rogers were frequent spectators, and actor Peter Ustinov has raved about the sport.

"I love to watch wrestling," he said. *"I feel it's the root of my profession. The other day, as I was going up in the lift, the liftman kept hitting me and poking me, for no apparent reason, and I was rather frightened. At the top, he said, 'You're my favorite wrestler!' He'd mistaken me for someone else, but I was terribly pleased."*

All the critics have not been rapturous. Brooks Atkinson wrote in the *New York Times*:

These mugs are terrible actors. They lack spontaneity. Once you have seen one meatball with blond hair step belligerently outside the ring and shake his fist at a jeering audience, you have seen them all.

Their fake rage and savagery have become repetitious and tiresome. The groans and snarls, the ferocity, the smashes against the turnbuckle, the slugging, the skull-crashes, drop-kicks, flying-mares and knee-drops, lack the fire of good acting. They represent the lowest level of ham.

A pan like that in the powerful *Times* might cause even a Neil Simon comedy to close, but pro wrestling has been taking heavy blows from sportswriters and others for decades, with no noticeable drop in attendance. The plots might be clichés and the players might be hams, but still the business prospers. And since it is a branch of show biz akin to burlesque, wrestlers generally follow the dictum of a veteran stripper in the Broadway musical *Gypsy*: "*You gotta have a gimmick.*" Burlesque has Candy Barr, wrestling has Ricki Starr; burlesque has Tempest Storm, wrestling has Gorilla Monsoon.

Very few grapplers have gimmicks as elaborate as Gorgeous George's, but any number of them have been elegant poseurs, even members of the nobility, including Lord Robert Duncum, Lord Charles Montague, Lord Albert Mills, Lord Jonathan Boyd, Sir Norman Charles, Lord Patrick Lansdowne, Lord Alfred Hayes, and the midget Lord Clayton Littlebrook. Lord Bertie Topham, a typical example, was transported in a chauffeur-driven Rolls-Royce and entered the ring wearing a heavy velvet cloak and smoking a cigarette in a long, aristocratic holder. Monocles are standard equipment.

When I was growing up in Los Angeles, we had a surfeit of blue bloods. My favorite was Lord James Ranicar Blears, who was seldom without his faithful second, Captain Leslie Holmes. At age twenty-six in an L.A. court, he had his name legally changed to Lord Blears. When he was just plain James Blears in World War II, he was a radioman on a Dutch vessel in the Indian Ocean when the ship was captured by a Japanese submarine. The enemy sailors started to slaughter the crew, so he dived overboard and managed to stay afloat fourteen hours until a U.S. cruiser picked him up. I say "managed to stay afloat," but that

Lord James Blears

is probably doing Blears an injustice, for he is an excellent swimmer (today he and his son are two of the finest board surfers in the state of Hawaii, where His Lordship is a wrestling promoter). After the war, he testified at an inquiry into Japanese atrocities.

Then there was Lord Leslie Carlton, an American whose real name was — depending on which rumor you believed — Tug Carlson or Leo Brooks Whippern. Perhaps both men used the title at one time or another. Anyway, Lord Carlton had a stooge, too. In New York, it was Sir James Hartley, whose costume included a Prince Albert (a long frock coat), purple cummerbund and monocle. He carried an ebony walking stick with a silver tip. In L.A., Carlton used a turbaned swami as his second, a role played by my dad's old wrestling teammate from the Los Angeles Athletic Club, Tommy Peratis, who would intrigue the fans by babbling in fluent Greek.

Never mind that swamis are supposed to be from India. Swami Peratis was probably a better wrestler than his master.

Third, there was Lord Athol Layton, a giant Aussie, who today is a combination TV announcer-wrestler in Toronto. When all these fellows and their seconds were working the territory, there should have been a local edition of *Burke's Peerage* to keep them straight. Instead, there was a stiff note from the British consulate-general in L.A.: *"No member of the British peerage is participating in any wrestling or similar exhibitions in the Los Angeles area ..."* The fans cared not a fig for what the consulate-general said; they formed a Lords of the Mat Fan Club, with a swell newsletter called the *Nobility News*.

In a category all by himself, but similar in some ways to the human orchids and noblemen, is the ballet artiste Ricki Starr, who enters the ring in salmon-pink tights and matching slippers, blows kisses to the crowd, and then uses the top rope as an exercise barre, doing *battements*, *pliés*, and *ronds de jambe*. Of course, this infuriates the grizzled thugs who usually make up his opposition. It is sort of like Little Lord Fauntleroy challenging a member of the Flaming Skulls motorcycle gang. But Ricki, well-built and the son of a pro wrestler, does all right. The last time I saw him work, in Houston in 1972, he twirled and whirled around and got Professor Boris Malenko furious and confused. At one point, Ricki got Malenko entangled in the ropes, then cart wheeled across the ring and slapped him in the face. The crowd loved it.

Starr grew up in St. Louis, studied a little ballet, and worked in a whole summer of musicals for the St. Louis Municipal Opera. He has had other professional experience and, believe it or not, has been featured in *Dancer Magazine*. As a dancing wrestler, however, not as a wrestling dancer.

"The stretches, the pulling, the extensions in barre work are terrific for me," he says. *"The average wrestler has short, thick, slow muscles. Ballet training pulls the muscles out, gives them elasticity, rebound. And it gives me balance in the ring — even in mid-air — so that I can't be clumsily knocked down."*

At the other end of the elegance scale are the hillbillies. Haystack Calhoun from Morgan's Corner, Ark., is the current favorite. He is fatter than two prize steers

"Look out below!" Haystack Calhoun, who needs about an acre of denim to cover his corpulent body, is about to use his 601 pounds to make a human pancake.

and it must take an acre of blue denim to make the bib overalls he wrestles in. When he starts to do a belly flop on his opponent's prostrate body, the poor victim had better say his prayers. In Detroit recently, Calhoun chortled and warned, "*There are going to be a lot of human pancakes around here before I get finished.*"

There are and have been many others. Hillbilly Spunky (Frank Robinson) and his pretty second, Daisy Mae. Man Mountain Dean (Frank Leavitt), supposedly from, and nearly as big as, Stone Mountain, Ga. Logger Larsen, Klondike Bill and Yukon Eric — all in Levis held up with rope belts. Farmer Marlin using his mule kick. Ike Eakins and his devastating pile driver, the "mountain drop." Bearded Elmer Estep lugging his jug of applejack. Farmer McKinley Pickins, Farmer Jack, and Farmer Martin. The Kentuckians, The Mississippi Plowboy, The Scuffling Hillbillies. Li'l Abner, Ike (Tiny) McNabb from the Ozarks, Elviry Snodgrass, Country Boy Humphrey and his cousin Jethro. All of them seem to be right out of Al Capp's inkwell.

Farmer Jones used to enter the ring leading his pet hog, Trooper, on a leash, but the best country mascot of all was Len Stecklin's raccoon. If the athletic commission permitted, he would bring it into the ring with him and leave it tied to a ring post while he worked. That ended, in Illinois at least, when the raccoon bit the referee.

The king of all the hillbillies was big, scraggly Leo (Daniel Boone) Savage, also known as Whiskers Savage, who claimed he rubbed possum oil over his beard to keep it looking good. Early in his career, he told people he was from Boyd County, Ky., a genuine hillbilly area next to West Virginia. Later he claimed Boone County was his home. That sounded even more like hookworm-and-corn-likker country until somebody looked at a map and saw that Boone County was smack dab next to the big city of Cincinnati. Anyway, Savage, or whatever his real name was, would arrive in a city and walk barefooted through the streets wearing a tattered blanket full of moth holes. He carried a lantern and was accompanied by a couple of hound dogs. Occasionally he kept pet possums under his hotel bed, or he would arrive early at the arena, tie his hounds to a telephone pole, sit down on the curb, and hee-haw over the funny papers.

As he moseyed down the arena aisle in his old blanket, pulled along by his hounds, he'd yell, "*Ee-yayhah, YOWIE!,*" treeing every coon for miles around. In the ring, he might park a chicken on a turnbuckle, where it would calmly cluck through the match. Or he would try to convince the referee to douse the house lights so he could scuffle by lantern light.

How old was he?: "*I don't right likely know. The house burned down — and the family Bible with it. It don't make no difference 'cause I can beat these ol' city boys anyhow.*"

Did his family root for him? "*Last time I counted, I had eight brothers and sisters, and ever' one of 'em, 'n' my mom 'n' pappy, are agin my scufflin'.*"

What was his favorite hold?: "*They ain't but one holt and that's the log-rollin' holt. That's the only one I need anyhow.*"

Promoter Paul Boesch was recently asked who was the greatest draw in the history of Houston wrestling, which has been a successful enterprise for more than fifty years.

"*Comparatively, you would have to say it was Whiskers Savage,*" he said, "*because he drew when nothing around the country was drawing very much, when the Depression was at its worst, when nothing was drawing in Houston either. With him on the card, they used to turn 'em away from the City Auditorium.*"

Whiskers Savage

"He was a great character. As far as anybody knows, he came from Boone County, Kentucky. If he didn't, he gave everybody the greatest snow job that was ever given anywhere. He came into town with a lantern and said he didn't trust these city lights. All this kind of stuff. And the people in Houston just went for it hook, line and sinker.

"... Whiskers Savage lived whatever he did twenty-four hours a day. Whether he was the most honest guy in the world or the biggest charlatan in the world, he was with it all the time. I remember one time in Dallas, he showed how he never let his guard down to anybody. I was going to take him downtown and there was a couple standing there, and it had just started to rain and the bus had gone by, so we said, 'C'mon, hop in and we'll take you downtown with us.'

"I said to Whiskers, 'Where you staying?'

"'Oh, I'm staying at the Salvation Army. You know, you sure meet a fine class of travelin' people there.'

"A little bit later he said, 'That Mr. McLemore [the Dallas promoter] is a nice man. He let me scuffle here tonight and he gave me fifty cents besides.'

"He would talk like this all day long. Just a rare individual."

Any wrestler from a western state is liable to be transformed into a cowboy even if he has never been on a horse. The villainous team of Dory Funk, Sr., and son Terry, who operated out of the Flying Mare Ranch on the edge of Buffalo Lake near Amarillo, Tex., entered the ring in cowboy hats, vests and fancy chaps. Cowboy Bob Ellis, often teamed with huge Tex McKenzie, used to wrestle in cut-off Levis, but now he has regular trunks carrying the brand of his own Texas spread. He claims he was "discovered" while bulldogging steers, so, naturally, his favorite hold is the "bulldog headlock," in which he grabs his opponent in a side headlock, runs partway across the ring with him, and then drops to the mat and slams his head down. Cowboy Bill Watts from Oklahoma has a horseshoe imprinted on the left buttock of his trunks and his favorite hold is the "Oklahoma stampede."

Where there are cowboys, there must be some Indians lurking about and, sure enough, wrestling has more than its share of Choctaws, Chippewas, Cherokees and Navajos, most of whom enter the ring in war bonnets, even if their particular tribes never did anything more warlike than shoo crows away from the corn. Under the feathers, there is likely to be a Mohawk haircut (head shaved except for a strip down the middle). They specialize in either the "tomahawk chop" or the "Indian deathlock," and they often go into war dances before or after their matches.

I wonder about the quality of tribal administration over the years because it seems a good percentage of the chiefs have been out wrestling somewhere most of the time. The list is long and gaudy: Chief White Owl, Chief Chewchki, Chief Kit Fox, Chief Little Wolf (nee Benny Tenario; he wore large sombreros, fancy vests and embroidered boots), Chief Big Heart, Chief Osley Saunooke (a 340-pound Cherokee from North Carolina who played football at Haskell Institute, an Indian school in Kansas), Chief Thunderbird from British Columbia (real name: Baptiste Paull), Chief Blue Eagle, Chief Suni War Cloud (real name: Sonny Chorre), and Chief Indio Cherokee and his aide, Princess Bonita. All women Indian wrestlers seem to be princesses, including Princess Tona Tomah, Princess War Star, and two gals who used the name Princess Rose White Cloud.

Among the wrestling braves over the years have been Don Eagle (Carl Donald Bell), an ex-lacrosse player and boxer from Canada who was merely the son of a chief (so why wasn't he a prince?), plus Jules Strongbow, Tiny Roebuck, Billy Two Rivers (a big star in Great Britain), Shoshone Wingo, Johnny War Eagle, Billy Red Cloud, Bobby Bold Eagle, Danny Little Bear, Jim Clinkstock, Little Beaver (a midget who slaps his opponents with a moccasin), Tommy Marvin and Joe (Little) Beaver.

"V" for victory, signals Danny Little Bear, who has applied a strange and wonderful hold on villain Rock Hunter. Hunter strains to avoid being pinned for the count of three.

Edward (Wahoo) McDaniel played football for Bud Wilkinson at Oklahoma and then for the Houston Oilers, Denver Broncos, New York Jets, and Miami Dolphins. Now he is wrestling full-time, entering the ring wearing a war bonnet, moccasins, and love beads. He is an especially big draw in Houston, where he has had a lucrative succession of matches against Dory Funk, Jr.

Of course, in addition to the Indians who aren't really chiefs, there are Indians who aren't really Indians. The prime example is a black man named Tiger Nelson, who for years has been the dressing-room attendant in L.A.'s Olympic Auditorium. He once wrestled in the Vancouver area as a member of the Blackfoot tribe!

"There was a guy out of New York that wrestled as an Indian," recalled my father, Brother Frank. *"One thing that I liked was that he would put on his whole Indian attire — feathers and all — and go to children's hospitals and pep up the kids. Of course, they were more interested in him being the Indian than being the wrestler, see. He'd read up on it. As a matter of fact, he knew more about the Indian laws and bylaws, and everything else around the United States, than most of the real Indians did, so he wouldn't be caught up on it. He didn't want to be caught as a liar, see. Even to most of the wrestlers, he'd swear he was Indian, but he wasn't.*

"This here Indian — a Jewish Indian — I was going to bend over backwards in Twin Falls, Idaho, to let him look good before I beat him. I didn't care about going up there. It was a long ways and it was just a so-so place.

"Well, I don't go for anybody kicking me in the butt, like when I'm getting up. Real showoff; when you're getting up, they come along and give you a side swipe in the butt. It's just like slapping your face and saying, 'You old coward.' I just told him, 'Don't ever do that again.' So, whenever I'm knocked down again and I'm getting up, he kicked me again. So I just beat him two straight falls.

"Afterward, I come up and told him, 'You ever kick me in the butt again, next time I'll break your arm or I'm going to kill ya."

Now, some of these fellows — Saunooke, Chewchki, Jules Strongbow, Joe Beaver — were heels, but all the wrestling redskins I know of today are more honest, faithful and courageous than Tonto. When Chief Jay Strongbow (no relation to Jules), supposedly a Cherokee from Oklahoma, finally gets tired of the villains misdeeds and starts taking his revenge, he goes into a simple little war dance, lifting his knees like pistons until his fringed, moccasin-like wrestling boots are just blurs, and his followers are filling the arena with war whoops. Said Strongbow of his fans:

"I'm just as proud as can be that they have taken to me as they have. Anytime that I wrestle, I'm out there wrestling for all these wonderful people."

A quote like that is enough to make anyone gag, but Strongbow has an even worse effect on some opponents. He once received a most-popular-wrestler trophy in a televised ceremony in Philadelphia, but before he could finish his humble thank-you speech, onto the set rushed opposition manager Lou Albano and two of his charges, Luke Graham and Tarzan Tyler. They ganged up on Strongbow, slapping him, ripping his war bonnet to shreds, and finally breaking the shiny new trophy over his head.

Colorful costumes are also *de rigueur* for the African warriors, the Scotsmen (Black Angus Campbell, Scotty Dawkins, The Great Scott, etc.), and especially the Hawaiians and Samoans, who go back in pro wrestling at least twenty years to Alo Leilani (Al Lolotai), an ex-football guard for the Washington Redskins and Los Angeles Dons, and Duke Keomuka, who used his "stomach claw" hold to produce stomach convulsions and cramping of the abdominal muscles in his unlucky opponents. Prince Maiava, wearing his necklace of boar's teeth, has returned to the ring after a long absence, this time without his aloha-shirted manager, Coconut Willie.

One of the most despised, and therefore successful, villains today is King Curtis Iaukea, a 360-pound ex-lineman for the University of California and the British Columbia Lions. After Iaukea gets his opponent lying helpless in the center of the ring, dazed or maybe unconscious from a series of sneak blows, he runs and does a bellyflop on him *à la* Haystack Calhoun. He calls this vicious move "the big splash."

"My great grandfather was an ambassador to Hawaiian monarchy," claims Iaukea. *"That's why I am permitted to use the title of nobility. If the United States had not come over to annex Hawaii, I would be a king there today."*

Turks, terrible and otherwise, usually having bald heads, mustaches and outfits out of *The Arabian Nights*, go back to the nineteenth century. We've had Ali Baba (Arteen Ekizian), Ali Bey the Turkish Terror, Mustafa the Terrible Turk, and Bob Managoff, the Terrible Turk. Managoff (nee Manoogian; look underneath the fez of a wrestling Turk and you find an Armenian) toured with the famous Frank Gotch for the Sells-Floto Circus in 1916. His son, Bobby, became a world champion in the early 1940s, and his daughter, Kay Armen, was one of the singing stars of the old *Stop the Music* radio show.

Youssouf the Terrible Turk, a big gate attraction around the turn of the century, was really a Marseilles dock worker with a smart manager. Legend has it that he did very well in the United States and sailed for home with $15,000 worth of gold pieces in a money belt strapped around his waist. The ship went down in the Atlantic and the "Turk" with it.

An example of the breed worked briefly for promoter Jack Curley.

"*I recall one who was known as Humid Kala Pasha, who was a Chicago boy by the name of Joe Rickard,*" he said. "*George Siler, the old referee, called him Humid because of his excessive humidity when he was wrestling. Humid was tattooed all over with ships and muscle-dancers and Cupids and one thing and another, and he was very interesting, but he was not a good wrestler.*

"*He got his training working in the gallery of the Trocadero Theater, a burlesque house in old Chicago, keeping order among the patrons, who were always very disorderly during the performance of the cooch dancer. In this work, he was very effective. He used a sawed-off pool cue for moral effect and several times he cleared the entire gallery alone.*"

Besides burlesque and western movies, there is another branch of show biz that wrestling uses as a source of inspiration: the circus freak show. My favorites in this wrestling subspecies are the hairy monsters, including The Wildman, The Beast, Farkas the Wolfman, The Wild Man of Borneo, and The Tree Man, who started his matches from an artificial tree set up in his corner and who once lighted a torch and set fire to the beard of The Mad Russian. There was Joe (Jungle Boy) Vertucci, the Human

Lou Bertucci, The Jungle Boy • 1950

Haystack, who claimed to have been reared in the tangled jungle of the Mato Grosso. Darwin should have lived long enough to study him. And I suppose I must include my father in his guise as The Thing.

Manager Gary Hart showed up in Houston one time with a Mexican protégé called Moon Man, whose hair stood out in all directions and completely covered his face. He could have clipped it off and had enough raw material for eighty fright wigs. Promoter Paul Boesch lost no time in getting him a bout. The original idea was to have him march down the aisle and cause an uproar, but then Hart and Boesch put their conspiring senses of drama together and decided to have Hart lead Moon into the ring with his bushy head hidden under a pillowcase. When the bell rang to start the match and Moon moved to the center of the ring, Hart held on to the pillowcase and WHOOSH, there was revealed suddenly under the bright overhead lights a weird creature who could have scared a pack of slobbering wolves back into their dens.

Among the other categories of freaks are:

Fatties: Haystack Calhoun, Haystack Muldoon, Man Mountain Dean, Elmer Wiggins, The Blimp (Martin Levy), and The Lady Blimp. Levy later actually worked in a freak show, sitting in a trailer playing solitaire, while the customers filed by to gawk at him. Brothers Billy and Benny McGuire from North Carolina claim to weigh more than 640 pounds apiece, but they still manage to ride motorcycles and, in Detroit and elsewhere, struggle up the steps to various rings without the aid of heavy-duty cranes. One of the newest dirigibles is dainty Heather Feather (Peggy Jones), 389 pounds of woman wrestler who trains on sausage pizzas. She enters the ring licking a lollipop and wearing a brightly colored ribbon in her hair. Lolita with lard.

Midgets: Some are indeed midgets and some are dwarfs, but in wrestling programs, they are midgets, period. Just about every one of them has a gimmick apart from his size. There is an Indian, Little Beaver; a human orchid, Fuzzy Cupid; a hick, Farmer Jerome; a cowboy, Billy the Kid, and a nobleman, Lord Clayton Littlebrook.

Giants: The current favorite, especially in Canada, is Jean Ferre (Andre Roussimoff), seven feet four inches tall and anywhere from 390 to 415 pounds.

Angels: They have been out of favor in recent years, but the nation used to be crawling with angels, who were usually huge, powerful men with gargoyle faces that "only a mother could love." The Golden Angel billed himself as "the man with a thousand holds." The Super Swedish Angel (Tor Johnson) was "the world's ugliest wrestler." We had The Polish Angel (Wladislaw Talun, also known as "old prune head"), The Czech Angel and Swedish Angel (Phil Olafsson), who later managed a riding academy in Salt Lake City.

The Swedish Angel • 1949

My dad, judo-expert Butch Madray, and The Swedish Angel once went in the same car from L.A. to the matches in San Bernardino, Calif. Since there was plenty of room in the car, Butch's wife Alice went along. Like most women, she was both fascinated and repulsed by Olafson's looks, and was a bit nervous around him at first. On the way home, she was fast asleep with her head on his shoulder.

"He had such a good personality," said Pop, *"that after a while, you never noticed his looks or his size. He got to be beautiful. He was one of the nicest, kindest guys."*

The man who probably started it all was The French Angel (Maurice Tillet). A disease in his youth, probably a glandular dysfunction known as acromegaly, distorted Tillet's facial features, and when he worked in England as a circus strong man, he was billed as *"that ferocious monstrosity, not a human being, but 20 stone of brutality."* An ex-U.S. wrestler, Karl Pojello, brought him to America and they had good financial success.

Time's writer described him, colorfully if not flatteringly, as having cordwood arms, a nose like a Bartlett pear, and fiddle-case feet. My pop remembers wrestling him once, shoving him in the face and being startled because *"my whole hand was just on his nose! Wide and big! His head was more misshapen than anyone's."*

Tillet, whose health was so bad when he worked in the U.S. that he had to use various ruses to get state licenses, died in France in 1954, only thirteen hours after he learned of the death of his close friend Pojello.

In 1958, a flamboyant wrestling promoter named Jack Pfefer introduced his latest sensation, The *Lady* Angel, who had not a hair on her head. Explained Pfefer:

"She is bald on account of she escaped from the fiends who invaded her native country by taking the guns from the secret police who came to arrest her and

The incredibly ugly French Angel punishes poor Rudy Dusek. Tillet's box-office success inspired a succession of imitators, almost one for every nation: "The Swedish Angel," "The Super Swedish Angel," "The Canadian Angel," and others.

members of her family and throwing them [selves] into river from vich there was escape. She lost her beautiful hair in the battle and decided to stay bald as that vas a good disguise — also it helps her wrestle. Any clown who tries a headlock on The Lady Angel finds it is like trying to hold a bowling ball dot has been covered vith butter."

Gee, uh, great, Jack. How about an interview with this buttered baldy? No? Why not?

"The Lady Angel comes from an old Central European family," he said. *"And members of the family vould disown her if they learned she vas wrestling. They think she is sending them money from vat she makes hanging by her hair in a circus act."*

Geneva Huckabee,
The Lady Angel

Another Jack Pfefer contribution to our culture — perhaps she was The Lady Angel using another gimmick — was The African Masked Black Pussycat.

Which brings us to the most popular and enduring props of all, masks. Red masks, black masks, white masks, green masks, purple masks. Phantoms, Terrors, Avengers, Flashes. Almost every wrestling territory in the country has at least one masked marauder, usually a villain of the most despicable type, looking as sinister as a hooded executioner on duty at the chopping blocks of Henry VIII.

Promoters can milk the gimmick in dozens of ways. If he loses tonight to Sonny King, then The Red Shadow will have to demask! Who is The Scarlet Pimpernel and why is he doing all these nasty things to people? Order your Dr. X T-shirts and Dr. X masks today! George Becker has vowed to rip off The Great Bolo's hood tonight in the Charlotte Coliseum and at last reveal that no-doubt cowardly countenance!

Alex Goldstein, a sort of French Pfefer, had a marvelous pair working at the same time in Paris and environs. The White Angel was as pure as homogenized milk and wore outfits of the same color. The Masked Man, exuding evil vibrations, dressed all in black to match his heart, except for a red leather belt which came in handy once in a while when he was in the mood to strangle somebody. At one point, The Masked Man offered a cash bonus to any foe who could remove his mask. Good guy after good guy came frustratingly close, until finally, before a huge crowd, The Masked Man was beaten and the hood ripped off — only to reveal a second mask underneath, glued to his face and supposedly impossible to remove!

A character calling himself The Invader used the same dirty trick in St. Louis recently, but naked faces are revealed quite often. In France, The White Angel, saintly and beloved, finally did get around to showing the fans what he really looked like. At the end of dramatic, slam-bang matches, he unmasked himself before packed houses all over the country.

"It isn't a sport anymore," said one disgusted fan. *"It's a striptease!"*

Another twist, told by The Mighty Hercules: He had Lou Thesz, champion of the National Wrestling Alliance, beaten — in fact, lying unconscious on the mat, cold as a Popsicle. But the irate fans screamed to the referee that Hercules had an illegal foreign object hidden under his mask. The ref ordered Hercules to remove the mask and prove that he was "clean." He refused and the title went back to Thesz.

"It was a ridiculous charge," said Herc with a snarl. *"A wrestler of my ability doesn't need to cheat."*

In Amarillo, Tex., in 1972, The Spoiler made a bet with babyface Red Bastien. If The Spoiler won, Bastien would have to shave off his mustache. If Bastien won, The Spoiler would remove his mask. Bastien won, and The Spoiler was revealed to the anxiously waiting crowd as Don Jardine.

"I shouldn't have agreed to that match," lamented Jardine. *"Bastien losing his mustache wouldn't have ended his career. Mine is over now. I just can't wrestle without my mask. It's part of me. That's like telling the Lone Ranger he can't wear his mask anymore."*

Just as with Terrible Turks, masked men are not new in wrestling. Perhaps the first big commotion caused by one was back during World War I at an international tournament held for a number of nights on the stage of the old Manhattan Opera House on Thirty-fourth Street, with the mat just behind the footlights. It is said that actor Douglas Fairbanks, probably scouting for some acrobatic new moves for his costume movies, seldom missed a bout.

Ex-lightweight champion George Bothner was the referee and the combatants included Alex Aberg, Dr. Benjamin Roller, Wladek Zbyszko (brother of the more famous Stanislaus), Pierre le Colosse ("Pierre the Giant"), Ivan Linow the Russian Lion, Sula Hevonpaa the Furious Finn, Demetrius Tofalos of Greece, and a young man from Wisconsin (Robert H. Friedrich) who called himself "Ed (Strangler) Lewis," a pseudonym borrowed from an earlier Wisconsin wrestler, Evan (Strangler) Lewis.

One evening, a gentleman in a dress suit stood up in the orchestra section, not to boo or cheer, but to shout that the best wrestler of all had been barred from the competition. Before he could yell very much, he, and a hooded hulk of a man sitting next to him, were hustled out of the place. He was a persistent cuss, however.

IS MORT HENDERSON THE "MASKED MARVEL?"

TWO PICTURES THAT INDICATE THE IDENTITY OF THE ALTOONA (PA.) EXPERT WITH THE MYSTERIOUS WRESTLER NOW COMPETING IN THE INTERNATIONAL WRESTLING TOURNAMENT, NEW YORK CITY.

The next night he and his protégé showed up in box seats and he got a little further with his accusation.

This went on for several nights, so that some spectators were yelling for the promoter, one Samuel Rachmann, to let the shadowy stranger enter the tournament. Finally, Rachmann bowed to public pressure and announced that The Masked Marvel would have his chance on the opera-house stage where, the promoter's tone of voice hinted, the poor bastard would do more sobbing then Enrico Caruso in "Pagliacci."

Well, Mr. Marvel was a sensation, at least for a while. Big and powerful as he was mysterious, he polished off several opponents in a row with little trouble and then faced Tofalos, the Greek who had been a champion weight-lifter in Athens. The Masked Marvel won easily. New York City loved him, not realizing he had been hired for $150 a week to don the hood and add a little spice to the proceedings. (He later had to sue for his money.)

Strangler Lewis was getting $200 a week and he proved that he was worth it. When it came his turn to meet the mystery guest, he beat him and sent him back to Altoona, Pa., where he was just plain Mort Henderson, railroad detective, chasing hoboes off the trains.

Since Henderson, there have been innumerable wrestlers who have performed incognito. In the late 1920s, Joe Stecher, who boasted that he had developed his famous scissors hold by practicing on sacks of grain, barnstormed the country battling The Masked Marvel, this time played by a Nebraskan named Pete Sauer, who later took the pseudonym Ray Steele.

The famous Golden Greek, Jim Londos (Christopher Theophelus), did not wear a mask, but he did use a disguise in his early days. In small towns, he would go to the matches dressed in the clothes of a construction laborer — very authentic-looking, right down to the plaster on his shoes and overalls. At the proper moment, he would stand up and challenge one of the wrestlers in the ring, quite often Ray Steele. Sometimes there would be bets involving some local sucker. Londos became known as The Wrestling Plasterer.

• Gino Garibaldi came out of retirement as a masked man called Zorro, but the longtime fans at L.A.'s Olympic Auditorium recognized his distinctive walk right away and called out, *"Hi, Gino."* Back into retirement.

• To add a touch of the macabre, a fellow billed as Fantomas (fantôme in French means "ghost") wrestled in a tight black outfit with a fluorescent skeleton painted on it.

• The Red Devil, circa 1934, wore a Satan costume with horns.

• The Russians, Ivan and Igor (Pedro Godoy and Juan Sebastian), were supposedly defectors from the USSR who wore masks to hide their identities from SMERSH. They destroyed opponents with a blow called the "Russian hammer."

• The Gorilla was wheeled up to the ring in a large cage as he shook the bars and raged at the fans.

• A nut calling himself The Clawman not only has his wife in a mask, too, but also has Clawchildren and Clawdog.

Benji Ramirez was one of several mummies who have tried their wrappings in professional wrestling. Of course, it is just a variation on the old Masked Marvel theme long popular in the sport.

"The man whose tenacity I admired most was The Mummy," said Houston promoter Boesch. *"The Mummy was a Mexican — no, he was a South American, then he came from South America and wrestled in Mexico a lot. Then he came to this country. But this fellow wore this heavy type of thing with bandages put around with tape.*

"It was cumbersome, and imagine wrestling in that thing for thirty, forty minutes, with this wild mop of hair sticking out the top. Damndest thing you ever saw. Just the inconvenience of it and the physical torture he had to go through!"

A plain old mask can be trouble enough, as George Linnehan found out.

"I wore a mask one time," he said. *"The promoter talked me into this in a town in New Jersey. The night I had the mask on, I was in with this handsome young fella, you know, and the match was about ten minutes old and I was fighting for my life — not with the fella, but with the people! I was trying to get out of the ring and to the dressing room, and when I got in, that mask came off and I never put one on since. In fact, it was coming off on the way in the door. I said, 'No more!' "*

Is the popularity of masks among pro wrestlers justified? *"Well, some of them have it and some of them haven't,"* said Boesch. *"It doesn't give them the ability and it doesn't give them the drawing power. A lot of these guys would be better off without it. We had one fellow here, Tim Woods, who called himself Mr. Wrestling. Tim was in a white mask, white suit. Everybody liked him, but underneath that he had a good-looking face and a great background. He was a great wrestler at the University of Michigan, he went to two or three different colleges, he had a degree in engineering. And I finally prevailed upon him to take off his mask and he became a better card with it off.*

"A mask doesn't give the man a real personality in most cases. You look at a man and judge his personality by the way he smiles or laughs, or whatever face he makes, and there you have just an impassive hood over his head and that's all there is to it.

"If you want masked men, you've got to go to Mexico because everybody in Mexico is a masked wrestler. I've often thought the way to make a fortune is to go into the wrestling-mask business and go to Mexico. They give fabulous attention to all of the details; the capes and the masks. Mil Mascaras is the most proud individual. You've never seen him go into the ring with a spot on a shoe or on a cape — on anything that he wears."

Isn't it a relatively new thing to have masked *heroes*?

"They're mostly Mexicans because there they're accepted for what they are, a certain character in this garb. El Santo — The Saint, what else? That's the way he comes in in the Mexican movies. He saves the day in a silver mask. Mil Mascaras along the same lines. The Blue Demon, El Olympico.

"The first Mexican wrestler we had here with a mask on was El Medico. He was the real daddy of them all in Mexico and he was a fine gentleman, really. In Mexico, El Medico was a greatly revered individual. They really went for him. He died of cancer. Pictures of him without his mask are very rare."

El Medico ("The Doctor") burst on the Texas scene in 1957 and was an immediate hit, and not just because there is a big Mexican-American population there. He had charisma, even though people couldn't see his facial expressions. He died in 1960 and the subsequent flood of mostly Latin imitators has included El Medico II, The Medics (one of whom died on a tour of Japan), The Interns, etc. South-of-the-border movie star Mil Mascaras ("Thousand Masks") and his brother, El Sicodelico ("The Psychedelic"), are two of the best.

Mascaras, as his name implies, has more masks than a large Halloween party, plus an excellent physique. He is so well-known and popular that, in 1973, the New York State Athletic Commission, which had banned masked wrestlers shortly after The Masked Marvel invaded the opera house, made an exception for Mil and allowed him to appear on cards at Madison Square Garden. The Black Demon (a non-Latin who is listed as coming from "parts unknown") and El Olympico have not been afforded the same privilege. They have to wrestle in hoods with their faces exposed. At one recent Garden match I saw, The Black Demon's opponent tried to tear off his hood, for what reason I can't guess unless maybe he wanted to expose a bald spot.

Mascaras has never been de-masked, but he had a close call in Los Angeles. He fought Black Gordman at the Olympic Auditorium, where a large percentage of the customers speak Spanish and probably had seen such Mascaras film epics as *Champions of Justice*. Before the match, it was agreed that if Gordman lost, he would have his great black head of hair shaved off. If Mil lost, he would have to remove his mask. He swore he would never wrestle again if that happened. Well, before a decision was reached, the bitter enemies collided in the middle of the ring and knocked each other out, and nobody won the bet. So, naturally, the Olympic management arranged a rematch under the same conditions.

Mascaras appeared in the ring with his mask patched together with tape. He explained to the referee that Gordman's co-conspirator, Bull Ramos, had tried to rip it off in the dressing room. Midway through the battle, Ramos passed Gordman a penknife from ringside and the villain used it to try to cut off Mil's mask, but our hero kicked the penknife out of Gordman's hand, beat the hell out of him, and pinned him. Gordman was sheared right there in the ring, a fitting end for a black sheep.

"... He only ripped the top open," said Mil, his career and secret identity still safe. *"A lot of fans saw my hair, but that was all."*

For a wrestler like Mascaras, or the late El Medico, who keeps his mask on much of the time, it understandably creates problems moving about in modern society. The Mighty Hercules told of having to call ahead to restaurants and warn proprietors that they were going to have a strange — and tough-looking customer. Mascaras once fled from some autograph seekers, ran out of the Houston booking office and jumped into a waiting car — only to see a policeman appear suddenly with pistol in hand, sure he had happened along in the midst of a robbery escape.

My dad tells of the night Wee Willie Davis ran into a highway roadblock in California.

"I don't know what he was going by, just The Masked Terror or something," said Pop. *"But there was a robbery by a masked man in a couple of service stations in Bakersfield. So there was a roadblock going out of town and here he comes with the hood on. He was driving away from the arena. They stopped him and he wouldn't take it off. He doesn't much like police, anyway, but it just happened to be there were eight or nine police cars, and he wasn't going to fight all those guys. Otherwise, he probably would have.*

"He continued to refuse, so they handcuffed him, picked him up, and put him in the Black Maria, a regular paddy wagon, and took him to jail, and in jail *he wouldn't even take it off.*

"He told them, 'Call the promoter.'

"So, they called the promoter to come down and identify him, tell them who he was. The promoter arrived and said, 'Take the God-darned mask off, for crying out loud!'

"He says, 'No sir, your town's going to be killed and it ain't going to be me that's going to do it.'

"He wouldn't take the mask off and he didn't *take the mask off, either. They finally let him go. That's the way I heard the story, anyway. Why they didn't rip it off him when they had him handcuffed, I don't know. Maybe they figured even a masked wrestler had civil rights."*

Davis obviously could have used some tips on smooth masked living from The Masked Man.

That arch-villain of France was on a train leaving the country. *In* costume. He wanted to take a nap and avoid any hassle with police and customs, so he pinned a publicity picture, with explanatory caption, to his coat lapel and went to sleep. Nobody bothered him.

Chapter 4
The Lady with the Cauliflower Head

In Titusville, Fla., near Cape Kennedy, a husband and wife came home late one night and caught a burglar in the act of ransacking their house. The panicked intruder lashed out at the man and knocked him down, but the woman stood in his path of escape and grabbed hold of him.

"*The first time I can't beat a woman,*" yelled the burglar, "*I'll quit!*"

The heroine, Mrs. Patrick Lynch, later described the scene for local reporters. "*Boy, was he surprised,*" she said. "*Patrick was hit in the stomach. He has a pacemaker and that guy could have killed him. It made me good and mad.*

"*I pinned the guy and knocked him good. His head hit the coffee table when I pinned him and there was blood all over my white living-room carpet. He finally got away, but the police ought to be able to spot him. His face was tore up real good.*"

Yes, the burglar had had the bad luck of tangling with an ex-woman wrestler, the former Ann Marie Antonelli, who said she was a ten-year veteran of the ring.

"*I wasn't ever famous or anything,*" she said, "*but I was pretty tough. I still am.*"

Women wrestlers have been in the forefront of the feminist movement since before Gloria Steinem bought her first pair of sunglasses or Ti-Grace Atkinson took her first karate lesson. Most of them are pretty tough and some of them are even pretty. The friendly neighborhood purse-snatcher has to make sure that his victim is not Natasha the Hatchet Lady. Get fresh with the beauty who looks like Yvette Mimieux and she's liable to be Maria Laverne, who can give the kind of body press a masher doesn't expect.

Women have had to fight for recognition and acceptance from male (and female) customers, male promoters, and those male chauvinist pugs, the men wrestlers, but their toughest opponents have been the do-gooders, lawmakers and bureaucrats, such as the Michigan athletic commissioner who asked in 1963, "*Would you like to see your sister wrestling?*" Or the Indiana governor who saw a filmed women's match on television and promptly banned similar shows in his state. Or the New Jersey officials who, in the early '50s, allowed women to wrestle only while standing up.

One of the funniest furors was in the Canadian city of Saskatoon, where the churches, Salvation Army, Women's Christian Temperance Union, and who knows what other groups urged the city fathers to ban the brawling broads. The local Roman Catholic bishop said that such shows were "*against the traditional Christian culture of which we are a part*" and that promoters were trying to "*feed the lower and baser appetites of those who watch.*"

"*Female wrestling is a crude, degrading spectacle, bound to have a coarsening effect on spectator and participant alike,*" said a Protestant clergyman, not to be out-bluenosed. "*We cannot conceive that such exhibitions would have no adverse bearing on the number of sexual misdemeanors among young people and attacks made upon women.*"

The obvious counter argument is that women should have the right to be crude, degrading, and coarse, too. Why should males have all the fun? And, as wrestler Betty Niccoli has argued, *"Men shouldn't be the only ones allowed to get hurt."*

"We found out long ago," said another, *"that if we can do wash, drive taxis, fly airplanes, play basketball, deliver mail, work as riveters and garage mechanics, we should be able to wrestle."*

In 1955, the Illinois Supreme Court upheld the right of women to wrestle in that state and said the athletic commission could not prevent Rose Roman from working at her trade unless the legislature enacted a law expressly forbidding it. California had passed just such a law in 1944, preventing women from participating in public combat for profit. (Scratch each other's eyes out at Hollywood and Vine, ladies, but don't charge admission.) That law is now off the books and women's wrestling is legal in the Golden State.

The most important bastion of male chauvinism to fall was New York, on June 5, 1972, when the state athletic commission knocked down its long-standing policy of refusing to issue wrestling licenses to women.

"There are many reasons why the commission acted at this time," said Chairman Edwin B. Dooley. *"Just a few months ago, I lifted the long ban on properly accredited and assigned female sportswriters, permitting them now to sit in the working press rows at boxing matches. Women wrestlers are licensed in about twelve other states and jurisdictions. In checking with the New Jersey State Athletic Commission, recently I found that lady wrestlers and wrestling in its state has been successful and has created no special problems."*

The principal supplier of women wrestlers is Lillian Ellison — alias Fabulous Moolah — of Columbia, S.C., whose voice and dipped-in-molasses southern accent call up visions of Scarlett O'Hara twirling her parasol. In the flesh, or I should say in her tights, she looks like what she is; a tough, middle-aged bird who has been women's champion for sixteen years or so. If a promoter wants to spice up his card with some females, all he need do is call Moolah on the telephone and place his order. Perhaps Moolah will send him Paula Kaye, or Susan Green, or Lilly Thomas, but if he puts up enough money, and if his state athletic commission doesn't have strict age requirements, he might even get Moolah herself.

For Madison Square Garden's first show after the ban against women was lifted, promoter Vince McMahon and his aide, Willie Gilzenberg, put Moolah in against Vicki Williams. Moolah won, as she always does.

(I should inject here that probably the most accomplished woman wrestler in history was a Tartar princess named Aiyaruk, daughter of Kaidu, whose feats were described, and no doubt exaggerated, by Marco Polo after his travels through the Orient. The king was anxious to get her married off, but she refused to accept any nobleman who could not better her in a wrestling match. According to Marco Polo's account, gallants from many lands accepted her challenge and her stakes. She wagered her hand in marriage, each opponent put up 100 horses. *"In this way, she had gained more than 10,000 horses,"* wrote Marco, which meant that more than 100 suitors had literally been "thrown over."

In A.D. 1280, Kaidu matched his strapping daughter with a handsome prince, who put up a *thousand* horses for the chance to be her husband. Kaidu wanted Aiyaruk to lose on purpose, but instead, she threw the prince to the palace floor just like all the rest. It sounds like a script for a *Wonder Woman* comic book. Princess Aiyaruk would be a perfect pseudonym for one of the women in Moolah's stable.)

Before she became Fabulous, Moolah was known as Slave Girl Moolah, the humble servant of a bushy-haired wrestler billed as Elephant Boy. In other words, a spicy prop. Elephant Boy entered the ring dressed like an Indian gentleman of immense wealth. Moolah followed along in a sarong, rather than a sari, and her main job seemed to be caring for her master's cloak, which, it was claimed, had once belonged to Catherine the Great of Russia and was insured for a million dollars.

Slave Girl Moolah & Elephant Boy

Her days as Elephant Boy's stooge are not mentioned when she gives out her own life story: She was the only girl in a family with thirteen children. Her mother, who died when she was eight, was Irish, and her father, a South Carolina building contractor, was full-blooded Cherokee. She fondly remembers being taken to the wrestling matches by her father. She was graduated from high school at age 14 and went off to South Africa with a brother who was a Golden Gloves boxer. He boxed there and she pestered a wrestling promoter into letting her make her professional debut, at the tender age of 15. She got her nickname because of her announced intention to wrestle for "*all the moolah I can get my hands on.*"

Not counting her days in "slavery," Moolah made her United States pro debut in Boston in 1954 and progressed so well that, in 1956, she was one of fourteen women invited to a championship tournament in Baltimore. She advanced to the final and beat the then-recognized champ, June Byers, in two straight falls.

Today she is the foremost female villain in the country — the high heel — doing anything she has to do to win.

"*There are places I'm really comfortable in, like Washington, Baltimore, and Dallas,*" she said. "*They hate me there, but they really love me, you can feel it. And my hometown, I can do anything there. But it all comes down to devotion. You have to have it in your blood; you've got to eat, sleep and live wrestling.*"

When women's wrestling was legalized in New Jersey, promoter Willie Gilzenberg brought her and Patti Neilson in to meet another pair of females. She ignited a free-for-all when she twice hit the referee, and the fans in the Elizabeth Armory loved it when all four wrestlers landed on the poor fellow at once.

"*It was fast, it was funny, and it lacked the suety, campy, often crude melodrama of the men,*" reported columnist Robert Lipsyte in the *New York Times.*

A woman sitting next to me at the women's Madison Square Garden breakthrough match in 1972 wasn't so kind. "*Moolah looks like an old, beaten-up broad,*" she said.

Beaten-up she may be, but, with her talent-booking operation prospering and the championship still in her possession, she has indeed fulfilled her wish to accumulate lots of moolah. She lives in her home state with her most recent husband and part of her stable of wrestlers.

"I have twenty-five acres at home in Columbia, South Carolina, with a ten-acre lake, and it cost a lot of pain to get that place," she said. *"Every bit was worth it.*

"I forget that I'm a wrestler when I'm not working. I dress conservatively, act like a lady, and associate with intelligent, well-educated people, many of whom have no idea of what I do for a living. I'm not like some of these egotistical peroxide blondes, male and female, who want to draw a crowd everywhere they go."

Gape away, let your eyeballs bulge! Mildred Burke in her prime was an amazing and awesome sight—wrestling her was a rotten way to make a living.

The other dominant performer in the history of women's wrestling, Mildred Burke, is now in her late fifties and should also be basking in fancy surroundings, but she isn't. She lives in a modest home in California's San Fernando Valley and works with her son for a soft-water company. On the side, she operates Mildred Burke's Private School of Professional Wrestling in North Hollywood. Inside the claustrophobic little gym, which consists of two stores with the separating wall knocked out, there is a photograph hanging on the north wall showing the young Burke flexing her impressive biceps. Time and sedentary habits have softened her muscles, and her figure is now more in keeping with the image of a grandmother who can cook a great pot of chili.

Out of her school has grown the World Wide Women's Wrestling Association, a relatively unsuccessful rival of Moolah's group. The WWWWA champion the last time I looked was Marie Vagnone, the daughter of two professional wrestlers. She is a fairly attractive blonde who grew up in Columbus, Ohio, and Norwalk, Calif. *"Her mother and I forced her into it a little bit,"* admitted Burke, *"but she has a very pretty body and is a very sweet girl."* Burke's other favored protégé is Princess War Star, a nice-looking girl who lives in San Bernardino, Calif., but claims she grew up on a Zuni Indian reservation in New Mexico. The princess is in awe of her teacher.

"I don't think I could beat her," said War Star. *"She's just a fantastic wrestler."*

Not such a fantastic booking agent, however. WWWWA girls are used regularly in Japan, Burke said, *"because I'm dependable, I've got the best girls, I keep 'em supplied with new faces."* They are also used by a promotion group in Kentucky, and occasionally in the Los Angeles area, but they seldom get hired by promoters elsewhere, even in San Francisco. Burke thinks it is a plot against her by the National Wrestling Alliance, a powerful association of promoters.

"*They don't have any girls who can touch my girls,*" she said, suddenly changing from the motherly "Millie" of her little gym into an angry, frustrated businesswoman with her claws out. "*I represent the years when the wrestler was* somebody. *I represent the years when the wrestlers got paid the way they should be paid.*

"*I represent everything they're* [the NWA] *trying to tear down.*"

Once she got warmed up, she started clawing Moolah verbally. Moolah simply ignores her, her school, and the WWWWA.

"*I have Moolah's girls try to come to me because Moolah treats 'em like dogs and they're prisoners,*" said Burke. "*I had one girl of mine that run off and went with Moolah. I don't think Moolah lured her off. She's wrestled as White Venus and all different names. She's changed about ten different times. Well, I took that girl — she was eighteen when I took her and had her sign a contract, but at that time, you weren't of age 'til you were twenty-one. Now they've got a new law.*

"*I made her a lot of money. I sent her to Japan, I sent her to Canada twice, she was making five hundred dollars a week ... When she came to me, she was a horrible-lookin' person. She was five feet eight inches and weighed two hundred thirty-five pounds and had her hair cut off short like a man's. She wasn't a lesbian, but she had all the appearances because she was built funny and had a big ol' body, but I saw in her very pretty features. So, we got her trimmed down, let her hair grow out, bleached it blonde, and she made a very, very good girl.*"

Then she ran off to join Moolah's troupe, where she is supposedly unhappy, but also where, Burke admits, "*they do work more because she's got an in with the Alliance. But right now, her days are to an end, at least here in California, because I demanded her age. I know she's as old as I am, and I'm fifty-seven. She hasn't wrestled here since I demanded to know her age.*

"*Really, I don't begrudge the girl wrestling. I really don't. What I begrudge is her keeping mine from wrestling ... The main reason I dislike her — when California*

Mildred Burke

opened up again for women, I had some girls training at the time, and I wrote to Moolah to let her know it was opening up and I said, 'Moolah, I'd like to work with you. You have everything on that side and I'll have everything on this side and we'll work together."

Her effort to divide the country failed, and now she has to settle for far less than half. Very unlike the old days when, for a long time, she and her second husband had it all to themselves.

Born Mildred Bliss in Coffeyville, Kan., she grew up in Kansas City, Mo., and Glendale, Calif. Her father never had a regular job, but did all right from time to time by inventing things, including a non-skid chain and a soap for mechanics. She dropped out of Kansas City's Manual High School and got married at age 17. While she and her mother ran a restaurant in Kansas City, she got pregnant, divorced her nonworking husband, and found her life's work at a local arena.

"Before I separated from him, he and I had attended a couple of wrestling matches," she said. *"At that time, Billy Wolfe was Missouri state champion and I saw him wrestling on the card. That was my first experience attending matches. It was really strange because then, in a crowd of three thousand or four thousand, you'd see maybe six or seven women at the most. They were probably the wives of the wrestlers or something. Women started attending wrestling matches when the women started wrestling. Anyway, there were very few in the crowd.*

"After I separated from my husband and had the baby, I kept going down to the arena and pestering this Billy Wolfe to teach me to wrestle.

"He said, 'You're too small. Even if you were good, who'd pay to see you?'

"I never was more than five-feet-two and I was one hundred fifteen pounds at that time. So I said, 'Well, give me a chance anyway,' *and I kept pestering him for three or four months. Finally, one day, he had hired a gypsy boy to take me up in the gym privately and slam me so hard that I'd quit bothering him. I think he gave him a whole dollar, which was a day's wages in those days.*

"Anyway, I'd never been in a ring before in any way, shape or form. He coached the boy a little, privately, and we came out from the corner, and the boy picked me up in a body slam, and he slammed me so hard the dust went about three feet high, I think, but when we hit, I managed to turn him over and pin him.

"Billy Wolfe said, 'Wait a minute, something's wrong with this. Get up and try that again.' *He goes over in the corner and coaches the boy a little more and then said,* 'Now do it again.' *This time, I'd learned a little something; I'd learned how he'd picked me up, so I picked him up and I slammed him and I didn't let him from under me. So I beat him twice in about ten seconds actual time.*

"… Then he brought in several larger girls that were girlfriends of wrestlers, or wives or something. They'd worked out a little bit in the gym. And he started putting those against me and I was defeating all of them."

Burke was just a good, natural athlete, and naturally tough. She remembered an incident from her grade-school days in California:

"The boys were playing against the girls one time, and the boys were eliminating all the girls out of the game by just kicking 'em in the shins. They weren't trying to kick the ball, they were just kicking 'em in the shins, and I was the most stupid one out there. I stayed in no matter how many times they kicked me in the shins. I wound up with what they call white swelling on the shinbone. And I was laid up a long time, but they never did get me out of the game. I was there or die! This comes out of stubbornness; I don't know what else you'd put it on."

Wolfe eventually realized he had something unusual and took her on.

Billy Wolfe instructing Violet Viann on the proper method of applying a leg scissors to one of her fellow students • Jan. 21, 1954

"*At that time,*" said Burke, "*he was running a show on a carnival every summer, so he took me out for two summers on the carnival, 1935 and the beginning of 1936. This was during the Depression years when ... if you had a top job, you only made twenty-five dollars a week. ... I had worked in a restaurant for four dollars a week, and that's seven days a week and twelve hours a day! Now, my real name was Mildred Bliss, but we're on the carnival one night. Bill's standing up there giving a big spiel about this great lady wrestler, and I'm standing down behind the tent ready to come out and he says, 'I now give you Mildred Burke,' and I'm looking around to see who the hell Mildred Burke is. He never told me he was going to give me that name. Then I went up the steps and got on the ball board. Why he chose that name, I don't know. He just told me he didn't think Bliss was a good name. He said there was an old saying, 'Ignorance is bliss.' He was right.*"

"*Now, you wouldn't believe this could happen, but it was this way. He was offering twenty-five dollars to any man within twenty pounds of my weight that could defeat me, say, like in ten or fifteen minutes. Well, actually, all I had to do was be defensive. I didn't have to beat the man. I wrestled almost two hundred men and the only time I was defeated — it wasn't because I was pinned — but I got knocked out. I was wrestling a collegiate wrestler in Omaha, Nebraska, and I picked him up to bodyslam him, and when I did, he managed to double his knee up in-between us, and when I fell, I fell on his knee which knocked all the air out of me. The next thing I knew, they had me outside the tent trying to revive me.*"

Female wrestlers had been on theatrical circuits before — Cora Livingstone was probably the most famous of these — but it was Burke who pioneered in the arenas. Her first bout was for Gust Karras, whose booking office was, and still is, in the old Pony Express town of St. Joseph, Mo.

"*The houses were empty,*" she said. "*People just didn't have money to eat on, so you know they weren't going to pay for entertainment. So I called Mr. Karras up and asked him if he'd let me wrestle in Bethany, Missouri, and he said, 'Well,* sure, I'll let you wrestle, but I don't know who you're going to wrestle. If you can find somebody to wrestle you, it's all right with me.'

Didn't Wolfe help her make this transition? *"Oh, I got it! I trained myself, too. Wolfe never taught me a hold. He always took credit for it, but he's got his first hold to this day to teach me! Anyway, he was a great manager and managed me out of everything I ever made, so he was good at managing, I'll say that.*

"So I went to the match that night in Bethany and there were, I believe, four men's matches on the card and then mine. We were supposed to be the third. The second match went on, was over with, and my opponent hadn't shown up, so they had to put the fourth match on. It was almost over and I didn't know what to do, so I saw a deputy sheriff standing outside the dressing-room door and I said, 'Do you know who it is that I'm supposed to wrestle here tonight?' *And he says,* 'Oh, sure, everybody knows him. He works in the restaurant down here.' *I said,* 'Well, what are we going to do? We're supposed to be on next and he's not even here!' *He says,* 'Not here!' *And the place was* packed; *standing room was sold out, they were standing on stepladders lookin' in the windows. It was unbelievable, nobody could imagine such a crowd.*

"The deputy took off and went down to the restaurant, and there was the fella still behind the counter workin', and he says, 'What are you doin' down here. You're supposed to be there wrestling that girl, and the place is sold out.'

"He says, 'I don't dare go up there. She's going to kill me, and then after she kills me, my wife's going to kill me. I just don't dare go.'

"The deputy said, 'Well, that's just too bad. You accepted it and you're goin'.' *So, he put him in the sheriff's car and hauled him down there. And he got to the arena. At the time I used to wear like a one-piece bathing suit and then a short bathing suit, like trunks. He said,* 'I can't wrestle. I don't have anything to wrestle in.' *I said,* 'Don't let that stop you,' *and I just pulled off my outside trunks and said,* 'Here, put these on.' *They were elastic and they fit all right.*

"They made him put them on and he says, 'Oh, my God. You're going to kill me, and then my wife's going to kill me for sure.' *It so happened he was a pretty wiry little fella. I was more scared of him than he was of me, but I just kept my bluff and my front up. I said,* 'Now listen, you just take it easy and you don't worry about anything. I'll make you look good out there before I beat ya.' *I didn't know anything and neither did he! I did want him to get in the ring because I wanted to have that match.*

"He put on my tights and got in the ring barefooted. It was comical as heck if you could have seen the whole thing. We got in the ring and there we stood, blocking each other, shoving around and everything. Pretty soon, I managed to drop and go behind him. I didn't want to beat him that quick. Actually, if he hadn't been so scared, he probably could have defeated me, but I just had my bluff in on him. I had several good chances to pin him quick and I let him back up and stood him around, then finally I beat him in about ten minutes. I don't remember the exact time.

"The crowd just absolutely went wild! He couldn't wait to get back to the dressing room. He said, 'Oh, my God, that was terrific. I want to do this every night. Can I go with ya and wrestle you again somewhere?'

"I never did wrestle him again, but he showed up through the years every once in a while at one of my matches. And his wife was even proud of it, you know.

"I had another funny experience in the second match, in Leavenworth, Kansas. They managed to get a local boy again to wrestle me there. The promoter or somebody got ahold of him. The same thing — the place was sold out again

*and I hadn't even set eyes on him. I didn't know
what he looked like or anything, so Billy Wolfe said,*
'I better wander over by the men's dressing room
and just kinda see what he looks like.'

"*The door was standing ajar a little bit and he saw
a whole lot of red in there and thought,* 'What is all
that red material?' *He kinda stuck his head in the
door and here this fella is sittin' there in long red
underwear!* Bill said, 'My God, fella, what have you
got that on for?'

"*He says,* 'Well, the men wrestlers said I couldn't
let my body touch hers and I couldn't find anything
else to cover me up.' *He came back and told me
about it, and I said,* 'For goodness sakes, go in there
and have him take it off. Don't let him go in there
lookin' like that.'

"*In that match we blocked each other. We were
really going after it and we blocked each other for
eight solid minutes. Neither one could get anywhere
with the other. After eight minutes, I finally got a*

Burke vs. Mae Weston

*break, went behind him, dropped him and pinned him. And for two years, they
said you could see him doing road-work for a return match. I never had that one,
either.*"

The next step, naturally, was to have women versus women. Burke and Wolfe
traveled through the South with a carnival and met a man whose daughter was
also doing a little carnival wrestling. Wolfe and the man went to see Chris Jordan,
the Birmingham promoter at that time.

"*Oh, good heavens. Girls?*" said Jordan. "*That would really kill the town. That
would* really *kill it. They wouldn't be able to do anything but pull hair.*"

Nevertheless, he was talked into it, and the match was such a success that he
couldn't get enough. He had sellouts all over his territory.

"*Chris was so impressed that he made up a belt for me,*" said Burke. "*A southern
championship belt, which I wore for awhile. Then the Midwest Wrestling
Association held a tournament out of Columbus, Ohio, and that's when I was
awarded the world's championship belt. Wilma Gordon, Mae Weston, Gladys
Gillam, Rose Evans — those were the four main names that I can remember.
Those were the four girls following right behind me into the business.*

"*People wanted to see women wrestlers and were willing to pay to see them.
They especially wanted to see the woman who had started this revolution, the
one and only Mildred Burke.*

"*Naturally I was flattered, but most of all I was delighted that my great idea had
been right. ... I became Mrs. Billy Wolfe, although we kept it quiet because Billy
felt that it might hurt my career if it was known that I was a married woman.*

"*... Male wrestlers at the time were making five dollars or ten dollars a match,
but the women could get up to a hundred dollars. The news of this kind of
money put hundreds of girls in training and the news of the full-capacity houses
excited every promoter. More and more girls came into the business.*"

Running the central booking office was Wolfe, who had quit wrestling himself
because of a bad back. He moved in with promoter Al Haft in Columbus and, by

1949, had between 150 and 200 women working for him, including Nell Stewart, June Byers, ex-softball pitcher Mae Young, Mars Bennett ("The Girl With the Iron Jaw"), ex-taxi driver Dot Dotson, barefooted Lilly Bitter, Mae Weston, and his own daughter from a previous marriage, Violett Viann. He paid prospects $50 a week while he trained them and estimated it cost him $1,500 to prepare a woman for a wrestling career. One he turned down, according to Burke, was Fabulous Moolah.

"She wanted to work for Bill, but even Bill couldn't have her 'cause she had a real funny body," said Burke, her claws unsheathed again. *"She was built all top and no bottom, you know what I mean? The legs were funny. Now, through the years, she's got heavier all over, kinda covered it up."*

Wolfe lived like a sultan, making liberal use of his harem during his wife's long absences. He had several illegitimate children by women wrestlers and took delight in showing off diamond rings, a jeweled money clip, and a jeweled belt buckle.

"A little hobby of mine, collecting ice like this," he said. *"Sometimes I've got fifty thousand dollars worth of diamonds on me at one time, and Mildred has the same."*

Burke stayed in the very best hotels, bought a new Cadillac, Lincoln or Packard every year, and liked to flash her $10,000 diamond ring, but she earned it all. She was on the road eleven months of the year, risking her 15½-inch neck in five or six matches a week and putting 100,000 miles a year on those fancy automobiles.

"I drove one time to western Canada," she said. *"I had a brand-new Packard and it came out a total wreck because they had five-hundred, six-hundred, eight-hundred-mile jumps every night, over gravel roads. When I finished up there after a week's work, I think I got fifty dollars for it on trade-in. I cracked the engine and the dust and dirt had actually seeped through the trunk and into the suitcases. Into the clothes!"*

She lifted light weights and practiced Charles Atlas-style dynamic tension (called isometrics these days) until, she claimed, her chest expansion was half-an-inch greater than Jack Dempsey's. After her first two years as a pro, her income was $50,000 to $75,000 a year.

Each December, she would knock off from the travel and spend the holiday season in Kansas City with her mother and son. Her son, who took Wolfe's name, traveled with her each summer. Most of the time, she was also burdened with Wolfe's son by a previous marriage, G. Bill Wolfe.

Mildred Burke in furs

"Bill kept his eyes on me pretty well," she said. *"When he wasn't there, he had his son with me. Not that I needed him 'cause I had to look after him. He was a confirmed alcoholic and he was a real problem. ... He was really sick, and time and time again, I had to put him in sanitariums while we were traveling because he'd drink so much. I never could let him drive the car; he'd kill somebody. I've*

driven as much as two thousand miles without getting out from behind the wheel, so you can hardly say he went along to manage me."

But her husband's philandering, her stepson's boozing, and her real son's loneliness could not detour her twenty-year ego trip. She was Mildred Burke, the high-school dropout from KC who had become champion of the world, and she played the role for all she was worth. She designed all her own extravagant clothes and bragged that she entered the ring to wolf whistles and left it to cheers.

"*Ninety percent of my wrestling was in white tights and white shoes,*" she said. "*Then I'd have some beautiful colored robe, maybe fuchsia or something, with white-satin lining. I had one robe that cost me eleven-hundred dollars. It was solid cut rhinestones. It weighed, I think, twenty-six pounds. There was nothing else in it; it was solid. ... It was clear to the floor from the shoulders. I got tired of carrying it because, you know, twenty-six pounds in the suitcase besides the tights and shoes and everything else. Then I had it cut in two and had two short jackets made out of it. Oh, it just glistened like diamonds! It was just fabulous.*

"*I always kept a real good tan. The white satin made it show up real good. I'm the first person to wear white in the ring; most state commission rulings said you couldn't wear white tights 'cause that looked too much like your own skin. So I said, 'I've got white on and I'm goin' to wear it.' That first night I got in the ring with white tights and a beautiful suntan, and the commissioner himself came back to tell me how absolutely gorgeous it was. He'd never seen anything look that pretty in the ring before. Now, everybody wears white. It's so common you don't even think about it.*

"*I was always either a main event, or part of a double main event, or a special attraction. What I preferred was to be on just before the main event. Now that's the proper place to put girls. To start with, they usually have a shorter match than the men. The girls work harder and faster than the men do. They gotta identify themselves and do it all in a few minutes and out. The two worst spots to be are the first and the last. The first one because the crowd's cold and they have to be warmed up. Then the last — well, just like my two girls who worked at the Olympic the other night, and I sent word down with 'em to ask the matchmaker to please don't put 'em on first. Well, they had three men's matches, then they had a six-man tag-team match, and then the girls to follow that. Well, it's always hard to drop from six people in that ring down to just two. No matter how good you are, it's a letdown.*"

Burke used to go to Mexico once or twice a year, usually to battle another member of Wolfe's troupe because, at that time, Mexican women were not allowed to wrestle. Burke was a favorite of the crowds, but it was apparently just as dangerous to be liked as to be hated. After her match one night, Burke and Wolfe left the stadium with an escort of six policemen. By the time they had covered the short distance to their car, all the hair in her fox-fur coat had been pulled out and Wolfe's pockets had been picked.

She made a movie in New Jersey called *Lipstick and Dynamite*, and that title aptly described what went on with the women. They were every bit as imaginative and roughhouse as the men. In Toledo, Burke kicked the referee, and a representative of the athletic commission immediately announced that she had been fined five dollars. A fan sent up a $10 bill to pay the fine, so, being five dollars ahead, she took another kick at the ref. In Texas, Mae Young got Burke's arms tangled in the ropes, then slugged her over the eye.

"*The first lick she hit me, it just swelled up; it didn't cut,*" she said. "*Then she hit again and it just laid it open. That was a twenty-foot ring there and the blood was shooting clear to the center. And I wore white satin, so you can imagine how all that red blood looked."*

G. Bill Wolfe watched her being sewed up afterward and passed out. No wonder he drank.

("What I like about the women is that they're as dirty as the men and they never stall," said a famous New York fan, Hatpin Mary. *"They pull hair, bite, kick, punch, and squeeze each other's heads between the ropes. And when one of them gets heaved out of the ring, she don't waste time crying for sympathy like some of them men pleaders do. No, sir. She climbs right back in there, punching and clawing.")*

One woman whom Burke hated to work against was Gladys (Kill 'Em) Gillam of Birmingham, who would believe anything the men wrestlers told her. One night, they convinced her that she actually had a chance to beat Burke for the title and that she should throw everything she had into it. What she decided to throw into it was her teeth. Burke got Gillam's head locked in a scissors and the challenger *bit* her on the inner thigh; just chomped down through the tights and the flesh and wouldn't let go. The referee tried to pull her away, but that just hurt Burke more. She finally opened up when the champ broke her nose with a forearm smash. Blood ran down inside Burke's tights and into her shoes. It took a year *"to heal it up."*

Serious injuries, though not from bites, are fairly common in women's wrestling. Toni Rose had both wrists broken and her head cut open twice. Evelyn Stevens suffered a broken collarbone. Fabulous Moolah broke three ribs in Washington, D.C., "cracked" her back in Sandusky, Ohio, and has a scar on her left cheek from being hit with a chair in Houston.

"See this scar above my lip?" asked Moolah. *"That happened fifteen years ago in Salem, Massachusetts. My opponent flew off the ropes and kicked me in the mouth. I was knocked unconscious. When I came to in the dressing room, my mouth was completely numb. I felt my teeth, which came through my upper lip. There wasn't a mirror for me to see how bad it really was. Anyway, I grabbed my lip and freed my teeth. Talk about a fat lip! I couldn't eat any solid food for two weeks."*

Most of the women, of course, live in dread of developing a cauliflower ear, into which few lovers would want to whisper sweet nothings. Burke has the suggestion of one on the right side, but she said she always stayed out of the ring for a while and gave her ears a rest if they were injured. However, the now-retired Ann Laverne had a lovely matching set of cauliflowers — big ones — and she was reportedly quite proud of them.

Even stranger, according to Burke, was Kill 'Em Gillam's "cauliflowered head." It seems that gullible Gladys never could learn how to take a fall properly and was always landing on the back of her head. It was a wonder she never broke her neck. Burke once knocked Gillam out of the ring and sent her plummeting to the concrete floor. She landed, as was her habit, right on her head. *"My God, I've killed*

Gladys "Killem" Gillem

her," thought Burke. But, no. Gladys got up immediately, climbed back into the ring, and started swinging. *"Her head was just mushy back there,"* said Burke, *"You could just push in on it."*

Gillam quit wrestling to become a lion tamer. Burke shook her head in wonderment, gave prayerful thanks, and thought, *"I pity the lions."*

The long years of Burke on the road and Wolfe at home tending the stable ended in 1952 when she sued for divorce and demanded her money. It was then that she learned that if ignorance was bliss, naiveté was Burke.

"I never did have it in my hands, you know," she said. *"He took everything I ever made. I was so dumb and stupid that I didn't even realize how much money I was making. Besides my own bouts, I was supposed to have a third interest in the business. I didn't know the amount my share had made until we separated and the government went and investigated the income tax. And in 1952, the stable had taken in two hundred fifty thousand dollars.*

"I'm ashamed to admit I was that dumb, but I was. My poor mother kept telling me, 'Mildred, you're really being taken. When he's through with you, you're going to wind up without a penny.' *And I just couldn't believe it. I had everything I wanted. I dressed well, had a new car and everything, but he made darn sure I didn't have twenty-five dollars in the bank. Anytime I would have demanded my money, it would have been a break. It should have been before I ever met him, probably."*

The National Wrestling Alliance considered the ensuing squabble bad for the business and pressured the combatants to settle ownership of the central women's booking office. Burke's story is that she borrowed $30,000 and paid it to Wolfe & Son to get out of wrestling permanently. But Wolfe married wrestler Nell Stewart and his son married wrestler June Byers, and they continued to operate in opposition, driving Burke out of Tulsa and Atlanta.

"Understand that all the time I'm broke," she said. *"I'm booking forty to fifty girls every night. I'm wrestling every night myself in a different town. I never went to bed for three years; I slept in the car is the only sleep I got."*

Well, at least she still had her beloved title. No one could take that away from her. Or so she thought. *"It was in Birmingham, Alabama, that I completely shattered my right knee; just shattered it. This was 1954. I'd had 'em both injured, but this time it was really serious. I was booked the next night in Nashville, Tennessee. I went up there on crutches and tried my best to get the doctor to shoot it so I couldn't feel it and let me appear in the ring, but he refused to do it. He said,* 'Oh, if I did that, you'd maybe injure yourself for life because you wouldn't be able to feel what you were doing to it.'

"I said, 'Well, drain it.' *It was swollen like this ... Nothing but* blood *came out of it.*

"During the two years that I had been managing the girls, Bill had taken June Byers off the road and was training her for nothing, only to beat me. She was a lot bigger girl, anyway. The most I ever weighed was one-forty and June ran normally about one-sixty--. So he took Ruffy Silverstein, who was one of the toughest men wrestlers, and he had him train her for two years just to beat me. She didn't have one match in front of an audience, always in the gym. They were feeding her nothing but certain foods, they were training her like a racehorse, and all this time I'm out working myself to death trying to run the business.

"So, the minute the word got out that I'd tore my leg out and I was helpless, practically, and ordered not to even appear in the ring, Billy Wolfe got to the Paul Jones office in Atlanta and told them to book me into a championship match with

June Byers. It was very foolish for me to accept it. Well, anyway, I'd never been scared of June. I'd beat her a hundred times. I just thought I didn't dare say I'm hurt 'cause then they'll think I'm scared of her. It wasn't a case of being scared at all.

"*It took place in Atlanta. My son was in California at that time and I sent for him to fly back there. I don't know why; I felt he was the only one who was really with me. My leg was in terrible shape, I couldn't hardly even lean on it, let alone do anything, so that week they booked me every night, and the night before the big match, they sent me on a trip that was about two hundred miles away. After you wrestle that late at night and drive two hundred miles back, it's almost daylight. Then they put me on an eight o'clock television show and a noon radio broadcast and they kept me up — I can see now how carefully planned it was. I didn't even get a night's sleep.*"

Burke had heard rumors that Ruffy Silverstein had taught Byers a special hold that was unbreakable. Once Byers backed her opponent into the ropes, she would apply the hold and, zingo, before you could say Stanislaus Zbyszko, the fall was over.

"*When she stepped into the ring, she weighed in at one hundred eighty pounds!*" recalled Burke. "*They had built her up twenty pounds of just nothing but muscle, not twenty pounds of fat. All she did was try to jam me backwards into those ropes. Well, I couldn't brace very well because of this bad leg. So, we shoved around, and every time she'd try to shove me into the ropes, I managed to switch it and shove her into the ropes. But I stepped back once and out went my knee, clear out of the socket. Well, she jumped down on me and I turned right quick, and my shoulders weren't down.*"

But Burke decided to give up "*cause I had to lay there and put my knee back in place.*" Then she hobbled out for the second fall, which, according to her, turned into a religious experience.

"For forty-seven minutes, we just stood there with neither getting anywhere, and that is a long time to block with somebody. I couldn't dive in. I had one leg; there was no way I could do that. All I could do was block her moves. And she couldn't do a thing to me, and by this time, you could hear her clear up in the balcony, wheezin' for air. I don't know why, but it was just like God had reached down and touched me with His hands because I was getting stronger. I wasn't breathing hard, I wasn't breathing deep, and my leg was holdin'. It was a miracle.

"*Pretty soon the commissioner and everybody at ringside says,* 'Either have a fall or we're going to stop the match.' *The ref repeated it to the girls. You can imagine how the crowd felt watching not a move, just locked arms.*

And I said, 'No, you're not stopping the match. You wanted this match, now you've got it. We're staying right here 'til one of us wins a fall.' *It went on about another five minutes and finally they got in the ring and they stopped it.*

I grabbed the microphone and I said, 'I am not leaving this ring. I am not defeated and I will refuse to get out of the ring until you … announce that I am still the world's champion. You booked this match, I didn't ask for it, but I'm here and now you're not going to stop it on me.' *So they got in the ring and announced right over the loudspeaker that I was still officially the world's champion. So then I left.*"

Burke claimed she was never paid for that night's work. Her son hocked a ring to get them as far as Louisiana, where New Orleans promoter Joe Gunther gave them the money to get the rest of the way home to L.A. Burke rested her leg and then toured Japan.

"*When I came back nearly six months later, they said the referee had changed his mind, had switched the decision, and claimed that June Byers won the match,*" she said. "*A referee couldn't possibly change his mind six months after a match is over, you know. To me, June Byers couldn't even wrestle a lick, because if she weighed one-eighty and I weighed one-forty, and standing on one leg, and she trained for two years to beat me, and she still couldn't do it — I don't think she could ever wrestle.*"

Billy Wolfe died in 1961. G. Bill Wolfe died the following year. Burke did not attend their funerals.

And two years after she had been given the championship, Byers lost it for good to Moolah in Baltimore, and a new era started.

Of course, there is no law that states a promoter must hire women wrestlers through Moolah or Burke. Vivian Vachon, young with blond hair, blue-green eyes, and a nice singing voice, can afford to be independent because her two brothers, Maurice (Mad Dog) and Paul (Butcher) Vachon, are promoters in Canada as well as top-flight villains. Vivian was with Moolah for a while, lost at least one title match to her (in 1970), and then moved out on her own. She has done very well in Canada and the upper Midwest.

"*I'm a girl wrestler because it's a great industry,*" she said. "*Lots of spare time. Good money. And a way to the top early.*"

Her competitors in the battle to supplant Moolah include tag-team partners Paula Kaye and Rita Boucher, who wear White Shoulders cologne into the ring, Yvette Mimieux-look-alike Maria Laverne, Ann Casey, Lovely Louise, Vicki Williams, Morgana Morgan, and Susan Green. These women claim that even the newest and least colorful among them earns $18,000 or $20,000 a year and that the stars can make more than $40,000. Perhaps that kind of earning power partly makes up for the fact that they have to keep their fingernails short.

Are there lesbians among them? Certainly.

"*Between you and me, the lesbians are by far the best girls in the ring,*" said a booker who requested anonymity. "*I don't know why it is. Maybe the more mannishness they have to them, the more ability they have to do this, but I don't like to have them because they're real headaches out of the ring. They get tied up with another girl and they don't want to go anywhere without that girl. Right away you got troubles.*"

There also is the problem of rapid turnover.

"*Most girls will tell you that they'll keep going as long as the body holds out, but they remind me of stewardesses,*" said New York promoter Vince McMahon. "*Soon as they meet the right fella, they get out.*"

Quite often, that right fella is a wrestler. The list of such marriages over the years is a long one, including Barbara Baker and Ripper Collins, June Byers and Sammy Menacker (he came after Billy Wolfe's son), Penny Banner and Johnny Weaver, and Joyce Fowler and George Becker. No burglar had better let himself get caught ransacking *their* homes.

For the ones who are staying in the "industry," like Ms. Vachon, all the new open territories seem to indicate nothing but continued prosperity and increased acceptance.

"*Listen,*" said Paula Kaye, "*there are three hundred fifty of us girl wrestlers and we're really not strange at all.*"

Chapter 5
Annals of Villainy

How delicious it is in the darkness of a movie theater to anticipate the scene in which the fiend will get his comeuppance. How we savor the moment when he dies — agonizingly, we hope, and preferably in slow motion. Jack Palance carefully pulled on his gunfighter gloves in *Shane*, then laughed as he shot down the brave, but foolish, farmer in the street. Because we despised Palance so much, Alan Ladd's fast-draw retribution was that much sweeter and more heroic. In *Goldfinger*, Gert Frobe left a gold-painted corpse for Sean Connery to find and avenge. Lee Marvin was a perfect scowling slobberlips in *The Man Who Shot Liberty Valance* until John Wayne snuffed his candle.

Satanic archenemies are necessary in our melodramas so that even the dimmest of us can see some clear contrast with the crusading knight. The characters we love to hate — the Professor Moriartys, the Fu Manchus — are played by experts. It is the same in wrestling.

One night in Vancouver, Ted (King Kong) Cox, who came from the California wine country and was its best customer, was mauling Dick Daviscourt, using every foul he could think of and inventing a few new ones. Finally, the referee stopped the bout because Daviscourt was lying in the middle of the ring howling with pain, unable to continue because of an injured leg. The crowd was on its feet doing some howling of its own — for Cox's scalp. Cox gestured for the fans to calm down, which they did when he knelt and gently lifted Daviscourt. He carried his battered opponent across the ring, stepped through the ropes while the crowd applauded his sudden change of character, and then deliberately dropped Daviscourt eight feet to the concrete floor. He was fortunate to reach the dressing room alive.

Heel Johnny Valentine gave Jerry Novak such an unmerciful beating in Michigan City, Ind., that the referee had to call for a stretcher to haul the victim away. The bearers were very careful to put Novak on the stretcher just so. They lifted it slowly. Then Valentine dashed over, upset the stretcher, and sent poor Novak crashing to the cement floor. Cowboy Bob Ellis came running out from the wings to take revenge and that led to a profitable series of Valentine-Ellis grudge matches.

"It's hard for customers to work up a fever week after week cheering some nice guy," said George Linnehan, *"but the world never seems to run short of boos."*

Linnehan, a charming, convivial fellow from Waltham, Mass., who now lives down on Cape Cod and does the public-address announcing at Boston Garden matches, was most emphatically not a nice guy in the ring. Most of the time, he was a heel, a villain, a bad guy like my father — disloyal, untrustworthy, unkind and irreverent. Not to mention sadistic and cruel. What he did to various square-jawed, wavy-haired heroes over the years was both a crime and a source of high income.

Must the ranks of pro wrestling always be divided into 50 percent heels and 50 percent babyfaces? Most of the time, yes, but there are exceptions.

Wrestling heels quite often need the ballyhoo aid of a second, and one of the best was Count Rossi, who stooged for dozens of despicables.

At the Houston Coliseum one Friday night, I saw Pedro Godoy try to maim clean-cut Gene Yates, Professor Boris Malenko try to maim Ricki Starr, Alaskans Frank Monte and Mike York the same to Red Lyons and Red Bastien, and Stan (Crusher) Stasiak ditto to Bearcat Wright. In the middle of the card was an offbeat match, Jose Lothario versus Dory Dixon. Lothario entered the ring wearing a big straw sombrero, shiny silver boots, and black tights. Dixon is a Jamaican with a Muscle Beach physique, like a Greek statue tightly covered with shiny black oilcloth.

"You're going to see some good clean wrestling here," said a wrinkled woman sitting behind me. She had been narrating the matches for her husband the whole evening, although as far as I could tell, his vision was just as good as hers. *"You see, they break when you tell 'em to, that's what I think's clean."*

Dixon and Lothario, the latter agile despite a somewhat bulging gut, threw each other around the mat, used the ropes to propel themselves like rocks shot out of slingshots, made improbably acrobatic getaways, and reversed each other's holds with clever, quick countermoves. Bing, bing, bing. Lots of fast action. At the end, sportsmanlike handshakes and generous applause. But no intensity of feeling in the audience; no sign of that fever Linnehan was talking about; no *heat*.

"Wrestling has lived because it has changed as the people have changed," said Houston promoter Paul Boesch. *"For your clean wrestling or anything else. When people want to see clean wrestling, then they get it because they turn out for it when it's advertised, but the truth of the matter is, if you put two guys on and say this is going to be a great scientific match — fast, speedy, nobody's going to get mad at anybody — they'll stay home."*

"Do you think people would come out to watch two nice guys fight each other?" echoed heel Jack Armstrong. *"Not a chance. You've got to give them a clear-cut choice ... Let's face it, a match between two very scientific wrestlers might be the greatest event ever. But boring! Who would pay money to watch it? The people want excitement and a choice, and I give them that."*

Since, as far as I know, there is no aptitude test yet developed for would-be wrestlers, how is it decided which ones will be heels and which ones babyfaces? Well, veteran wrestlers and promoters know, for instance, that a handsome, well-muscled young man just off the football field of some Big Ten university is going to appeal to the audiences more as a babyface than a heel, so when they break the new kid into the business, they teach him no foul tricks.

Conversely, the older, uglier, and fatter a man is, or if he is a foreigner or a masked man, the more likely that he will be a heel. There have been some old, homely babyfaces (How's that for a contradiction in terms?) and there have been a few handsome villains — Terry Funk and Nature Boy Buddy Rogers spring immediately to mind. And a fellow might misbehave all over the country, leaving a trail of opponents' blood and disgraceful disqualifications from the Greensboro Coliseum to the Cow Palace, yet be a model citizen in his home area. Thus, ex-pro football star Ernie Ladd is a babyface in Texas, a heel everywhere else.

Ernie Ladd

(The fact that Ladd, a black man, can be a villain where and when he chooses is something of an advance in wrestling, although it probably would still be unwise and unsafe for a black to go into Meridian, Miss., and mistreat some white man. Black wrestlers in the past — Jim Mitchell, nicknamed The Black Panther, Jack Claybourne, Seelie Samara, ex-UCLA football player Woody Strode, Tiger Conway — were almost always good guys. That includes the late linguist Reginald Siki, who wrestled Stanislaus Zbyszko in 1925 and whose name was borrowed by the current peroxide-blond Negro heel Sweet Daddy Siki. The heroes today are Bearcat Wright, Dory Dixon, Bobo Brazil, Sonny King, and, sometimes, Thunderbolt Patterson.

(Ladd, a former tackle for the San Diego Chargers and other teams, is still one of the few black heels, and at about 290 pounds and six-feet-nine inches, he makes a formidable one. His appetite is legendary. In 1963, he won the first Golden West Eating Contest before a crowd of 1,000 in a hotel dining room. Some of his football teammates at the time held up a placard that read, "*Eat his arm off, Big Ern.*" He won a heifer calf and a red-velvet championship belt. He probably ate the calf that night for a bedtime snack, and maybe the belt, too.

(To continue for a moment this parenthetical detour through Harlem, the reader might like to know that the first black pro wrestler was probably Viro Small, known as "Black Sam," who was born a slave near Beaufort, S.C., in 1854. He became a foundry worker in Richmond, Va., at about age 15, after the Civil War. Later, he was a laborer in a New York slaughterhouse, then a hoister of sauerkraut barrels and beer kegs at a Bowery tavern called Owney's Bastile. He made his wrestling debut as a substitute in Owney's back room, a place well known to showman P.T. Barnum and the staff of The *National Police Gazette*.

(Now, back to villains and how they get that way.)

"*The crowd really dictates it,*" said Jack Armstrong. "*Most nights I'm the villain. I became a heel pretty naturally, I guess. The crowds seemed to hate me, so why not follow up on it?*

"*Image is the most important thing in my job. If people don't like me, I play it for all I can. The more people I can put in the seats, the more I make.*"

Every once in a while, a heel will become a hero, a miracle of nature comparable to a caterpillar's metamorphosis into a butterfly. Fred Blassie did it in Los Angeles, Ray Stevens in San Francisco, but they both retained their hard-earned nasty reputations elsewhere. Perhaps the most complete convert of the last few years is gargantuan Gorilla Monsoon, who had a series of battles against good-guy Bruno Sammartino before he went straight. He has a blubbery, ugly physique that only a killer whale could love, yet today he is a favorite of the fans, and on the side, he manages babyface Chief Jay Strongbow. (He also is reputed to own the ring used in Madison Square Garden. I can imagine him telling promoter Vince McMahon, "*Either you let me play or I'll take my ring and go home.*")

Much more common are the good-into-evil transformations of such wrestlers as Black Jack Lanza, Don Evans, Paul Jones, Bobby Shane, Dale Lewis, and Johnny

Valentine. Their usual explanation is that they got tired of losing matches to people who used dishonest tactics, tired of working under the handicap of being gentlemen, so they decided to start breaking the rules themselves. The more likely explanation is that they, or some promoter, figured they could draw bigger crowds and make more money as villains.

An example is Cowboy Bill Watts, an ex-University of Oklahoma wrestler and football player who was making big money as a babyface and tag-team partner of Sammartino when he suddenly and inexplicably went bad. Instant dry rot in the conscience. Overnight hardening of the heart. It happened early in 1965 in New Jersey before TV cameras and a packed house. He and Bruno were involved in a tag-team match versus Smasher Sloan and The Golden Terror. Sammartino was in the ring getting the lasagna beaten out of him and trying desperately to tag Watts and get some relief. But, to the audience's astonishment, Watts pulled his hand out of reach and let his friend suffer. When Sammartino was finally defeated by foul tactics and was lying helpless on the canvas, Watts at last came through the ropes — and kicked him! Then he grabbed the microphone and shouted to the audience: "*In my estimation, you're nothing but a bunch of pigs!*"

Cowboy Bill Watts

There followed a series of big matches against Sammartino, and Watts has ever since been a split personality — still a babyface in some places, a heel in others. He even donned a mask in St. Louis and called himself Dr. Scarlet. Up until April 1973, there had been seventeen masked men in that territory since World War II and Watts was the only one who unmasked of his own accord. For four months, no opponent was able to take it off.

"*Everything I do gets a crowd reaction,*" he said. "*If I blow my nose, they howl, because I* project. *I make 'em feel my loathing for them.*"

Sammartino, by the way, enjoyed plenty of revenge. He mutilated Watts' cowboy hat and antelope-skin jacket and was disqualified in February 1965 when he wouldn't stop kicking the turncoat.

"*If that's what they teach you at the University of Oklahoma, you can have it,*" roared Sammartino afterward. "*I don't need a rematch. I'll fight him without a ref. Then we see who does the kicking and gets away with it. He's the most hated bad guy in the ring today. He's lost the respect of all the people.*"

"*They can boo all they want,*" answered Watts. "*I'll laugh all the way to the bank. I think I'll get a Cadillac. No, maybe a Chrysler Imperial.*"

The last I heard, he was in the upper Midwest teaming with Wahoo McDaniel as a cowboy-Indian good-guy combination.

The most easily recognizable heels are the foreign menaces, and the most easily recognizable of these are the Japanese, who have numerous advantages over others trying to curry the fan's disfavor. We have been conditioned to hate, or at least distrust, Orientals by such spy-thriller and comic-strip villains as Fu Manchu, Ming the Merciless (Flash Gordon's old rival), Dr. No (in the sixth James Bond spy novel and the subsequent hit movie) and dozens more, and by various wars against the Japanese, Red Chinese, North Koreans, and Vietcong, in which slant-eyed soldiers have been portrayed as consistently sneaky and sadistic. We have had a few fictional Chinese heroes — Honolulu police detective Charlie Chan, Chop Chop in the *Blackhawk* comic books, Connie and Big Stoop in the *Terry and the Pirates* comic strip and radio program — but clever spy Mr. Moto, created by the late novelist John Marquand, has been one of the few good guys from Japan. Oh yes, there was the Green Hornet's faithful aide Kato, but he was magically transformed into a Filipino right around the time of the attack on Pearl Harbor.

In wrestling, Japanese heels predate World War II. While rummaging through an old scrapbook filled with yellowed, tattered clippings from the '20s, I found an article about a wrestling card in Houston. Marin Plestina, the original Paul Jones, and Joe Malcewicz were working that night, but the description of the opener was what caught my attention: *"The fans didn't even know the first bout had started, when it was over. Kazou Yoshimi, weighing 140 pounds, threw Tommy Henderson, 175 pounds, in twenty-eight seconds, with what is technically known as a 'Japanese arm-and-head hold.' Ringsiders claimed that Kazou wrapped his kimono around Tommy's Adam's apple and hung on until the Oklahoman said 'uncle.'"*

Since the war, we have had Japanese villains coming off the assembly lines — in Hawaii as well as Tokyo — as fast as Sony transistor radios and Honda motorcycles: The Great Togo, Harold Sakata, Hiro Matsuda, The Great Yamato (and his personal geisha, Hanako San), The Great Togo, Tojo Yamamoto, etc. (On the other side of the Pacific Ocean, the Japanese are mostly the good guys, and the Americans, with those strange round eyes, are the sneaky ones.)

The all-time great inscrutable serpent was Mr. Moto — known to his friends as Charlie — who was nothing like the tiny Marquand espionage agent. Moto had a crew cut, which is standard for nasty Nipponese, and a thin beard and mustache. He entered the ring wearing wooden clogs and a fancy ceremonial robe, and gave a hypocritical little bow. His stooge, Fuji, followed him carrying a tray of burning incense. Moto or his stooge would sprinkle salt in the four corners of the ring, a custom borrowed from the traditional sumo wrestling in Japan and intended to drive the evil spirits away. Very handy to throw in opponents' eyes, too.

At New York's St. Nicholas Arena in 1954, without his stooge and without his salt shaker, Moto tried another method of banishing evil spirits. He attempted to motion his opponent, Antonino Rocca, to one side while he gestured with his hands and stomped his feet on the canvas. Rocca kept rushing at him every time he tried to perform the ritual until,

Fuji & Mr. Moto

finally, the bell rang and referee Johnny Garon, Jr., started counting Moto out for not wrestling. Poor Moto thus had to take on Rocca and the spirits, and they were too much for him.

Charlie Moto is now clean-shaven and using salt only for his food. He lives in a house near the beach in Orange County, Calif., drives a Maserati, and handles the matchmaking for the Olympic Auditorium and other Los Angeles-area clubs. Seldom are his Olympic cards without one of his cheating protégés, perhaps

Kenji Shibuya or Masa Saito. Moto's old stooge, Fuji, is a prosperous dealer in L.A. real estate.

His dirty tricks live on in the ring. In the East, Professor Toru Tanaka and tag-team partner Mr. Fuji are constantly throwing salt in people's eyes. In February 1972, Tanaka was disqualified for throwing salt at Pedro Morales, missing and temporarily blinding the referee.

In the West, Shibuya, Saito and The Great Kojika have used the karate chops and sleeper hold (in which blood is cut off from the opponent's brain just long enough to render him unconscious, but not long enough to kill him). Kojika (beard, mustache, crewcut) once put Mil Mascaras to sleep on the Olympic canvas. The attending ring physician entered the ring to wake up Mascaras, but Kojika put him to sleep, too. Promoter Mike LeBell then jumped in the ring and ordered Kojika to revive them both or he would be fined and banned (like an evil spirit). He woke up the doctor, but refused to help Mil, so the doctor had to do it.

Those Japanese who know English are never hesitant to speak minds about Americans. *"Japanese wrestlers are far superior to American wrestlers,"* says Shibuya. *"An American wrestler has no guts and they cry like babies when you chop them."*

To show that World War II is perhaps fading a bit in people's memories, we have had at least one Japanese babyface in the last few years, although his visits have been infrequent. His name is Shohei Baba, and since he is six-feet-ten inches tall and weighs 319 pounds, he is called Baba the Giant.

"I guess because I was Japanese, a lot of fans figured I'd be like the rest of the Japanese wrestlers who've come here," he said. *"I'm glad I was able to change that image and show we're not all bad guys."*

Actually, the bad guys are not so inhuman either — outside the ring. They do not toss babies in the air and catch them on their bayonets. Toru Tanaka once gave a show for a group of retarded children in Houston, and for its amusement, tried to break a cement block with his head. It split open — his head, not the block.

Then there was the time The Great Togo and his "brother," Tosh Togo, appeared on Dave Levin's wrestling interview show on Los Angeles television.

"The Great Togo got up on a rubbing table with a sledge hammer and a wood-splitter — a wedge — and Tosh knelt down in front of that rubbing table and had a cube of wood on his head," recalled Levin. *"It was twelve by twelve by twelve. He didn't have a cushion, just a little piece of plywood under it so when the wedge went though, it wouldn't hit him in the head.*

"He knelt down in front of the table and The Great Togo takes the hammer, puts it on the wood, gives it a few taps to get it set, then goes up with the sledge hammer. ZANGO — you know how they holler? And down with the sledge hammer and it didn't split. So he had to do it again. Well, it took five slams of that sledge hammer and poor Tosh was getting an inch shorter each time he hit him. And finally the wood split and Tosh stood up ... and who was the guy who took the bows? The Great Togo with his hammer!"

Even more common as foreign menaces are the goose-stepping, heil-Hitlering, swastika-bedecked, jackbooted, monocled Nazis, often sporting names that smack of the Third Reich: Killer Karl Krupp, Otto Von Krupp, Karl Von Hess, Fritz Von Goering. They remain seated during the "National Anthem", turn their broad backs on the U.S. flag, and issue outrageous statements like these:

"I'm gonna win the world championship, take it back to Germany, and keep it there."

— Hans Schmidt, a 240-pound heel whom the Chicago *Tribune* discovered was really a French-Canadian from Montreal named Guy Larose

"We're still the master race and we will prove it."

— Karl Von Sholt

"Pain. I love dishing out pain. It's beautiful. Vunderbar. Nothing makes me so happy as when my opponent is squealing in terrible pain. Then I like to grind my heel into his face and give him even more pain. But as much pain as I give, I can never give as much pain as was given to my country."

— Killer Karl Krupp

From Stuttgart, or so he claims, comes Baron Fritz Von Raschke. He wears a nobleman's monocle and cape, the latter decorated with either a swastika or an Iron Cross. His boots are decorated with red swastikas. He was started in wrestling by Minneapolis hero Verne Gagne, but his true master-race psychosis soon came out. In 1970, he met Gagne in Chicago's Comiskey Park for the championship of the American Wrestling Alliance. The co-feature was Mad Dog and Butcher Vachon versus Dick the Bruiser and The Crusher. Almost 30,000 fans showed up and the card grossed about $148,000.

Kurt and Karl Von Brauner

America has also been infiltrated by Kurt and Karl Von Brauner, Karl Von Stroheim, Hans Mortier, Baron Von Sieber, Karl Von Brock, Siegfried Stanke, Kurt Von Poppenheim, Karl Von Schoeber, and Count Von Zuppie, all of whom presumably got off with light sentences, somehow, at the Nuremburg trials.

Von Zuppie was my father's favorite; he knew him around Wichita in 1946.

"Count Von Zuppie, a great wrestler and he only weighed 165 pounds," said Pop when he came across the count's photograph in a scrapbook. *"Drunk all the time. Sober, he taught more fellas wrestling than almost any guy I've ever heard of. A great guy, but he just couldn't let the bottle alone. He had a pigeon chest. He'd put it out and he'd look like a banty rooster. I used to get him matches; I felt sorry for the guy. He cost me a lot of change, for dinners and stuff like that, but he was my pet. And he liked me, too."*

Perhaps the most successful of all the wrestling storm troopers is Fritz Von Erich, whose press releases used to say that he was born *"in Berlin, Germany, and was raised to manhood under strict, Prussian, disciplinary rules."* His chief weapon is "The Iron Claw," in which his big meat hook of a right hand clamps onto an opponent's face and squeezes until the poor guy's features could seemingly be covered by a watch crystal. To have some semblance of control over that vicious claw, he holds the wrist tightly with his left hand. He has claimed that his right hand is insured for $1 million.

These days Von Erich restricts his wrestling pretty much to the Dallas-Fort Worth area, where he has a big say in the promotion and is a good guy in the ring, perhaps because many of the people remember him as Jack Adkisson, who played tackle on a conference-champion Southern Methodist University football team with the immortal Doak Walker. Or as the man who set an SMU record in the discus throw. He is involved in many businesses in Texas — gas stations, wrestling films, Laundromats, apartment houses — and owns a home on Lake Dallas.

The rest of the country can keep on enjoying Von Erich villainy, though, because Fritz's brother, Waldo, still makes the rounds, still espouses the cause of the Fatherland. That not every fan takes his act seriously is demonstrated by the song composed by a fellow in Boston, a tribute to Waldo to the tune of "God Bless America."

The tradition of Russian heels, carried on today by such men as Professor Boris Malenko and Ivan Koloff, goes back to way before the Cold War and John Foster Dulles' policy of "brinksmanship." Blond-bearded Sergei Kalmikoff, the Siberian Gorilla, used to attract attention by parading down Broadway wearing a gold-braided Cossack tunic with cartridge belt, boots and Astrakhan hat. His favorite hold was "the Russian bear hug." In 1936, he went back to Russia, but there has been no shortage of his comrades in U.S. arenas: Al Karasick, The Russian Lion, who once knocked out a referee in Astoria, Ore., and was for years the promoter in Honolulu; Ivan Poddubny, who sported a handlebar mustache; Kola Kwariani, the bald chess master, and Mastros Kirilenko, The Terrible Cossack.

And, of course, Americans playing Russian roles: Ivan Bulba, who was really Johnny Shaw from Texas; Ivan Kameroff, one of three wrestling brothers from New Haven, Conn., and Ivan (The Terrible) Mikaloff, a 260-pound giant. One of the most imposing was Ivan Rasputin, The Mad Russian, whose matted body hair made him look more like a gorilla, Siberian or otherwise, than Kalmikoff ever had. But Rasputin was from Boston and his real name was Hyman Fishman.

"*I grew the beard on a bet in 1938 and folks said I looked like Ivan Rasputin,*" admitted Fishman when his guard was down. "*The handle stuck and here I am.*"

(The original notorious Rasputin was named Gregory Yefimovich, not Ivan, but let us not quibble about a little poetic license by his wrestling namesake.)

The most fiendish heel in the Detroit-Toronto area is The Sheik, who looks like a thick-necked Vincent Price, and who spills as much of his victims' blood in various rings every month as Price has in numerous horror films. The Sheik enters the ring half-hidden in a burnoose (a hooded cloak worn by Arabs, Moors and other mysterious folk of the desert) and has a camel imprinted on his trunks. His favorite hold is "the camel clutch," but before he goes about applying it, he kneels on a Muslim prayer rug and bows toward Mecca, a religious observance that invariably draws boos, hisses and thrown objects.

Although The Sheik is rumored to be the behind-the-scenes promoter in Detroit, he pretends to speak no English, using instead a talkative stooge, Abdullah Farouk (Ernie Roth), to represent him. (In other territories, fronting a bevy of other villains, Roth is known as The Grand Wizard, but he usually wears the same type of outfit: wild sport jacket, turban, sunglasses.) A few years ago, The Sheik was attended by a veiled female, Princess Salima, who seemed to have stepped right out of a Baghdad harem or the Broadway cast of *Kismet*.

Minus his burnoose and his aide-de-crime, a little weasel who passes him illegal weapons, "The Sheik" shows off his wounds after a Detroit match. He is king rather than sheik in Michigan, a state that doesn't allow harems and probably shouldn't allow this dastardly villain's dirty tricks, either.

"I was pledged to him as a child," she said. *"I am his wife. It gives me joy to serve him."*

The Sheik has no patent on the gimmick. There was a villainous Sheik wrestling in Boston in 1938, and handsome, haughty Sheik Lawrence was terrorizing opponents with his "Arabian airplane spin" in the '40s. Today, along with The Sheik, we have The Great Mephisto, who has a camel figure on his trunks and a slave girl named Salina, and Abdullah the Butcher, an obese, bald-as-an-eight-ball black man whose manager claims that his wrestler is (a) from The Sudan, and (b) insane. Abdullah's real name is Larry Shreeve.

In addition to adding pageantry to the proceedings, these costumes and roles are sort of a shorthand means of communication between the wrestlers and the fans. Monocles, turbans, swastikas, oriental eyes, burnooses — they all usually mean identification as a villain the instant a bad guy starts strutting down the aisle. The heat radiates toward the heel right away, instead of later, when he refuses to let the referee check his body for grease or when he uses dirty tactics in the match itself.

Too many homegrown heels use a tired, overworked means of instant identification; bleached-blond hair. It is, I suppose, a legacy from Gorgeous George. The loathsome list is endless: Fred Blassie, Eddie and Jerry Graham, Rip Hawk, Ripper Collins, Dusty Rhodes, Johnny Valentine, John L. Sullivan, Larry Hamilton, the Fargo brothers, etc., etc. Without these valued customers, the peroxide industry in the U.S. might collapse.

Blassie, for one, does not need the help of peroxide to attract notice or be hated. He knows his job very well and has been working at it with enthusiasm since his debut in St. Louis in 1943. Connoisseurs of villainy could fill ten scrapbooks with descriptions of his adventures: the time he was fined $500 and suspended sixty days for tearing off a referee's shirt in the Olympic Auditorium; the time he called Las Vegas women "pigs" and Las Vegas children "juvenile delinquents" on a local TV show and was forced to apologize by the state athletic commission (*"I didn't mean nothing personal by what I said"*); the time he supposedly broke Edouard Carpentier's knee; the innumerable times he has used his "razor-sharp" vampire's teeth to cut open an opponent's forehead.

His conceit is colossal, illustrated by his statement after winning over Bruno Sammartino by disqualification in 1964: *"The only ones I'm afraid of are the ladies. They molest me."* Perhaps Blassie's finest moment as a heel came in a small Pennsylvania arena, where he was supposed to wrestle an exhibition versus Pedro Morales, then champion of the World Wide Wrestling Federation. Morales appeared and inspired the usual cheers, and then Blassie came out in street clothes, his arm in a sling.

"I can't wrestle," he told announcer Vince McMahon, Jr. *"My arm's busted."*

He climbed into the ring to show Morales the note from his doctor, but as he did, his manager, Lou Albano, slipped up behind the Puerto Rican hero and hit him over the head with a chair. Then Blassie ripped off the sling and started pummeling the stunned Morales with the supposedly broken arm. Morales was rescued by Gorilla Monsoon and Chief Jay Strongbow and carried to the dressing room unconscious. When he came to, he demanded that Blassie be made the top contender for the WWWF title, and thus his next opponent, jumping ahead of King Curtis, which Freddie claimed is what he wanted all along. A subtle tactician, as you can see.

The Dirty Duseks: Rudy, Joe, Emil & Ernie

Multiply Blassie by four, subtract the Marilyn Monroe hair, and you have a pretty good picture of the Dirty Duseks, Rudy, Joe, Emil and Ernie, also known as The Riot Squad. (At one time the nation was absolutely infested with Duseks. Danny Dusek was really Sid Nabors, no relation. Wally Dusek was really Charles Santen, no relation. Dick Dusek was supposedly a nephew.

Actually, the Duseks *themselves* weren't really Duseks. Their real surname, also Bohemian, was Hason. Rudy was the first to turn pro and took a neighbor's name; three of his brothers and several imitators, including my father for a short time, followed suit.) They were the sons of an Omaha fisherman and butcher who was, perhaps, relieved that they did not carry his name into the ring. Wrote a newspaperman after seeing Ernie in action one night in Camden, N. J.:

> *"Dusek was the winner after wrestling the dirtiest match, beyond all doubt, this city has ever seen …"*

Time chronicled one week in the lives of the Duseks in 1935. The magazine ran a photograph of Joe clenching his fists and snarling at the fans in hometown Omaha; he had just been tossed out of the ring and the fans had laughed at him. In Boston, Rudy watched Danno O'Mahoney get a decision over Ernie, then leaped into the ring, tried to attack the referee, and started a free-for-all. Rudy had five bouts of his own that week and Ernie was hospitalized after some idiot in the balcony in Camden — they adored him in that town, apparently — threw a heavy object and hit him as he returned to the dressing room.

"Never a dull match with a Dusek" was their slogan, and they were not exaggerating.

The Dirty Duseks are all dead or retired now — Rudy died at age 70 not too long ago after being a successful promoter, Joe is the promoter in Omaha — but my father, also the son of a Bohemian butcher, remembers them fondly.

"Oh, they were funny," he said. *"You'd get Emil and Ernie and tell 'em to sing "Sioux City Sue," and they'd sing it* 'Schlioux Schlity Schlue.' *They had a crazy lisp. The older brother, Rudy, had a little bit of a lisp, too. They all had it.*

"They say the old man, whenever they came home visiting, they'd get down and wrestle all over the place, and the old man was still the papa of the family, for years and years. They all had big, wide feet — Bohemian feet, you know. Not long but wide."

Only one notch below the Duseks in the hierarchy of infamous families were the Zaharias brothers from Pueblo, Colo., George, Chris and Tom, plus a nephew who performed as a fourth brother. Their real surname was Vetoyanis. George rose from being a shoeshine boy in Pueblo to rank as one of the esteemed villains of his time, a man who lifted the fine art of begging for mercy to such heights that he was nicknamed The Crying Greek from Cripple Creek (Cripple Creek was a town in his home state; Pueblo created rhyming difficulties). At first, like most young wrestlers, he was a babyface.

"I was changed overnight," he said. *"One night in Memphis in 1930, I threatened to quit.* 'Look at my eyes, they're all cut,' *I said to an old promoter.* 'Nobody wrestles by the rules.'*

"'Hit them first!' this old promoter told me.*

"So, I became a villain and saw to it there were always fireworks when I wrestled."

Too much fireworks one time. In a tank town, Zaharias entered the dressing room after a match and began to put on a show that the patrons outside could not see, but could certainly hear. His crashing around and yelling and overturning chairs made it sound like D-Day was taking place in that little room. The old building couldn't take it and the dressing room partially collapsed, bringing lumber and plaster down on the wrestlers' heads. After rescue by firemen and police, George groused: *"Why don't you folks demand that the commission build decent dressing rooms for the wrestlers?"*

A policeman pulled the last bit of debris off Zaharias' corpulent body and replied, *"I happen to be the commissioner and you're getting a bill for a new building tomorrow."*

George defeated plenty of wrestlers in his career, but he seldom if ever hurt one. The late Herman Hickman, an All-America lineman at the University of Tennessee and a professional wrestler before he became a well-known football coach, told New York columnist Ben Epstein about his barnstorming days with The Crying Greek.

"Herman loved you, George," Epstein later told Zaharias. *"Before he died, Herman told us one night that, even though it looked to everybody as if you were killing him, it was like being caressed by your girl."*

Zaharias shook his head. *"No, old Herman said it another way,"* he corrected. *"He said that rassling me was like being caressed by your mother."*

In 1938, Zaharias met the famous woman golfer Babe Didrikson at the Los Angeles Open and, later that year, they were married. The obese villain and the mannish Babe didn't make any most-beautiful-couple-of-the-year lists, but their marriage was a very happy one through the tail end of his active wrestling days, his promoting in Denver, his operating a clothing store in Beverly Hills, and their semi-retirement in Florida. Babe died of cancer in 1956 and George has never recovered from the loss. He married again in 1960, but it didn't last.

"*She was a wonderful woman,*" said Zaharias, "*but she couldn't stand always being in the Babe's shadow.*"

I thought I could go on and make a life of my own. I found I couldn't. We were a team. I dedicated my life to her. Now I can't break the chain. I think of her every day."

In 1967, Zaharias visited the West Coast to help honor ex-champion Jim Londos at an awards program. "*I could never be the champion because Londos wouldn't let me,*" he told the audience, "*so I finally married a champion.*"

**George & Babe Didrikson Zaharias
July 31, 1953**

There are plenty of American and Canadian heels who have continued the mayhem where the Zahariases and Duseks left off. Stan (Crusher) Stasiak, who borrowed his ring name from an earlier heel who died from wrestling injuries in 1936 in Massachusetts, has made good use of his "heart crusher" punch. If nothing else, it gets plenty of ink and gives other wrestlers something to complain about during TV interviews.

"*This man is inhuman, his hold is inhuman, and he doesn't care if he walks across a carpet of bodies,*" screamed Ernie Ladd. "*He is interested only in himself.*"

It gives Stasiak himself something to yell about on television, too:

Stasiak: "*Last week here, as you recall, I wrestled Tommy Siegler, and I deliberately, in front of the camera, applied my 'heart crusher,' just to put an end to any controversy about it, to prove it is not a punch, but the palm of the hand, which you yourself saw — the palm of the hand — you had the nerve to argue with me last week. Why, you saw it ...*"

Announcer: "*No, I didn't see the palm of the hand. It looked to me like you used the fist.*"

Stasiak: "*Why, you ... you're blind. There's something wrong with your eyes. And you're stupid, just like the others who say that. If anything should be barred, it should be Fritz Von Erich's 'claw' ... Look at the scars on my face from where he applied 'the claw,' literally clawed me. Every time he applies it, I get — I bleed. THAT should be barred.*"

And so on until the commercial break.

Just as vicious appearing is the "throat stomp" employed by a homicidal-looking matman named Wladek (Killer) Kowalski, a giant heel from Hamtramck, Mich., who usually appears in purple tights with lightning bolts on the sides and glittering gold wrestling shoes ... the better to stomp you with, my dear.

"*I was on the floor and he just jumped up in the air and landed feet-first on my windpipe,*" said Verne Gagne in a strained voice after meeting Killer one night. "*It knocked the breath out of me. It's a pretty rough hold if his aim isn't just right. He tore off a guy's ear with it one night, fellow named Yukon Eric.*"

Actually, a man Kowalski's size landing with his full weight on an opponent's Adam's apple would be a murderer making his nickname come unhappily true. What Kowalski does is land with one foot on the throat, one on the mat. The victim hopes the latter lands first. Gagne's statement about Yukon Eric Holmbeck is true. Kowalski's foot tore off part of Eric's ear, an ugly incident that wrestlers often refer to when talking about the dangers of their profession.

Ex-Boston promoter Abe Ford, who still takes vitamins recommended by Kowalski, recalls a show he staged at the Framingham, Mass., Armory. Afterward, a major sent word to a surprised Ford, inviting him and the hated Kowalski to dinner at the home of a judge. At the end of the evening the judge told Ford, *"I'd like my son to grow up and be a gentleman like Kowalski is."*

Few people would guess that the perpetrator of the throat stomp was not a homicidal maniac after all, nor a laboratory creation of Dr. Frankenstein, but — outside the ropes, anyway — a warm, sympathetic human being, a true gentleman. Not only that, but a deeply religious person.

Killer Kowalski

"Probably the most sincere of all the people who have gotten religion in wrestling is Kowalski," said promoter Paul Boesch. *"He was at the top of the wrestling heap, really. He was making fabulous money. All of a sudden, he decided he was doing the wrong thing. He went into this religious retreat, he went on a strict vegetarian diet, he lost about 100 pounds. He almost died, as a matter of fact, and this went on for a couple of years. He would spend his days meditating and reading, playing deep music and listening and thinking. The inactivity and the diet and everything — the loss of weight almost killed him.*

But then somebody convinced him that he could live with religion and that religion wasn't meant to kill you. Finally, he came around, to some extent ... He's in the sport, but he carries his books with him, he reads his religion. If you want to discuss it, he'll talk for hours about it, and each year he takes a three-week hiatus and goes on a retreat out near Mount Shasta in California."

In descending order of vicious nicknames, we leave Killer, skip over Killer Tim Brooks, The Crusher and The Stomper, and stop at Dick the Bruiser, who was known as Dick Afflis when he played football for the University of Nevada and the Green Bay Packers. The Bruiser is an extraordinarily mean man. On a TV show around 1961, the announcer told his audience that the big, luscious birthday cake at ringside was for Cowboy Bob Ellis. It seems that some orphans had scraped up their last pennies, emptied their piggy banks, and bought the cake for their hero. The Bruiser came out, stomped on the cake, and presumably made the orphans cry. Another time, his babyface opponent got a cake from a little girl all dressed up in her Sunday finest. The Bruiser vaulted into the ring, pushed the girl aside, and mashed the cake into the hero's face. Conveniently, that was also before TV cameras.

Another bit of brawling ballyhoo ended up costing The Bruiser some money. In 1963, he was scheduled to wrestle football player Alex Karras in Detroit's Olympia. At that time, Karras was on suspension from the National Football League's Detroit

Lions because he had been caught betting on games. He was doing some wrestling for Detroit promoter Johnny Doyle and helping run the Lindell A.C., a tavern of which he was part owner. A few nights before the match, The Bruiser came strolling into Karras's bar and, the story goes, spat out some insults and was refused a drink. A brawl ensued, involving The Bruiser, Karras and *eight* policemen. One cop suffered a broken wrist, another torn ligaments in an elbow, and The Bruiser got a cut under his left eye that required five stitches to close. He pleaded innocent to charges of assault and battery. Later, he was fined $400, and still later was sued by the two injured cops.

As for the match itself, Karras entered the ring in blue tights emblazoned with a silver lion and was seconded by Major Little, forty-three inches tall. About 7,000 fans, fewer than expected, showed up, despite the banner headlines on the brawl in the Detroit newspapers a few days earlier. The Bruiser pinned Karras in less than twelve minutes.

Karras took away $4,500 for his short shift, but quit wrestling the following month, turning down a $40,000-a-year contract from promoter Doyle. Ten years later, Dick the Bruiser is still antagonizing the fans and fouling opponents.

"People give me a laugh," he said, *"They form fan clubs for me and I cut 'em cold. They put up signs cheering me on and I rip 'em down. They come to me for autographs and I steal their pens. They send me money for pictures and I keep it. The slobs don't know any better. They still go away happy.*

"... In the ring I use anything that comes to me. All I want to do is get the job done, give the fans some action, and get out and drink some beer."

"Anything that comes to me" is the key phrase there. By that, he doesn't mean just thoughts that happen to cross his warped mind. For instance, there was the time he was wrestling Bobby Managoff in St. Louis. He left the ring suddenly, overturned a table at which State Commissioner Mike Cleek was sitting, wrenched a leg off the table, and went after Managoff. The good guy took the illegal weapon away from him, so The Bruiser resumed his attack with two chairs.

Items such as chairs and table legs are frequently used in professional wrestling. The Bruiser once attacked Bruno Sammartino with a lighted cigar. In Charlotte, N.C., 9,000 people saw Ernie Dusek, trying desperately to unmask The Great Bolo, grab a spectator's crutch and flail away at his opponent. In Richmond, Va., an elderly gentleman, perhaps a planted accomplice loaned Art Neilson his cane. In San Antonio, Duke Keomuka ripped a piece of two-by-four lumber from the ring and battered Prince Maiava over the head with it, but Maiava wasn't above using similar tactics. He once tore off his sarong (he had regular trunks on underneath, so don't be shocked) and used it as a noose to try to hang Bull Curry from the ropes; Curry retaliated by dumping a snow cone on Maiava's head.

One time in a small southern town, Chief Chewchki, the pseudo-Sioux, jumped out of the ring and pulled a high-heel shoe off the foot of a woman seated at ringside. He jumped back in the ring and proceeded to batter his opponent over the head with it. The woman's male companion climbed up on the ring apron and demanded that the villain return the shoe, at which point Chewchki went into one of his regular routines, taking off the man's straw hat and taking a bite out of the brim. He wasn't called Chewchki for nothing, you see.

The man shocked the crowd, and the chief, by pulling out a .22 revolver. Chewchki fainted — or pretended to.

When the crowd had calmed down and Chewchki was safely back in the dressing room, he was asked if the pistol had scared him. *"Of course not,"* he replied. *"The straw hat poisoned me."*

You can be sure that anything and everything that could conceivably be brought into a ring, has been. For one thing, wrestlers love props. The Kangaroos, Al Costello and Don Kent (formerly Al Costello and Roy Heffernan), carry boomerangs to underline their Australian backgrounds. Johnny Kace and Nicoli Volkoff used to enter the ring with a large, leather-padded log which they would hang in their corner before a tag-team match, and then pound with awesome-sounding forearm smashes — WHOMP, WHOMP, WHOMP, WHOMP. Brother Jonathan, my dad's old partner in crime and the father of the current big-time heel, Don Leo Jonathan, used to carry around with him a snake named Cold Chills, which he claimed was a 155-year-old Mexican rattlesnake.

As far as I know, Cold Chills was used strictly for photographs and show, but not so with a certain garter snake in Mexico City. At the Arena Mexico, Chico Casasola and Bobby Bonares were wrestling The Blue Demon and Caveman Galindo. At ringside was Esmeralda, a well-known singer on Mexican radio. A nicely dressed and apparently well-meaning man passed up a cup of what looked like orange juice and asked Esmeralda to hand it to Galindo, who was on the ring apron. He took it from her, poured out the liquid, and extracted from the cup a twelve-inch garter snake, then grabbed Casasola in a headlock and beat him in the face with the poor snake until the referee disqualified him. Esmeralda, her mother, and her sister were bombarded with fruit and other debris, and Esmeralda was even hit on her bouffant hairdo by a brick. A police riot squad finally rescued her.

In a Columbus, Ga., television studio, Mario Galento was battling Billy Hines.

"We were going at it nip and tuck," said Hines. *"Neither of us was very popular, so the big crowd was about evenly divided. Suddenly Mario grabbed me in a headlock and pulled something from his trunks. It turned out to be a roll of pennies. He hit me with it just above the right eye. Pennies flew everywhere, and I had a cut that later took seventeen stitches to close."*

The chief of police was watching at home, said Hines, and issued a warrant for Galento's arrest, but it turned out that Galento could not be arrested because the mugging took place in a wrestling ring.

• Chief Chewchki once hit upon the idea of dusting his trunks with sneezing powder, then getting a scissors hold on his unsuspecting opponent's head. It was also Chewchki who would often hide a loop of wire in his corner and use it at climactic moments to try to strangle his foe, and Chewchki who was caught in Indianapolis with two sheets of sandpaper studded with carpet tacks hidden in his trunks, and Chewchki who so frustrated Whitey Hewitt with hair pulling that Hewitt showed up for their next match with his head shaved.

• Out of the referee's sight, Count Dracula used to pull out from somewhere a handkerchief and a bottle clearly labeled "chloroform." He would soak the handkerchief with the liquid, then put his opponent to sleep while the angry crowd tried to tell the ref where the bottle was hidden. A nice audience-participation stunt.

• Harry Finkelstein was fond of bringing a piece of soap into the ring and rubbing it in his opponent's eyes. Just as the referee was about to catch him soapy-handed, he would hide the bar under one arm or the other.

• Dr. X (Jim Osborne) has been known to hide a piece of metal in his mask to make his headbutts more effective. He beat Dan Hodge that way in Tulsa, but several of Hodge's babyface buddies jumped up on the apron to explain to the referee what had happened. Just then, Dr. X started to hide the object in his mouth, but Dennis Stamp hit him on the back, he was forced to spit it out, the ref saw and reversed the decision.

• Killer Tim Brooks wears an elbow pad, sometimes on his left arm, sometimes on his right, which his enemies claim is loaded with some heavy illegal object. The Great Mephisto has a steel-lighted boot he uses the same way.

• Professor Toru Tanaka, perhaps out of salt temporarily, pulled a rope out of his trunks and choked Pedro Morales. Fred Blassie did the same thing. It's amazing how much storage space there is in those late-model trunks.

• In Erie, Pa., Fidel Castillo, the evil Cuban Commie rat, was caught carving a road map in Luis Martinez' forehead with a fish hook. (Somehow, it is usually the forehead that gets cut open, seldom any other part of the face or head.) Probably the most prolific and blatant user of illegal weapons — cola cans, ballpoint pens, pencils, knives, razor blades, pieces of metal, tables, chairs, microphones — is The Sheik. This is mainly because his manager, Abdullah Farouk/The Grand Wizard, is the acknowledged master at secretly passing objects to his villainous protégés. It is nearly always the heels who have managers — Farouk, Lou Albano, Playboy Gary Hart, The Black Baron, Crybaby Cannon, Pretty Boy Bobby Heenan. The babyfaces usually have to fend for themselves, with only the ineffectual referees to help.

Passing illegal weapons into the ring is just one function of a manager in professional wrestling. Perhaps more important is ballyhoo, the art of blathering entertainingly during TV interviews. Farouk, Albano, Bronko Lubich and others are pretty good at this, but the all-time master mouth was Wild Red Berry, who fronted for the Kangaroos, Gorilla Monsoon (when he was still a heel), Waldo Von Erich, and probably everybody on the FBI's Ten Most Wanted list.

Berry, a tough but small guy from Pittsburg, Kan., was a pretty good spieler when he was still an active villain, too. He sold Wild Red Berries (candy drops) to the kiddies and had funny feuds going with everybody. Bill Welsh, a Los Angeles TV announcer who covered a lot of wrestling back in the late '40s and early '50s, rates Berry as his all-time favorite.

"*My famous feud with Berry was probably the dramatic highlight of early TV,*" he said. "*Once, Berry had friends report that I was maligning his ability as a wrestler. He was not going to appear at the Hollywood Legion until I was fired. We started gathering signatures of fans who wanted me to stay and we got at least fifty thousand names. It was unbelievable! Berry showed up, but he brought a device which he claimed could pick up the announcer's comments. I was always saying derogatory things when he had the earphones on, but it ended when one of his opponents smashed it over his head.*"

"*Wild Red Berry started his talking career here,*" claimed Paul Boesch of Houston. "*Of course, he was at a point then when his wrestling career was just about over and, one night, we were going to have an interview. He said,* 'Look, I want to say something real smart. You know, to sound big.' *I merely said,* 'Well, just go out and say, *'May the better man emerge victorious.'* 'Hey,' *he said,* 'that sounds good.'

"*So Red then went out and said it and he really took his own hook. Afterward he said,* 'Tell me more.' *So, we used to ride to Dallas and Fort Worth together; Red was good company. And I bought a couple of little books with quotations —* Bartlett's Quotations, *I had — and he'd look them over and he'd write things down. He has a tremendous memory, this is the thing about Red.*

"*He learned little poems and he learned other things, and he'd come out and he'd spout them, but then when he left here, he went to Los Angeles and he already had started this thing, and the* pros *picked him up there. They wrote speeches for him. 'He has the sagacity of a chipmunk and the jaws of a lion,' and all that kind of stuff."*

"They'd write these speeches for him and he'd go to the Kiwanis and he'd give this big, long speech. And then some people started asking him what certain words meant, and Red got hung up a few times, but then he went and memorized the definitions of the words! See, he couldn't write a thing ... but he sure as hell could remember it."

"Here are a couple of samples from *Berry's Familiar Quotations:*

"Let these hams primp their feathers and strut their plumes. I will proceed to maltreat and obliterate them. I will turn loose such terrific voltage and velocity and elliptical trajectory that when it lands on the cleft of the chin, it will tear loose their medulla oblongata from the pericranium, cure them of chronic dandruff, and knock out four of their impacted wisdom teeth."

or: *"Some of those abusive, obstreperous, pernicious rumor-mongers who have sought to smear, besmirch, and destroy my reputation, will never be able to take away my spirit of optimism because I will always be a ray of sunshine, a creator of gladness, and master of myself. I have been a successful champion wrestler because I'm brave as a lion, strong as a mule, tough as a pine knot, and sharp as a razor."*

No wonder The Kangaroos hired him to do their talking for them and issue all the challenges to the "insidious mugwumps" who stood in their paths to titles and title shots.

If ever a Pro Wrestling Hall of Fame is built, there should be included — besides Mr. Moto's salt shaker, The Sheik's burnoose, Count Dracula's chloroform bottle, and a recording of the Dusek brothers singing "Sioux City Sue" — the old, faded, warm-up jacket that Wild Red Berry used to wear into the ring. Sewn on the back were the words: *"I am right."*

Houston's Paul Boesch is one of the old hands at broadcasting wrestling matches, thus he is used to having behemoths land in his lap, as almost happened in this scene from Sydney, Australia, in 1940. That's Boesch next to the fallen grappler. Note he is still yakking into the mike despite the near catastrophe.

Chapter 6
Carnival Impresarios

Back in the mid-'30s, six men were simultaneously claiming to be the legitimate heavyweight wrestling champion of the world. However, the sport has matured and modernized since those chaotic times and nothing so ridiculous as six title-holders could happen. No, in these chaotic times, there are only three world champs.

The top dogs in the three strongest alliances, the NWA, AWA and WWWF, are the current claimants, and professional wrestling also has WWWWA, WWA, NWF, Grand Prix, Southern, Texas, and Central States champions, among others, but no single accepted king of the hill as in boxing. The reason is simple. Rival promoters and factions control these various titles and refuse to give them up. They cannot see how having one universally recognized champ would put more money into their pockets, and perhaps they are right. Yet they get annoyed at all the jokes about buying championship belts at F.W. Woolworth's for fifty cents a dozen.

"Sportswriters around the country have poked fingers at the fact that wrestling has more than one champion," said an indignant mid-western promoter. *"Wrestling was smart enough twenty years ago to have more champs. Now other sports are doing it. Baseball and football leagues have broken up into smaller divisions so there'll be more winners. They have taken a chapter from wrestling, though no sportswriter admits it."*

What the promoter failed to mention was that at least the baseball and football leagues eventually decide a champion each year. Wrestling is sliced up into separate kingdoms with never a championship joust between them.

Here is a quick tour back and forth across the borders:

The *National Wrestling Alliance* (NWA) covers the most territory. Formed in the late '40s, it includes Mexico, Australia, parts of Japan and Canada, the entire West Coast from Seattle to San Diego, Texas, Oklahoma, Kansas, Missouri, and almost all the South. St. Louis promoter Sam Muchnick, an ex-newspaperman, has been president for all but about four years of the organization's history. The NWA has an annual convention to discuss common business problems and the brass from other alliances usually attend.

The current NWA champion is ex-Oklahoma State star Jack Brisco, who travels to the alliance's major cities defending his belt before big crowds, just as Dory Funk Jr., Lou Thesz, and others did before him. The NWA traces Brisco's heavyweight championship back to Frank Gotch in the early 1900s.

The *American Wrestling Association* (AWA) was formed in 1960 and calls itself "the major league of professional wrestling." It includes Minneapolis-St. Paul (the headquarters), Milwaukee, Chicago, Indianapolis, Omaha, Denver, and parts of Japan, and it is moving into Hawaii. The AWA seems to ride on the back of Verne Gagne, who has been its promotional brain, and, for most of the fourteen years,

Pop retired from the ring in 1959, the same year this bull of an Italian, Bruno Sammartino, entered the business. The city of Pittsburgh has been somewhat more proud of this product, shown here after winning the championship of the mis-named World Wide Wrestling Federation.

its champ. Naturally, the AWA claims that its title carries the most prestige and authenticity.

"It goes back to 1959 in Omaha, Neb., and I won it from Edouard Carpentier," said Gagne. *"He had won a decision over Lou Thesz, the NWA champion, in Chicago. Many promoters felt Thesz was getting himself deliberately disqualified too often so he could hold onto his title. A group of them got together and said, if he got disqualified against Carpentier in that match in Chicago, Carpentier would be awarded the title. That's exactly what happened."*

The *World Wide Wrestling Federation* (WWWF), not to be confused with Mildred Burke's World Wide Women's Wrestling Association (WWWWA), covers the eastern seaboard from Washington, D.C., Baltimore and Philadelphia, north into New England, which is impressive if not precisely "world wide." But then Gorgeous George wasn't really very gorgeous, either, and Lord Blears wasn't a noble. The WWWF's most important showcase is New York City's Madison Square Garden, which is packed once a month for Pedro Morales' or Bruno Sammartino's title defenses. The booking agent for the whole territory is Vince McMahon, an old-timer in the promoting business whose father was the matchmaker for boxing promoter Tex Rickard. McMahon commutes to the East from his home in Florida, as does his chief Garden aide, Willie Gilzenberg.

Those are the big three, overshadowing the National Wrestling Federation (NWF) (which is so un-national that it is practically unknown outside Buffalo), the World Wrestling Association (WWA) in the Midwest, and the Grand Prix in Montreal.

Japan is also fragmented. The NWA used to be affiliated with the Japanese Wrestling Association, but recently switched to the All-Japan Pro Wrestling Alliance, a group formed by the popular wrestler Baba the Giant. There is an outfit that concentrates exclusively on women and midgets, plus an AWA-affiliated group, International Wrestling Enterprises, and the New Japan Wrestling Alliance.

The father of "puro-resu" in Japan was Mitsuharu Momota, alias Rikidozan, the son of a Kyushu farmer. He was discovered by some big-city sumo scouts when he was thirteen and taken to Tokyo for training and fattening up. He quit that ancient and ponderous Oriental form of wrestling in the summer of 1950, shed some blubber, and soon went in for American-style catch-as-catch-can. It was a big success and, as more and more Japanese giants quit sumo to join him, the sales of television sets zoomed, just as they had in the U.S. a few years before because of programs featuring Gorgeous George and others. Rikidozan did some wrestling in the States — he once had a draw with Lou Thesz — but he didn't really need to stray from the Far East. He became a wealthy man, bought himself a racy yellow Jaguar, built a $200,000 wrestling center, and got in all sorts of public brawls — he was once stabbed in the stomach during a nightclub fight, staggered to the microphone, and screamed obscenities at the management. He died in 1963 at age 39.

American stars like Bobo Brazil, Johnny Valentine, Bruno Sammartino, and Dick the Bruiser, and Mexican stars like Mil Mascaras and The Medics have made the lucrative trip across the Pacific. U.S. babyfaces appearing in Tokyo and Osaka often behave like heels — round-eyed foreign devils from across the sea.

Wrestlers, who have no International Brotherhood of Amalgamated Bodyslammers to negotiate for them, tend to think in terms of "territories," rather than alliances. If Killer Karl Krupp is not making enough money in Los Angeles and its auxiliary towns — Long Beach, San Bernardino, Costa Mesa, etc. — he might head back to Buffalo or down to Miami and their satellite spots. The man who books the talent for a territory usually also promotes weekly or monthly shows in the main city — *e.g.*, LeRoy McGuirk in Tulsa, Paul Jones in Atlanta, Nick Gulas and Roy Welch in Nashville. Promoters in the smaller towns give the booker-promoter a cut.

The traditional trust and respect that flourishes between promoters and wrestlers can be illustrated by the poignant and perhaps apocryphal tale of Jack Pfefer, a frail little Russian immigrant who once staged wrestling shows in New York, and Hans Steinke, a 240-pound oak of a German who was featured in *Believe It or Not* for winning a thousand matches in succession. It seems that Pfefer (pronounced "feffer" and pronouncedly stingy) had given Steinke one too many lousy payoffs and was confronted by the angry hulk in the booking office, a utilitarian place decorated with advertising posters for Brooklyn's Ridgewood Grove and other arenas. Unsatisfied by the discussion, Steinke picked up Pfefer by the ankles and hung him upside down out the tenth-floor window overlooking Times Square. They came to terms fairly quickly.

An authoritative book published in 1937, *Fall Guys, The Barnums of Bounce*, was written by Marcus Griffin, a newspaperman who had worked for Joseph (Toots) Mondt's booking office in New York and then turned traitor, exposing the machinations of various promoters and cartels of the '20s and '30s. He portrayed Pfefer as one of the world's foremost chiselers and gave this example: Wrestler Herb Freeman, not long out of City College of New York, lost a match against Jim Londos in Madison Square Garden and went around later for his payoff. Pfefer slid the check over to him, face down, and had him endorse it, then paid him $1,500 in cash. However, the check was for $2,500.

"He never made dot much before in his life," said Pfefer, defending his deception, *"so now he is richer and so am I, for being his meneger."*

Of all the promoters and matchmakers[1] who have ever drawn up a card or dreamed up a salable gimmick, Pfefer was perhaps the screwiest, a legendary character inside the business. He is retired now and living in the Boston area, but he is spoken of in the past tense because he no longer returns phone calls or sends Christmas cards to old friends. And he is spoken of in awe because of his

LIFE IS JUST A SHOW

THE SHOW MUST GO ON

COMPLIMENTS FROM
JACK PFEFER and JOE TOOTS MONDT
BROADWAY'S WRESTLING ATTRACTION
BIGGER AND BETTER THAN EVER

For years, skinny Jack Pfefer and tough ex-wrestler Toots Mondt were the bosses of New York City wrestling, allies at times, enemies at times. Both made a peck of money out of the business, both are now retired; Pfefer in Boston, Mondt in St. Louis.

large collection of wrestling photographs and memorabilia and, more enthralling to most, his reportedly vast collection of dollar bills.

At first glance, the only things notable about Pfefer were the large diamond in his pinky ring and his large nose (writer A.J. Liebling described him as "corvine," or having the appearance of a crow).

"*He was about five feet tall, skinny as a rail,*" recalled ex-wrestler Dave Levin, "*and he had a diamond that was half as big as he was on his pinky finger. It was big as a dime, really. A diamond as big as that. And he was so scared wearing it all the time that when he rode the subways — even back in those days when they were fairly safe — if it was an empty or near-empty car and he wasn't protected by a crowd, he stood by the door so he could jump when the door opened, if need be. He wouldn't even sit down. He always stood there picking his nose, and he had plenty of nose to work on.*"

Matchmakers are often burly ex-wrestlers — men like Toots Mondt, who could, and would, beat up disobedient employees to keep them in line, or Joe Malcewicz, the ex-Utica Panther, or Professor Roy Shire, Paul Jones, and dozens of others. Pfefer, who came to the U.S. as a stagehand and porter with a Russian ballet company, controlled his men — with the notable exception of Steinke — by other means. Fines, for instance. Pfefer was always fining the boys for some infraction of his rules. And by screaming non sequiturs at the top of his voice.

Pfefer had a sort of wacky, Gracie-Allen logic in almost everything he said. "*Give me a cup of tea in a glass,*" he would tell a waitress. Or he would autograph a photo with his motto: "*Life is just a bowl of pickled herring. You must taste it to like it.*" He used front men rather than apply himself for a promoter's license, reasoning, "*If I don't have a license, dey can't take it avay from me.*" He often juggled two telephone conversations at once: "*Mike, ya son of a bitch! Vare da hell are ya? Not you, dahling. Get over here, ya son of a bitch! No, not you, dahling.*"

He didn't know how to drive and, in fact, did not have the slightest conception of how mechanical contrivances worked. Bobby Managoff, later to become world heavyweight champion for a time in the early '40s, was on his way to a Brooklyn arena by subway, but a train wreck held him up. He thus violated Pfefer's first commandment: *Thou shalt always be in the dressing room an hour before the matches, thou son of a bitch.*

"Bobby, vot happened?" screamed Pfefer.

"Jack, I couldn't help it," said Managoff. *"I got the train at the right time, but there was a wreck."*

"Vy didn't ya get da train in front *of dot one?"* asked Pfefer.

The little promoter's favorite whipping boy was George Bollas, an elephantine wrestler who had been NCAA heavyweight champion for Ohio State in 1946 and who worked most of the time behind a mask as The Zebra Kid.

"One time we were going from Toledo to Akron," remembered Dave Levin. *"We generally stopped midway at a certain restaurant, and just before we got there, we saw The Zebra Kid, who was supposed to wrestle the opener, pulled over to the side with a cop, evidently getting a ticket. Pfefer was riding with me in the car.*

"'Look at dot son of a bitch,' *he said.* 'He's leaving late all da time, now he gets a ticket for speeding.' *And he's raving on about Bollas.*

"We got to the restaurant and were eating and in walked The Zebra Kid. "'Hey, ya son of a bitch, ya got a ticket for speeding, didn't ya? Vy don't ya leave earlier?'

"'Well, Pfefer, I didn't get a ticket for speeding,' *said Bollas,* 'I just got a warning ticket. It wasn't anything. The reason I was late, I had a flat tire.'

"'A flat tire!" *hollered Pfefer.* 'Vy don't you think of dose things before ya start out?'

"Now, from anybody else that would be a wisecrack, but Pfefer was sincere. He figured you had to fix your flats before you began a trip! Another time, I was driving to Grand Rapids, Mich., and Pfefer was with me, and Ivan Bulba, a Russian with a big beard. In those days, beards were unusual. All of a sudden, there was a terrific snowstorm and it was really coming down. And what happened? My car really started to get the willies, going so slow I couldn't get any power out of it.

"Pfefer said, 'God damn it, Ivan here's in the opener. Ve vill hikehitch. It isn't so far. Ivan, come, ve vill hikehitch. Davey, ya make it as soon as ya can.'

"They got out in the snow — the little weasel Pfefer and great, big, bearded Ivan Bulba. They looked like the most unholy two you ever saw walking down the highway in the storm. I said to myself, 'Who the hell will ever pick *them* up?' *Would you believe it? The first car that passed by me pulled over and those two got in. How could they be that lucky?*

"Well, it was only a few blocks and I got to a service station. I had the car fixed and went on into Grand Rapids. There was The Zebra Kid sitting in the locker room and he's got a scowl on his face. I said to him, 'What the hell's the matter with you?'

"'Oh,' *he said,* 'that goddamned Pfefer. I'm driving along the highway and there I see Pfefer and Bulba walking on the side. I pick 'em up and I bring 'em here, and all the while they're riding in the car, he's chewing me out for being late!' "

Pfefer loved to change names and nationalities, and even religions, partly to suit New York City and all its ethnic neighborhoods and rivalries. John Emerling became

Ray Schwartz. The fellow who was Terry McGinnis elsewhere was Max Martin the Romantic Wrestler for Pfefer. Giuseppe Mazza became Joe Bommerito. Johnny Iavanna was changed into Salvatore Balbo. Johnny Shaw became the above-mentioned Ivan Bulba, and Paul Boesch suddenly turned into a Jew, although his friends continued to see him go to a Lutheran Church on Sunday mornings. George Wenzel reluctantly became Dave Levin and was amazed a few months later when Pfefer changed Dutch Schweigert into George Winchell. Why, he wondered, couldn't Schweigert be Levin and Wenzel be Winchell?

"He had a Polish fella come over here," said Levin, *"and the guy must have had a Polish name of some sort, but Pfefer decided to give him a real jawbreaker, Felix Lavakoski. Pfefer was calling the promoter in Bridgeport. He was telling him,* 'Next veek, I got for ya a' new sensation, a Polack. Felix Lavakoski.' *So the guy evidently asked him,* 'How do you spell it?' *So Pfefer said,* 'L-a-v, L-a-v ... oh to hell vith it. Don't book him!'"

Harry Finkel strolled into the booking office one day to check his schedule and saw that he was to wrestle Joe Bommerito, who had borrowed $2 from him and not repaid. *"I'm not going to wrestle that son of a bitch,"* said Finkel.

"Vy the hell not?" demanded Pfefer.

"Because he's a welsher, that's why."

"A velsher!" said Pfefer. *"Vot da hell difference does it make if he's a Hungarian or a Chinaman?"*

Jack Pfefer

Over the years, all round the country, promoters have been almost as full of schemes, fun and foibles as the nuttiest of wrestlers. Joe Malcewicz of San Francisco always tried to have a main event in Salinas that would appeal to the many Filipinos in that town because they have narrow rear ends and he could squeeze more of them into the little arena. Ray Fabiani, the late violin-playing Philadelphia impresario, once on the same night, although miles apart in location and culture, promoted an Antonino Rocca-Johnny Valentine match and a Handel opera starring Renata Tebaldi.[1]

One of my dad's favorite promoters was Bill Lewis in Richmond, Va., a fat man who took pride in escorting special friends down to the local mortuary and having the undertaker haul out the custom-built Lewis coffin with a mattress in it. No tight quarters in the afterworld for him.

"He had two towns, Norfolk and Richmond," recalled Pop. *"And he rode back and forth in an ambulance. He'd lease it and his wife would drive and he'd sleep in the back. And he had an itch and a skin rash all the time from nerves. Any kind of pill you'd take, an aspirin or anything like that — he wouldn't even know what it was — he'd say,* "What're you doin'?' *And he'd take one, put it in his mouth, and drink it down with water. Any kind of pill you had!*

"One guy would say, 'Bill Lewis, what a goddamned shitty payoff this is!'

He'd answer, 'Wait a minute, wait a minute.' *He'd run out, come back in, and have eight or nine different pills in his hand. He'd say,* 'Lookit heah, I'm a sick man, and this man is going to beat me up. You heah, you heah?'

"He could actually cry. Tears would run down his face. He could cry at will. He was the damndest guy you ever met in your life."

The summer of 1956, when I toured Tennessee and Alabama with Pop, he told me the story of Bill Lewis's infamous raffle. For about a month, Big Bill ran a raffle for a pony that had been foaled right on his own Virginia farm. Finally came the big night of the drawing, Lewis himself to draw the winning ticket.

"He reached in the box and pulled out a ticket," said Pop. *"He says, "Well, wouldn't you know who won the pony! My son Blue. My son Blue won the pony!' He'd used that old gimmick where you palm the ticket. He just couldn't give that pony away, and he had a* ranchful *of ponies. And, oh, the people were sore. It killed the town for a while."*

The rest of that summer, whenever Pop or I thought we were being conned or kidded ("swerved" in the wrestlers' lingo), one of us would turn to the other and say, *"Well, wouldn't you know who won the pony!"*

The most interesting and gracious wrestling promoter I've met, and one who seems reasonably sane, is Paul Boesch of Houston, who is actually a promoter-matchmaker-wrestler-poet-author-war hero-broadcaster-art collector. That he was, and on rare occasions still is, a wrestler is evident by his wonderfully puffed-up pair of cauliflower ears, which are his trademarks. He gives out miniature-cauliflower-ear cufflinks as mementos. He would have to be dragged kicking and struggling to a plastic surgeon to have them fixed, and even though Boesch is in his '60s, I would rather join a police-department bomb squad than try to be the dragger.

In World War II, as the commander of a rifle company, he was the recipient of mementos: shrapnel wounds, two Silver Stars, two Bronze Stars, two Purple Hearts, the Croix de Guerre and, for helping take the pivotal town of Huertgen in the Huertgen Forest, the Presidential Unit Citation. He started wrestling again when he got back to the U.S., even before he received his discharge papers.

"And it really felt good to have somebody kick me in the face again," he said.

From his war experiences, he wrote a book, *Road to Huertgen*. A slim volume of his poetry, *Much of Me in Each of These*, is full of verse about war and soldiers, but also touches on clouds, dawn, happiness, angels, and a blind boy pianist. He has read his poems to audiences at the Texas Hall of State in Dallas and at Rice University in Houston.

"I find nothing incongruous in writing poetry," he said. *"When people ask me why, I say, 'Why not?'*

"… I'm still defensive about it. When people ask me what I've written and I say a book of poetry, I still look at them out of the corner of my eye, as if to say, 'Go ahead and make a crack.' "

Boesch has been broadcasting wrestling matches in Houston for more than twenty-five years. He was describing the weekly main event on radio station KLEE when the owners obtained the first Houston television license, so Boesch moved over to their Channel 2 and became the first TV sportscaster in town. He has been doing it ever since, although the program has moved from Channel 2 to 13 to 39 (UHF). He has also had shows in Dallas-Fort Worth, San Antonio, and Port Arthur.

"At least I haven't rubbed raw to where people don't watch the program anymore," he said. *"That's the only attribute that I have, taking it easy. Not only that, I try to be articulate and intelligent and not speak down to people. I realize a lot of my audience is not well educated. Some of them are Mexican people who speak*

Spanish and may have some difficulty understanding me, but for me to break it down into little words would be wrong."

For him to inject a little color into the proceedings, however, is perfectly fine. He once complained about the garlicky fumes emanating from tag-team partners Ivan Kalmikoff and Karol Krauser in pre-match and post-match interviews. When they wouldn't lay off the garlic, he conducted the next interview wearing a gasmask. And when Duke Keomuka was punishing opponents with a hold called the "stomach claw," Boesch and Larry Chene devised the Larry Chene Protective Shirt, with a front padding of foam rubber.

Wrestling has been forced to shift channels and time slots in Houston because of various other programs considered more appealing. Boesch delights in gloating over his show's longevity.

Paul Boesch

"As I always say, I wonder what happened to the Friday-night fights? Whatever happened to Robert Taylor in The Detectives*? Because of that program, they said,* 'We gotta shift you up a half-hour. This is the most important program in the world.' *And all these programs have died and we just keep going along and going along, because we must give the people something they're looking for."*

Boesch did the TV and, for almost twenty years, worked as an assistant to Houston promoter Morris Sigel. When Sigel died in 1967, Boesch compensated his widow and took over the Gulf Athletic Club, which was in bad shape because Sigel had been too ill in his last few years to pay close attention to his business. Boesch started giving tickets away — but only once to any one group — and changed the television show to Saturday from Friday, when the matches had been running live on the tube and damaging the gate at the Coliseum.

Today, pro wrestling is thriving on a weekly basis in Houston, and Boesch has time to get involved in practically every charity in town and entertain visitors in his photo-filled office on San Jacinto Street, on the edge of downtown. He is proud of his collection of wrestling statuettes, *e.g.*, Jacob wrestling the angel, two grappling bears made of whalebone, two ceramic frogs wrestling on a lily pad (which wrestler Mike Paidousis brought back to him from Japan).

Promoters like Vince McMahon in New York and Verne Gagne in Minneapolis are reluctant to grant interviews to any reporters, except those from the non-critical wrestling fan magazines, but Boesch and Sam Muchnick of St. Louis will talk about their favorite sport with anyone, defending it very well if need be. In no time, Boesch can have the listener believing that the annual NWA convention is really a meeting of the College of Cardinals.

"I am proud of wrestling and especially proud of Houston wrestling, where so much of my own time and effort has been able to color it," he said. *"I neither step on other sports nor do I step down when it comes to matching our place in the community.*

"Wrestlers are human, good and bad like everybody else, and with fewer eight-balls among them than most other sports. I trust wrestlers. In some sports, you

have to have iron-clad contracts. Our business is done on handshakes and telephone calls. It's also done in the majority of cases by people who have their own code of honor, their own set of rules that they feel are honest and fair, and I think this is great."

It's also done, he could have added, by the biggest bunch of zany ballyhoo artists since P.T. Barnum, by men who love to lure the customers through the turnstiles with the most outrageous and outlandish attractions their vivid imaginations can devise. Boesch is not at all embarrassed by this aspect of pro wrestling. In fact, he has played a great part in it, going back to the matches staged in mud which drew lots of attention, laughs and gasps before World War II, when laughs, at least, were needed.

"The first mud match ever held in this country was in Seattle, Washington, 1937," said Boesch. *"Actually, nobody knew what a mud match was. It wasn't intended to be a mud match. But we had a Hindu wrestler, Bhu Pinder. Now, in India, they wrestle on the ground and they prescribe a big circle, something like sumo, but the object is to put a man's shoulder and hip down at the same time, and, of course, the symbolism is there. If you beat a man, you've ground him into the dirt. They wet down the dirt in order to keep the dust from going all over. The dirt is churned up and kept soft. It's the cheapest medium available.*

"We thought this was a great idea for when the regular card was over. Bhu Pinder, he was there, and we had Gus Sonnenberg, former world's champion. So they were going to wrestle Hindu style, wrestle on the earth. ... It drew a great crowd. Of course, we put a little too much water on the thing, so there was, in a sense, some idea of mud. They got smeared with this stuff, but it was still a Hindu-style match.

"Well, in the crowd that night was Joe Malcewicz. He was up in Seattle for something and he saw this thing, and he said, 'Hey, that's a great idea. Can I borrow your Hindu?'

"He took Bhu Pinder to California, to San Francisco, and the first match they had with him was with Sandor Szabo [Oct. 5, 1937, in the Dreamland Arena]. Only, they just filled that ring with dirt and water until they had soft, slimy mud, and they also had newsreel cameras there. And then the newsreel cameras shot this picture and it showed all over the country.

"Well, all over the country, there were wrestling promoters in the middle of the Depression who were wondering how in the hell they were going to fill their houses. And everybody said, 'Hey, mud match!' The Hindu match was gone. The fact that Bhu Pinder was a Hindu was gone. Everything was lost in the translation.

"In places they used dirt, this was fine. Some places, like in Florida, they filled the ring with shaved ice. ... In places in West Virginia, they filled the ring with coal. Up in Wisconsin, they filled the ring with fish. That wasn't the only thing that smelt!

"The crowning irony of this whole thing was that, during the war, in a town in Germany, I was in a room in a house where a wall had been knocked out, and artillery was falling, and we were waiting for orders to move on. I was idly thumbing through a book. It was in German and I came across a picture of a couple of girls wrestling in mud. This was a scene from the United States.

"I had a German-speaking medic and I said, 'What are they saying?'

"So he read it. 'Well,' he said, 'this is a propaganda sheet. It says here, "This is the way the decadent Americans treat their women."'"

Mildred Burke vs. Leona (Babe) Gordon in a mud match
Akron, Ohio • January 23, 1938

"*I thought,* 'Oh, my God. I started the war!'"

The photos probably were of the early-1938 mud match in an Akron, Ohio, armory between Mildred Burke and Babe Gordon, watched by about 2,500 customers and covered by *Life* and numerous other publications. Burke's manager-husband, Billy Wolfe, talked her into it.

"*It was the first women's mud match in the world as far as I know,*" said Burke. "*They had had the men, but not the women. I know the promoter said to Bill one time,* 'I know how we can make some money, but you wouldn't do it.'

"'What's that?'

"*He said,* 'Put Mildred in a mud match.'

"*And Bill said,* 'What makes you think I wouldn't do it?'

"*Oh, it was really a mess, too. To this day my hearing's not too good from getting mud down in the eardrums. You put cotton in there, but sometimes it slips out, and other times, maybe you forget to put it in 'cause you have to put it in the last minute 'cause otherwise you can't hear 'em introduce or anything else too well.*

"*But I really fixed Bill up on that. He was getting way in the back so no mud got on him, and there was all this sloppy, slimy mess. So when the match was over, they had to wipe my face off to see who won. They couldn't tell with two big blobs of mud*

Mildred Burke after the mud match in Akron, Ohio

standing there, me and Gordon. I walked over to the corner and Bill was coming over very carefully to hand me a towel, trying to keep from getting too close where the mud had splattered, and there was a big, sloppy puddle right close to the corner, and I just threw both legs up in the air and came down in it and scooted, and I absolutely, completely covered him with mud. And that wasn't just for the crowd. I did it for myself!

"*I said, 'Now think again when you put me in a mud match!'*

"*Then I was in one in a little town in West Virginia ... Bluefield I think. We got in there and we were completely caked from one end to the other with mud, and then we didn't find out 'til the match was over that they didn't have showers. We weren't even checked in a hotel. We had just stopped there on the way and dressed. They handed us a bucket. All you could see was the whites of our eyes. ... It took about twenty buckets of water before we finally got enough of the mud off even to go somewhere else to wash, but we did have to stop at a motel — after that, anyway — because there was just no way of getting it all off.*

"*One other match I had was in Jacksonville, Florida, and this one was about the worst of all. I didn't know anything was really wrong until I went out there and there was this terrible odor. Oh, this really stunk and I thought, 'My gosh, where did he get this mud from? This smells so bad.'*

"*There was no time then to say anything; you had to get in the ring and wrestle. And nobody could walk! I slipped down the first thing I got in the corner. The other girl slipped down in the other corner. The referee fell down, he couldn't stand up ... We couldn't even get out to the center to get hold of each other! We finally had to crawl out there, it was so slippery. Mud really isn't that slippery — if it was just mud. So after the whole match was over — nobody could do anything but roll around — we asked the promoter, 'What on earth happened to that mud that made it so slippery like that?'*

"*It turned out he'd gotten these big five-gallon cans of lard and melted 'em and mixed 'em with the mud, and the mud itself he'd gotten out of the old swamps down there. That was my last mud match. Never again.*

"*And I had one more after that.*

"*It was recently. I wrestled Steve Allen in the mud on TV here in Los Angeles, when he had his own show by the Hollywood Ranch Market. They called me up for it and I agreed to wrestle. I told him to be sure that they sifted the mud because there could be glass and stuff in there that could just cut you to pieces. I said, 'Be sure now they get that mud sifted.'*

"*We came out and, while we were wrestling — me five-feet-two and him six-feet-two — we didn't feel anything so much, you know, in the excitement of the match and the mud going in all directions, but when we got to the showers and washed off, we were just covered with blood. We were cut to ribbons! I was just cut all over. Nothing deep, but they just kept bleeding all over, and when I got my clothes on and I came back out to the stage, he was back out there with a bathrobe on. Because he was bleeding so bad, he didn't want to put his clothes on anymore. He was just cut all over.*

"*I never even talked to him after that because he went on with the program and I went on and left. ... He said something to the audience, 'I was told to sift this mud and I told them, but they didn't do it. Somebody's going to get it!'*"

Mud matches spread to England in 1938. At the Winter Gardens in Clapham, Mary Brewer of Brixton beat Elmo Marcel of France. Columnist Art Buchwald saw two women, The Blonde Tiger of Flinsburg and Ushi of Dusseldorf, wrestle topless in a mud pit in Hamburg. After the bout, Buchwald said, waiters went from table to table in the nightclub cleaning up the patrons. The Olympic Auditorium in Los Angeles staged a mud match and provided ringside reporters with raincoats. *Time* reported "female wrestling on a mat of liquid mud" in Osaka as late as

1947. The great Strangler Lewis even once participated, albeit reluctantly and quickly:

"Lewis told me one time he wrestled this great Gama in India," said ex-wrestler George Linnehan, *"and I guess he didn't know about it when he went over there, but they wrestled in mud. He was a very neat man, a fine dresser. He got in there with this fella and he saw this mud and he was thinking, 'Ugh!' He told me, 'I got in that mud and I couldn't get down quickly enough, to get out of there. I took the money and came home.'"*

Whatever substance is possible to wrestle in, you can be sure that somewhere, sometime, two or more screwballs have wrestled in it:

• The Baskin-Robbins Bout: On Sept. 10, 1938, two pistachio nuts named Joe Reno and Roughhouse Ross battled in Minneapolis in 250 gallons of vanilla, chocolate and strawberry ice cream. The referee almost drowned, but what a way to go! Another time, promoter Bill Lewis was stopped from staging a match in fifty gallons of vanilla ice cream.

• The Molasses Battle Royal: Twelve men in the ring at once in Lake Worth, Fla., 1941. Feathers were added to the molasses just to make it more yucky. The sticky winner was Wild Bill Ludlow.

• The Tomato Bowl: Again in imaginative Lake Worth. It took a ton of tomatoes to fill the ring up to a foot, and then they were trampled by six wrestlers battling at once.

• The Blueberry Bowl: In the town of Manistique, on the upper peninsula of Michigan, in 1939, a half-inch-thick bed of berries served as the squishy, colorful battleground for Tiger Multhabet and Bulldog Lanier.

If the wrestlers don't actually perform *in* some offbeat substance, it might be smeared over them afterward. In Austin, Tex., in 1964, Verne Bottoms met Maria DeLeon in a grudge match. The loser was to be tarred and feathered. Wrestler Jack Donovan, Verne's husband, was her ringside second and, at a crucial point in the match, he jumped up on the apron, swung at DeLeon, and accidentally hit his wife instead, enabling DeLeon to win. Bottoms was so mad, she dumped the pail of tar over Donovan's head and DeLeon added the feathers.

Irish Danny McShain and Bull Curry wrestled on St. Patrick's Day once and the crazy penalty that time was that the loser would be painted green. Houston staged another match after which the loser was painted yellow.

"Tony Borne once called McShain a jackass, or a dirty jackass, or something like that," Boesch recalled. *"So it all ended up in an argument where the loser had to give a jackass a bath in the ring after it was over. We've also had a match where a guy called another wrestler 'dirty,' which wound up with the loser having to take a bath in the ring. I've got some slides of that. Tremendous, tremendous.*

"I must tell you what happened with the jackass. Borne had a manager named Leo (The Lion) Newman. The match ended with McShain losing and lying there unconscious. They brought the jackass into the ring and McShain wasn't able to rise up. All of a sudden, a couple of wrestlers came into the ring and they pointed to Leo Newman, and the people screamed, 'Yes, let him do it!' I've got some of the starkest-looking pictures you ever saw of poor Leo trying to get out of giving the jackass a bath and, eventually, the jackass literally kicked him in the head. And here's McShain lying on the canvas, with one eye open, watching it all."

Nobody else I know of has ever tussled with a jackass inside the ropes, but there have been plenty of wrestling bears, an idea that goes back at least to the

Middle Ages. Gorgeous Gus, Black Ozzie, Victor, Sonny, Terrible Ted, and Not-so-Gentle Ben are some of the bears who have prowled around American rings. Baron Von Raschke and Bobby Heenan versus Terrible Ted drew about 10,000 fans recently to Detroit's Olympia. Ted was supposedly trained by The Beast, who took off the real beast's muzzle partway through the match and forced the two heels to flee to the dressing room.

"*Bears are used mostly through the South,*" said my father. "*In Atlanta they had one ... Ginger I believe the name was. That was a funny one. They had to put leather gloves on the front paws by law because it had claws. They muzzle 'em, too. You never have to worry, really. This old Ginger, she was in heat, and this guy was starting to wrestle and Ginger kept curling him up into a little ball; would roll up this guy underneath and start humping. This guy was fighting for his life trying to get away. The people were going crazy, in hysterics. But the commission didn't think it was so hilarious. From then on, no bears in Atlanta or around Georgia.*"

Fred Kohler, later to become the successful promoter in Chicago for many years, once toured through the Midwest with a 700-pound bear. "*It kept outthinking me,*" he said. "*I finally won a match with it in Dubuque, Iowa, and turned to wrestling more orthodox opponents.*"

The most popular novelty attraction — actually it is so common that it is now no more a novelty than doubles in tennis — is the "Australian tag-team match," called that although, in all probability, Australia and Australians had nothing to do with its creation. Houston's Paul Boesch claims that his town was the first to have four men in the ring at once.

"*I had nothing to do with this,*" he said. "*This was back about 1937 or '38, and Morris Sigel's nephew — Morris was promoting here — was in the bathroom sitting on the pot one time when he got an inspiration. He came out and said to his uncle,* 'Uncle, if you can put two men in the ring to wrestle, why couldn't you put in four men? Have two men against two men?'

"*And Morris said,* 'Great idea!'

"And that's how team matches were born. Of course, that spread around the country. Then somebody got the bright idea of putting one member of each team outside and having the tag, which was infinitely more exciting. After a while, the other got kind of dull. They exhausted all of their possibilities.

"*Strangely enough, Houston does not particularly take to tag-team wrestling as a main event. Very, very rarely do they go for it. They like to see them, but if we were to give them a diet of tag-team* main events, *we'd go out of business. I've learned it from bitter experience. And as much as you'd think that,* 'Oh, my God, this is the combination that's got to do it,' *it seldom is.*

"*The two redheads, Red Lyons and Red Bastien, are a great team, but to put them in against any other two in the main event wouldn't work. After Johnny Valentine and Wahoo McDaniel had wrestled against each other for umpteen times, knocked each other's heads off, they kissed and made up and we put them in as a tag-team combination.* That *appealed to people. But it's very rare, very rare.*"

If four men in at once — which often happens when the referee loses control — adds some riotous variety to a card, why not eight men? That has been tried. For instance, in the Houston Coliseum late in 1971, the team of Ernie Ladd, Dean Ho, Jose Lothario and Nick Kozak met Johnny Valentine, King Thunderbolt, The Spoiler and Buddy Wolfe. Ladd and Valentine were the "captains."

And, if state law allows, why not mixed doubles? Tanya West and The Executioner met Lucille Dupree and Lou Klein in Detroit not long ago, but, as usual, in these matches, the men and women wrestled only each other. There had to be simultaneous tags. Chattanooga Memorial Auditorium had Rita Cortez and Tojo Yamamoto versus Barbara Galento and Pepi Rocco, wrestling under the same restrictions.

Mixed doubles can lead to some silly gags and gimmicks. My old man was guilty of one while working the Nashville-Birmingham territory. "*I had an instance in the South where I had a woman partner in a tag-team match,*" said Pop, "*and every time she'd get hurt, she'd come crying to me, 'Ooh, my arm's hurt,' and I'd kiss it and pat it for her and tell her, 'Get out there, you're doin' good.' Then she got hit in the chin and I'd kiss it real nice and console her. Nice-looking little gal.*

"*Then she got kicked in the ass and came running over to me holding her ass cheek and I said, 'Oh, no,' and I turned my back to her, and the people just roared. It was just one of those things that came along that we just took advantage of.*"

One thing Pop would never go for was a battle royal, where a promoter gets ambitious and puts ten or twenty men inside the ropes at the same time, and hopes thousands of ticket buyers will want to see the resulting melee. "*I never was involved in any free-for-all,*" Pop said. "*I said, 'I've only got one eye and I'm not going to get it knocked out.'* That's what I always was afraid of in wrestling. I'd get hit in this eye sometimes and I'd be blurred for maybe two, three days.*"

Los Angeles Battle Royal

The Olympic Auditorium in L.A. has put on a twenty-two man battle royal once a year since 1970, with the survivor supposedly winning $11,000. Bruno Sammartino, in his first Los Angeles appearance in five years, won the '72 version, which drew 11,772 fans and also had three closed-circuit theaters. Victor Rivera won in '73 over such stars as Bobo Brazil and Freddie Blassie. The City Auditorium in Atlanta staged a twenty-six man "over-the-top-rope battle royal" in 1973. In order to be eliminated, a wrestler had to be thrown out of the ring over the top rope. Ox Baker, The Assassin, Jesse James and El Mongol were among those who exited — and excited — that way. Other recent biggies: a fourteen-man battle royal in the Greensboro Coliseum, fourteen men in the Milwaukee Arena, twenty men in Philadelphia. Back in May 1946, Houston had a battle royal with just five men;

Dizzy Davis, Bob Wagner, Jack McDonald, Tug Carlson, and Jules Strongbow. Inflation obviously has set in.

Bill Lewis was credited, or blamed, for inventing the boxing battle royal, in which six men slug it out with one boxing glove apiece. Gloves are used every so often in wrestling as a gimmick, usually by two opponents who have done everything possible to each other in a series of regular matches.

"*I put up my southern title in a boxing match,*" said Pop. "*We had big crowds all the time in Birmingham. That's where I won my title and that's where I lost it. The promoter's brother, Herb Welch ... I wrestled him a few times and beat him in there, and then he told me he'd fight me.*

"Fight you! I'll kill ya boxing," *I told him.*

"*Because I beat one guy boxing already. In a little town, I cold-cocked one of the promoters, who also wrestled, which led to a boxing challenge. That's when I soaked my glove in a bucket of water and I hit him with a wet glove and, boy, the water went* splat *and looked terrific! I can't even think of the guy's name.*

"*Anyway, Herb Welch jumped in the ring and challenged me to a fight. This was when I was just about ready to get out of the territory. I told Nick Gulas, the boss of the territory along with Roy Welch, that this could be a hell of a deal. I'd put up my title, belt and all, that I could beat him boxing. And we had a hell of a show.*

"*Somebody was holding me up in the ring. I went out on the apron and they were holding me up. Every time they'd push me to go in the ring, he'd hit me again. Out I'd go and they'd start counting all over again. He must have hit me eight or ten times out of the ring, then when I finally fell in the ring, then I was counted out. That's how I lost. My two seconds were helping push me in the ring and they were the ones who lost it for me.*

"*It was all fighting, just a regular boxing match. It was easy. A boxing match is ten times easier than wrestling, because you can go all night long fighting. Easy. Oh, the fans went crazy! They loved it!*"

The Jares-Welch fight was typical — another one was Bob Orton versus Eddie Graham in Florida in the mid-'60s — but there once was a vicious variation in Salem, Ore., something called a West Virginia-coal-miner's-glove match. No time limit, no disqualification, winner take all. Atop one of the ring posts was a glove with steel inside. The first man — Bull Ramos or Dutch Savage — to get to the glove could use it as he pleased, or the other fellow could wrest it away and do likewise. Good, clean, bloody fun. The athletic commission in Oregon must not be a namby-pamby bunch.

Then there is the "brass knucks" match, another innovation that Paul Boesch claims for Texas.

"*We had Bull Curry here some years ago, and Bull, of course, was the toughest-looking and toughest coot there ever was,*" said Boesch. "*He still is. ... I remembered reading in Jack Dempsey's memoirs that he had boxed Bull in Detroit. I was trying to show how tough Curry was in his own style of wrestling. This is when we thought of brass knucks as being the ultimate in savage-type wrestling. It was back in 1960, somewhere around there.*"

Lots of wrestling territories today, in addition to a regular championship, a tag-team championship and maybe even a TV championship, have a brass-knucks trophy, which goes to the top dog in a roughhouse, anything-goes category. Brass knuckles are not used, although sometimes, as in LeRoy McGuirk's Tulsa-Little Rock territory, the competitors tape their knuckles.

Chain and strap matches are very big these days and come in, it seems, a variation for each nationality and taste:

• The Russian Chain Match:

Wahoo McDaniel had one versus Mr. Houston. They were chained together by their right wrists and used the chain to choke each other and batter each other bloody. Sometimes in these affairs, the chain comes loose and one of the wrestlers wraps it around his fist for what *Wrestling Monthly* called "a super brass knuckle." Whitey Caldwell and Ron Wright had a spectacularly bloody Russian chain match in Knoxville, afterward claiming 274 stitches between them.

• The Indian Chain Match:

Billy Red Cloud had one against Bobby Heenan in Detroit in 1972. Red Cloud wound the chain around the villainous Heenan and then yanked, spinning his victim like a top.

• The Indian Strap Match:

Less dangerous than a chain match. In this one, the opponents are attached by eight feet of rawhide. Great for choking, but not nearly as bloodletting. Wahoo McDaniel met Stan (Crusher) Stasiak in a strap match in Houston in July 1972, and McDaniel has had many others.

• The Mexican Death Match:

No time limit. A Jose Lothario specialty in which the winner gets one minute in the ring with the loser with no referee present.

• The Hindu Death Bout:

Leather straps again (but no mud). Tiger Jeet Singh had one against The Sheik at Cobo Arena in Detroit.

• The Italian Chain Match:

Tony Marino had one versus Killer Tim Brooks in the Cleveland Arena. Brooks' sneaky manager, Eddie Creachman, was handcuffed at ringside to Marino's temporary second, a wrestler named Psycho, so he couldn't pull any monkey business. The match ended in a draw when Marino and Brooks knocked each other out simultaneously.

• The Chair Death Match:

Tex McKenzie versus The Sheik with wooden chairs permitted as weapons. The chairs were soon broken and the two rivals used the remaining sticks and splinters to cut and jab. McKenzie even stretched those elastic rules and used the press table as a giant bludgeon. Nero would have loved being ringside, except he would have been annoyed at the gore splattered on his toga.

• The Roman Gladiator Match:

An invention of Freddie Blassie, or so he claims. A gladiator match is over when one man is unconscious or helpless and is dragged completely around the inside of the ring.

It is Blassie who is probably the biggest exponent of cage or fence matches, but he was not the originator. Once again, Boesch claims that honor for Texas, and I begin to suspect that this charming man has a bit of Irish blarney in him, a compulsion to claim his adopted state started or invented everything from the cotton gin to the flying mare. But, on second thought, Texas wrestling is just wild and nutty enough that it is possible he's not kidding me.

"It wasn't totally my idea," he said. *"We had kind of a wild match in Galveston. Bull Curry was involved in that, too. Bull was always involved in something wild.*

A fellow named Norman Clark was promoting there. I was refereeing, and he said, 'Golly, I wish I had some way to keep those guys in the ring.'

"*And I remembered that in Dunedin, New Zealand — Dunedin is a town on the south island down there — they wrestle in a ring out over the chairs in a town hall. To keep the wrestlers from falling out into the laps of people who are sitting right around the ring and can't move, they put a net — like a tennis net — around the ring on the outside of the poles. You'd get in the ring and then they would bind this thing around.*

"*Well, it was a great idea in Dunedin, New Zealand, and it drew a big crowd in Galveston, but it didn't keep the guys in the ring. We used a fish net because this was typical of Galveston, being a fishing capital. Then we decided — this was the middle '50s, somewhere around there — to make it into a fence match in Houston ... What we did first was build a frame and use chicken wire, and then we put barbed wire up on top of the thing to keep them in — some strands of barbed wire. We were actually saying they would wrestle inside a barbed-wire fence, and that did attract a hell of a crowd. It drew a big gate because it was something new and, of course, because of somebody being behind a fence and not being able to get out.*

"*But the fence was a little inadequate because you have twenty feet of fence and you stretch chicken wire, and even though you have a two-by-four frame, eventually it got busted by somebody's head. So then, you say, what do you do, go to a cyclone-fence guy? Yes. We had a fellow who donated this fence, made it for the ring. We're still using it.*

"*Eventually the commission said,* 'We frown on the idea of barbed wire. How about cutting it out?' *So, we cut out the barbed wire part.*"

Buddy Colt tries to climb over the top of the cage to escape the wrath of Paul Jones at the Bayfront Center Arena in St. Petersburg, Florida.

The fence idea naturally spread. The way wrestlers wander from territory to territory, there is no way to keep a secret even if a promoter had reason to. In 1961 at the Olympic in L.A., Blassie met Mr. Moto with the ring encircled by chicken wire. In October 1972, Dory Funk Jr. put his National Wrestling Alliance belt on the line against Fritz Von Erich inside a cage. Fred Curry, Bull's son, wrestled The Sheik outdoors in Cincinnati in a cage, the sides of which were about thirty feet high.

"It was a wild battle," said Curry, *"and after a while, we hit one side of the cage so hard we broke through, got cut, and bled so badly they had to stop the match."*

The opposite of a cage match is the lumberjack match, in which there are not even ropes. A number of other wrestlers are stationed around the ring to throw back in anyone who is tossed out or who tries to escape. John Valentine met Crusher Stasiak in Houston in 1972 with an "eight-man posse" guarding the exits. In Pittsburgh that same year, Manny Soto, Waldo Von Erich, the Fargo brothers, and others were stationed around the ring when George (The Animal) Steele met Bruno Sammartino. Hampton, Va., staged one in which the guarding wrestlers were given canes to use as weapons, except for the Royal Kangaroos, who used their boomerangs.

Apart from the fun and games and gimmicks, promoters must attend to straight business matters: credits and debits, advertising, arena rentals, labor costs, insurance, and, yes, competition. And not just competition, but outright territorial wars.

Almost every territory has had at least one. In the 1930s, Toots Mondt's group in New York forced out Jack Pfefer, so Pfefer gathered some light-heavyweights and started running opposing shows, advertising "no fat bellies." Sam Muchnick, the man who was to become NWA president, battled Lou Thesz and his father for control of St. Louis in the 1940s. Johnny Doyle challenged Aileen and Cal Eaton in Los Angeles and lost. George Becker failed in an attempt to move in on Jim Crockett's Charlotte territory, and so on.

The current important battlefront is Atlanta, where ex-wrestler Paul Jones has been promoting since 1944, running shows every Friday night in City Auditorium and providing talent to other Georgia and Florida towns. One of his partners in ABC Booking, Inc., wrestler Ray Gunkel, died of a heart attack in 1972 after a match in Savannah. In November of that year, Gunkel's pretty widow, Ann, opened a rival booking office and hired away twenty-five of Jones' wrestlers.

The spectacle of an ex-fashion model becoming a wrestling promoter and battling the cauliflowered establishment brought the press running. It turned out that Mrs. Gunkel was not fighting alone. She had a partner and matchmaker, Tom Renesto, who had once wrestled as a masked villain, one of The Assassins, before becoming an assistant to Mrs. Gunkel's late husband.

"I didn't know a thing about it until Monday morning," said Jones, the week he found himself wrestlerless. *"The whole thing just happened overnight. They just took my wrestlers over. But Paul Jones is still in business. I'm not retiring and I'm not quitting. I'm just going to out-promote them. This town isn't big enough for two wrestling promotions."*

His remaining partner, ex-wrestler Lester Welch, was even more determined. Since Jones is in his seventies and not in good health, Welch has carried the burden of the fight. The two formed Mid-South Sports, Inc., and abandoned ABC Booking, of which Mrs. Gunkel owns a part.

"When you spend your whole life working for something," said Welch, *"and you invest it and somebody tries to take it away, you're going to fight."*

"She's carrying on the dream of her husband," said wrestler Dick Steinborn, defending Mrs. Gunkel. *"Ray had wrestled in the tank towns in the early days. He knew how bad it could be for the wrestlers, how the wrestler could be treated badly by promoters.*

"She has opened up something new and exciting for us. The conditions are much better. We're all working out harder, we're better oriented, sleeping better, and we're happier with our families."

One thing Gunkel Enterprises insisted on was a physician on hand at all matches. *"My husband died on a dressing-room floor in Savannah,"* Mrs. Gunkel said. *"It was an hour before a doctor arrived. I'll never be able to forget that. I'll always wonder if he could have been saved if there had been a doctor there."*

Late in 1973, the Battle of Atlanta was still going on.

Another important business concern of promoters is television, without which the wrestling industry would certainly wither and maybe die.

When television came along in the late '40s, promoters of wrestling didn't know how to handle it, nor did anybody else in sports. It was quickly discovered that television matches would pack taverns, sell sets, and move advertised merchandise, and stations were signing up promoters right and left. In Los Angeles in August 1951, for example, set owners could see wrestling workouts on Sunday mornings, regular matches every week night and Saturday afternoons. By February 1953, the market was even more saturated: nine live wrestling programs plus two or three more that had been "canned" elsewhere.

Announcers, as well as wrestlers, became national celebrities. Dick Lane called his first match in 1945 for an experimental station in L.A. (and is still at it almost thirty years later, still yelling "Whoooa, Nellie!" into the microphone when the action gets wild).

"Some of the names for holds weren't very delicate," he said, *"so I had to think up new ones. I'd just make up a name describing the way it looked to me. Like the crotch-locked leg strangle — and that's the delicate name! In a few years, my names became the proper nomenclature."*

Dick Lane—you might remember him as the Boston Braves' manager in *The Babe Ruth Story*—has been broadcasting wrestling matches in Los Angeles for almost thirty years. Here he managed to elicit a few comments from behind a sinister hood. Lane invented many of the terms for wrestling holds, including the "crotch-locked leg strangle." *"And that's the delicate name!"* he says.

In the East, Dennis James made a reputation for himself by using sound effects to match or mock the action on the mat: twisting a cracklebone (a rubber dog bone with steel wires inside) when a leg was being twisted, playing a waltz record when the two wrestlers were gouging each other's eyes. Ringside announcer Guy LeBow used to put on an air-raid helmet when the action got furious. Once a German heel rolled over to the edge of the ring and clapped his gargantuan hand on the helmet. LeBow heard bells the rest of the night.

But by the mid-'50s, the novelty had worn off and the party was over. TV stations were offering different fare. Wrestling was a classic victim of overexposure. Luckily, the promoters hit on a new formula, a way to *use* TV, rather than be drained dry by it and discarded, like boxing or an old Brillo pad.

"In wrestling today, even though it's on TV, the fan is never shown the match he really wants to see," said Willie Gilzenberg of the WWWF. *"He has to come in person to see that. If you give it away for nothing, why should anybody come to the arena to pay to see it?"*

For example, AWA TV-studio matches are shown live locally in Minneapolis-St. Paul and the tapes are sent to TV stations in Duluth, Fargo, Chicago, Honolulu, Japan, etc., where the AWA stages regular shows. Tapes made in Tulsa are seen a few days later in, among other places, Little Rock, with spliced-in locker-room or ringside interviews ballyhooing an upcoming Little Rock card. Wrestling interviews are very transparent hard-sell, as shown by this Fort Worth conversation between Bearcat Wright and announcer Dan Coates:

Bearcat: *"But the big thing is, Dan, I'm here to announce that the main reason for me coming back to Texas was to obtain a match with Crusher Stasiak. That match has been made."*

Dan: *"Yeah, you don't mean it!"*

Bearcat: *"You bet. That match is in the bag. For once and for all, all the derogatory remarks that Stasiak made regarding me — I'm going to push 'em right down his throat, Dan. Now I don't want to stand here and sound like a big braggart or anything ..."*

Dan: *"You don't, keep talkin'."*

And Bearcat did until Stasiak's manager stuck his nose into the interview and precipitated a brawl.

From WTCN in the Twin Cities comes this gem from heroic Verne Gagne:

"As for Mr. Bockwinkel's contention that I'm over the hill, Marty, and that I'll be beaten so badly tonight that I'll be humiliated into retirement ... well, all I can say is let him prove it in the ring. If I've learned one thing in my many years in wrestling, Marty, it's that words are meaningless unless they're backed up in the ring."

Gagne was wrong, Marty. For hyping the gate, words mean a hell of a lot in pro wrestling today.

A 1968 interview with Bobo Brazil and Gene Kiniski on the set of the Los Angeles TV wrestling program turns into a free-for-all.

Chapter 7
The Fans
"Killer Kowalski Believes in Sauerkraut"

Notes on a night at Madison Square Garden:

Promoter Vince McMahon puts on shows here about once a month, usually on Monday nights, and they resemble my image of street festivals in Spanish Harlem. There are so many Puerto Ricans in the crowd that the concessionaires should sell *cuchifritos* rather than hot dogs. Lots of untucked-in shirts, just like I have seen on the streets of San Juan and Ponce. Teen-age Latin kids in sneakers, some of their older brothers wearing tank shirts, their sisters equipped with Kodak Instamatic flash cameras. They are here to cheer for their countryman, Pedro Morales, the latest in a line of dark, swarthy stars in New York wrestling — Jimmy Londos, Antonino Rocca, Bruno Sammartino — and the very first Puerto Rican champion.

As I walk in, the loudspeaker says children under 14 are not allowed to watch wrestling exhibitions, by state law, which seems silly. Well, OK, it isn't exactly Sesame Street or a Disney movie, but matches are regularly on television, accessible to anybody who can get UHF channels on their sets, so why not here? I remember seeing babies in their mothers' arms in the Houston Coliseum and little kids crawling under the seats.

Here vendors are selling fifty-cent programs containing no articles and an incorrect card. They are also selling little American and Puerto Rican flags to wave, large posters of Pedro, and plenty of beer. Some of the people in the seven dollar ringside seats don't look like they can afford it, but there they are, some of them with their wives and two or three kids, who go up to the ring and pound on the blue mat to see how hard or soft it is. I talk to some ringsiders.

"*In an article when Pedro and Bruno were great, real friends,*" says a 14-year-old Puerto Rican boy, "*Bruno told Pedro,* 'When you wrestle, make the match real exciting as much as you can because some people have gathered money all month just waiting to see you in action.'"

"*Mr. Fuji and Toru Tanaka, I don't like them guys at all, not at all,*" says a teenager from Queens. "*They always come and they start puttin' salt in people's eyes. It can blind 'em; it's not a fair fight at all.*"

"*It's a good sport,*" says a man from Linden, N.J., "*better than sittin' in a tavern. I watch it at home, Saturday evenings, six-thirty. A lot of it English, too.*"

"*I just like the real live matches,*" says a teenager from Long Island. "*On TV, it just loses some of the flavor. You don't get to yell and scream. That's the fun part. It's not just watching, you've got to get into it.*"

At eight-twenty, the fans start whistling, getting into it early. Shortly after eight-thirty, the first two wrestlers appear and climb into the ring.

Juan Caruso vs. Mike Graham.

Fat, bearded Caruso wearing a black tank shirt and black tights, swinging a bolo. A man behind me says Sonny King wrapped it around Caruso's neck on TV last night; I discover I'm missing many of the nuances because I haven't been following the TV-studio build-up matches on UHF. Graham is much trimmer and younger, wearing white trunks. Caruso chokes, bites, pulls hair, begs for mercy, appeals to the audience for support that never comes. Young Graham gets the advantage and an authority sitting behind me says, "*That's a submission hold, I think. I think so.*" Yes, by golly, Caruso gives up. "*I told you it was a submission hold,*" the authority tells his girlfriend. "*I knew it!*"

Joe Nova vs. Flying Fred Curry.

Nova, in purple tights, weighs 275 pounds and should drop fifty of them. "*He needs a bra,*" says a lady down the row. The trimmer, younger, nicer Curry bounces around like Antonino Rocca used to. During the match, Nova tries the old, tired "*shake hands and let bygones be bygones*" routine and the crowd yells "*No, no*" to babyface Curry. Curry pins him and a young, handsome hero has won again. "*Isn't he fantastic?*" says the authority.

Gorilla Monsoon vs. The Black Demon.

The Demon in a black hood, but his face is not covered, again by state law — or at least by state-commission ruling. Monsoon is from Manchuria, says the program, although he looks no more Oriental than an Italian-American who lives in New Jersey, which, in fact, is what he is. The Black Demon is from "parts unknown." Certainly not from a good wrestling school. Monsoon beats him easily.

Pedro Morales vs. George (The Animal) Steele.

By now, the Garden is almost packed to capacity. The *Times* will give the attendance as 19,512. The main event is on early for some reason. Steele has a bald head, black tights, and a hairy back. Morales bright red trunks, championship belt, brilliantined hair. When the referee scolds Steele for some dirty, illegal trick, The Animal gives a marvelous, slack-jawed, drooly stare at the ceiling. Finally, the hero has taken enough and makes his two-fisted comeback. Sweet vengeance. Hysteria in the crowd, a roar like ten Knick championships. People standing on seats, on backs of seats. Cameras flashing. A woman behind me loses her balance, claws the air in desperation as she falls and gives me a four-inch slash on the neck. If her fingernails aren't clean, I'm liable to develop a hell of an infection. Steele uses the old hidden-weapon gimmick, sometimes putting whatever it is in his mouth to hide it from the referee. Firecracker goes off somewhere in the audience. The shrieking never ceases. Pedro finally gets Steele groggy — or maybe Steele is a little sick from taking a bite out of a turnbuckle — and leaps at him chest-first from the top rope, then pins him. The whole spectacle takes fifteen minutes and fifty-nine seconds and the crowd has been standing and screaming the whole time. Steele tries a sneak attack as Morales celebrates, but Morales bashes him out of the ring, and Steele, creepy, crawly thing that he is, scurries for the dressing room like a loathsome bug escaping the light. Flags wave. "*Viva Puerto Rico,*" yells a man in front of me.

"*My God,*" I say to the authority after I slump back into my seat and blot the blood off my neck wound, "*what if Steele had beaten Pedro?*"

"*He'd never get out of here,*" he says with a grin.

I believe him.

Ernie Ladd-Toru Tanaka vs. Sonny King-Indian Jay Strongbow.

King, tall and dark, balances the match — a good-guy Black on the team opposite a bad-guy Black, Ladd. Strongbow in a war bonnet, King in flowered pink trunks, Ladd wearing a crown, Tanaka in bare feet. All they need is an Arab referee to make this a United Nations coffee klatch. Crown and war bonnet shed, they go after each other. Ladd, in trouble against Strongbow, kneels and begs for mercy, but Strongbow just goes into his high-stepping war dance. Audience war-whooping, and if you've never heard thousands of Puerto Ricans war-whooping, you haven't lived. Tanaka keeps indicating in sign language that Strongbow is crazy. Babyfaces win the first fall, heels win the second. In the third, Tanaka throws salt in the Indian's eyes and the ref gives the heroes the match on a disqualification. Tanaka gets in some sort of ruckus en route to the dressing room and a teen-age girl behind me yells, "*I hope they kick his ass!*"

Vicki Williams vs. Fabulous Moolah.

Barefooted Vicki is a peroxide blonde. Moolah has "World's Champ" on the back of her short robe. Lots of wolf whistles. At one point, Moolah stands on the bottom rope posing for the crowd and Vicki drop-kicks her in the buttocks. Moolah goes over the top rope and out of the ring. Undaunted, Moolah climbs back in and wins as usual.

I leave during a second tag-team match, *Eddie Graham-Don Curtis vs. Terry Funk-Dory Funk, Sr.* I'm worn out, mostly from getting up and down dozens of times, trying to see over and around all the people in front of me who refuse to stay seated. If I'm tired, I wonder how the small, elderly, gray-haired woman in the front row must feel. All evening she has been on her feet, pounding the mat, shouting abuse at the heels, alerting the referee to foul tricks he missed. Time after time, a cop has to gently lead her back to her seat as she fusses and fumes.

I learned later that the woman was Mrs. Georgette Kriger, 73 years old. She and her sister, a couple of years younger, take a bus north from Baltimore every month in order to see the Garden wrestling exhibitions. They have been making the trip for fifteen years.

> **Woman Wrestlers Headline Program at Garden Tonight**
>
> Women wrestling for the first time in New York is the main attraction on tonight's exhibition card at Madison Square Garden. Women had been prohibited from appearing on a New York mat until last month when the State Athletic Commission lifted the ban. The scheduled participants are Fabulous Moolah and Vicki Williams.
>
> Second-billing on the program goes to Pedro Morales, who will meet George (the Animal) Steele. Morales is undefeated in 14 consecutive Garden appearances and he has a large and devoted following in New York.
>
> In what might be another first, a father-son team will appear in a tag-team exhibition when Dory Funk and his son, Terry, oppose Don Curtis and Eddie Graham. The program begins at 8:30 o'clock.

**Madison Square Garden
July 1, 1972**

"*We love it, that's all I can say,*" said Mrs. Kriger. "*Sure, I like to see the good guys win. But you have to have bad guys, too. They make life exciting.*"

Mrs. Kriger and her sister are merely the latest in a series of wrestling zealots in New York City. At Ridgewood Grove in Brooklyn, there used to be a man of 70-plus nicknamed Piccolo Pete who serenaded losing favorites with a tune on his piccolo, hoping to revive them. On the less constructive side, and far more famous, was Hatpin Mary.

Mrs. Eloise Patricia Barnett of the Bronx had been going to wrestling matches for years before TV announcer Dennis James called attention to her, and ordered his cameras aimed at her, in the late '40s. An anonymous lamp-shade braider, she got her first notoriety when the cameras caught her jabbing a hatpin at Stu Hart and Eddie King at the Winter Garden in the Bronx.

James ran a contest to give her a nickname and, after going through more than 2,500 entries, he picked "Hatpin Mary." The athletic commission spoiled her fun a bit by ordering her to either leave the hatpin at home or stay home herself. From then on, she was limited to yelling or offering a baby bottle to crying villains, although she once rubbed a Popsicle on George Linnehan.

(In 1956 in Albany, Ore., wrestler Doug Donovan came out of the ring and into the vicinity of a 73-year-old widow. Suddenly, he let out a bellow and kicked the woman. She sued for $75,000, Donovan's attorneys produced a two-inch needle

Everybody's grandma loves wrestling, or so it seems. At Topeka, Kansas, these grandma-aged twins [Mertie and Gertie Hite] take exception to some miscarriage of justice in the ring.

found on the floor near her seat. Donovan didn't have to pay a cent, except for legal fees.

(Speaking of suits, L.F. Pierce of Lee County, N.C. was seated at ringside at a local arena in 1963 when a 240-pound wrestler landed in his lap. He sued, but the state Supreme Court upheld a lower-court ruling that Pierce, as a longtime wrestling fan, should have been aware of the dangers of sitting so close. *Sports Illustrated* commented, *"So now it has been established that if you are hit by a flying wrestler in North Carolina, you have only yourself to blame; you have to pay your own medical bills and you don't even get to keep the wrestler."*)

Wrestling addicts, the true believers, are among the most ardent sports fans on earth. When ex-First Lady Bess Truman was asked what she missed most about Washington, D.C., she replied, *"Wrestling on Thursday nights."* A Peoria man was watching his idol, Verne Gagne, get mauled on television, and finally got so worked up that he got out his .38-caliber pistol and shot at the screen. The glass took the full impact, luckily for him, because otherwise, the picture tube would have exploded. It has been proven over the years that the addicts will buy anything with their heroes' names on it — the life story of Bruno Sammartino on a long-playing record, candy drops called Wild Red Berries, magazines, photographs, Dr. X masks, Baron Michele Leone's health booklet, Sandor Szabo's Hammerlock recording of *It's All in the Game*, and a boxed game called *"Grapplin', a fast-moving, exciting game of professional exhibition wrestling"* (one card says, "Your opponent misses a body block, hits his head on the ringpost and is down. You may try for a pin").

Sometimes a wrestler, even a rotten no-good heel, can be an inspiration, as in this case in Boston: *"Wrestlers are health faddists,"* said a fan. *"Killer Kowalski believes in sauerkraut. It's good for bursitis, arthritis and neuralgia. Juices are good for you. And every time he gets an injury, he puts Saran Wrap, like on his knee. It holds so tight, you know. You put that on your face and you die; it's better than a cast. Saves him a lotta doctor bills. It worked for me."*

There is not much doubt that most of the true believers are old people or people from the lower-income and education brackets — the so-called blue-collar workers. Puerto Ricans in New York, Mexicans in Los Angeles, factory workers in Detroit, miners in West Virginia, everybody's grandmother.

"Lower status and older age generate a whole complex of social and social psychological conditions which both ready most spectators for the harsh violence of the match and lend a credibility to the performance, which is difficult to comprehend in other social circles," said Professor Gregory Stone of the University of Minnesota.

Well, professor, then shouldn't the promoters also try to appeal to the higher classes and thus widen the market? No.

"The promoters have cornered a market," he said, *"and are quite content to keep that market because they know it is going to last. If they try to expand their*

market into the higher economic strata, they will be in trouble. But I think they are too smart for that."

Professor Stone himself didn't behave too intelligently one time in a Wisconsin bar. He tried to convince the patrons that wrestling was fake and got chased out of the place.

The fans believe, worship, hate and yell. They always yell.

"*It's been a satisfaction for a lot of people,*" said announcer Dick Lane. "*I see wizened little men, all week long browbeaten by wives and bosses. For their admission, they can vent their spleen on that one guy.*"

"*... People who enjoy it and enter into the spirit of the thing receive a very beneficial catharsis from watching a good match,*" said a veteran ringside physician in Denver. "*Society prevents most of us from giving physical expression to our anger. We can't usually whip an impertinent truck driver, or the big guy who kicks sand in our face at the beach. So, we let two other guys work out our hostilities for us. It's safer that way.*"

Safer, that is, until the spectator just stops yelling and becomes a combatant himself. Freddie Blassie once found a knife sticking in his calf during a match in a small town. He went back to the dressing room, extracted the knife, poured iodine on the wound, and left. Art Neilson was stabbed in the right side in Chattanooga and had to undergo two hours of surgery. Billy Edwards was stabbed in Waco, George Linnehan in New York and New Haven, Pedro Zapata in Florence, Ala.

In 1960, mean Angelo Savoldi was "boxing" Dan Hodge — another one of those "let's put on the gloves" challenges between wrestlers — in Oklahoma City's Municipal Auditorium. Hodge had been NCAA 177-pound champion thrice for the University of Oklahoma and had been undefeated in three years of collegiate varsity competition. Savoldi and Hodge were in the fifth round when a 50-year-old man from Perry, Okla., Hodge's hometown, climbed into the ring and stabbed Savoldi in the back and arm. The assailant was William Edward Hodge, Dan's father.

"*I had him beat, but the guy had to use his family to try to win,*" said Savoldi after about eighty stitches closed him up again. "*I just can't wait until I'm well enough — six, seven weeks, however long it takes. Then I'll meet him again. The fur will fly, too, I promise you. They will have to carry one or the other of us out of there.*"

Ballyhoo even from a hospital bed.

Blackjack Mulligan, a tall, mustachioed heel, has a two-foot scar on his arm and leg from a fan attack in Boston — it took 200 stitches to close the wound. "*I had just pinned Pedro Morales, the world champ, when this guy comes into the ring,*" said Mulligan. "*There must have been twenty or twenty-five cops around the ring, but this guy comes through the ropes. He had a knife and hit me on the arm and drove the knife down to the canvas. I looked down. I really thought I was going to watch myself die, there was so much blood. Funny though, I wasn't scared. I climbed out of the ring and the crowd parted suddenly and I walked myself to the dressing*

Fan Stabs Son's Foe

OKLAHOMA CITY, May 28 (AP)—A 10-round boxing match between wrestlers Angelo Savoldi and Danny Hodge ended in the fifth round here last night. Savoldi was loser to a knife wielding fan.

Police jailed William E. Hodges, 50, father of Savoldi's opponent. Savoldi, 39, was hospitalized in serious condition from knife lacerations across his back and arms.

"I just stood it as long as I could," the elder Hodge told police who booked him on assault with a deadly weapon. "If he whipped Danny fair and square it would have been all right."

The unrehearsed action came midway in the fifth round when Savoldi appeared to be getting the best of young Hodge, a former Olympic wrestler.

Oklahoma City, Oklahoma
May 27, 1960

room. Fortunately, there was a doctor there who put on the tourniquets, and I got to a good hospital right away. I was only out of work for two months."

And the attacker? He got away.

"Gorilla Monsoon, Morales' tag-team partner, saw what was going on," said a ringside observer, *"and he picked up the guy with the knife and threw him right at the feet of the cops, and the cops just looked at him and laughed and let him get away and never caught the guy."*

The police do not always shirk their duty, as proved in this incident related by ex-wrestler George Linnehan (who, coincidentally, was the ring announcer the night Mulligan got stabbed):

"One night in Brooklyn, I was wrestling outdoors with Michele Leone, before he became Baron Michele. When the match was over, there was a young fella about 17 who jumped up in the ring and motioned for everybody to come in with him, so I pushed him off to get him outta there. And when I did, everybody started coming. The police were there and they did a very good job, but one of 'em had an awful time because this fella grabbed for his gun and he tore the leather holster on him, but the cop got the gun away from him. He'da shot me, he'da shot me.

"I saw this other man get up in the ring and he just stood there and I kept watching him. A tall man he was, in a light suit. I backed up a little bit and he said, 'George, I'm Lieutenant So-and-So. Come over here.' *So I backed right up to him and I stayed there and I was all right.*

"But then I had to go down to the police station. They were going to have me arrested for hittin' the kid! But I wiggled out of that.

"Another time a guy came into the ring with a knife, but he got away. This was in San Antonio. And when I got into the dressing room, I said to this cop friend of mine, 'Boy, what a friend you are! Where were you when this fella came in with the knife?'

"He said, 'He wouldn't of touched ya.'

"I said, 'Are you kidding? I'm in there almost naked and this knife looked awful big to me!'

"He said, 'I'd of shot that thing out of his hand the minute he lifted it.'

"I think he would have, too."

In Baltimore one night, Dick Daviscourt had a headlock on Gino Garibaldi when a local grocer took justice into his own hands, jumped into the ring, and slugged Daviscourt under an ear. In San Antonio a fan snatched away the timekeeper's hammer, climbed up on the ring apron, and clouted Johnny Valentine on the head, knocking him out. In West Springfield, Mass., in 1972, rioting fans had their own cans of tear gas to use on the police. In Cleveland, a Tony Marino-Killer Kowalski match sparked a riot in which a flying chair broke several of the lights above the ring. Marino fell on the broken glass and it took more than seventy stitches to fix him up.

The late Johnny Doyle, who promoted in L.A., Detroit, Boston and Australia, among other places, and announcer Dick Lane agreed that the worst riot they ever saw was in 1949 in the Olympic Auditorium in Los Angeles, set off by Gorgeous George. George was wrestling Jim Mitchell, The Black Panther, and threw Mitchell out of the ring. He wouldn't let him get back in, even kicking him in the face as he tried to crawl through the ropes. The Olympic exploded into a riot. Down an aisle and first into the ring was a big black man bent on making Gorgeous into something ugly. George leg-dived him, yanked him off his feet, and managed to jump out of the ring and into the tunnel underneath that led to the dressing rooms (since closed up). Timekeeper Jack Smith threw a chair in front of the entrance to block it. In the melee, a man from Azusa was stabbed in the shoulder and another man had his thumb broken.

Gorgeous, Panther Sued for $30,000

LOS ANGELES—INS. Professional wrestler "Gorgeous George" (George Wagner) and "The Black Panther" (Jim Mitchell), who make their living throwing each other around, may have to pay $30,000 damages — for throwing each other around.

A suit in that amount was on file Thursday by three spectators as the outgrowth of a riot at Olympic Auditorium last Aug. 24 when the Gorgeous One threw Mitchell out of the ring.

Complianants Claude Bullard and his wife, Esther, and Charlie W. Morelock also named matchmaker Babe McCoy, booking agent Johnny Doyle and Alvah M. Eaton, described as doing business with the Olympic Wrestling Club, in their damage suit.

Bullard charged that in addition to injuries received when Mitchell fell on him, he was stabbed in the riot that followed.

December 2, 1949 article

The eastern equivalent happened at Madison Square Garden the night of Nov. 19, 1957. Antonino Rocca and Edouard Carpentier had just been declared the winners over Dr. Jerry Graham and Dick the Bruiser. Graham, always the sore loser, slugged Rocca when he was taking his bows and drew blood. Rocca, in frenzy, then banged Graham's head against a ringpost until he, too, was bleeding. The fans went berserk.

Two policemen were injured, somebody stole Graham's sequined robe, more than 500 chairs were damaged, and three overzealous customers were fined or jailed.

Dr. Julius Helfand, chairman of the State Athletic Commission, was less than tickled. He canceled the next Garden wrestling show, fined Rocca and Graham $1,000 apiece, Bruiser $500 and Carpentier $100.

"I'll never forget one time in Bluefield, West Virginia," said Reb Russell. *"I was wrestling the local boy and I defeated him in a very unsportsmanlike manner. After I had him pinned from a slam, I helped him to his corner and slammed him again. This was too much for the crowd and they came like a wall of human flesh into the ring after me. I had to fight like a man possessed to get to the dressing room.*

"I had long ago learned that you should never let a crowd get you down on the floor because they'll kick you into unconsciousness. And I didn't desire that. But, in reaching the dressing room, which had walls of plasterboard, I had to climb out through a window and run out into the cold February night in my tights. I told the other two wrestlers who had taken me to the match that I would see them on the main road.

"There was a forest of trees and brush near the main road and that was where I headed for. Some kid that saw me go out the window notified the fans coming out of the arena and they started in pursuit. They beat the bush for me, and one fellow pressed so close that I could have reached out and touched him. They looked all over for me, but due to the cold, they didn't keep up the search. I was almost freezing.

"An hour later, I walked out on the road and joined my friends near a gas station. I knew it was them because they blinked their lights from time to time to make sure that I observed them. I was never so glad to see anybody in my life. I was purple from the cold and took a good snort of whiskey, which warmed me considerably.

"Another time, in Ottawa, Canada, I had to fight for my life. I was wrestling a young French wrestler from Montreal named Larry Moquin. It was VJ night and there were a lot of the French from Hull, across the river; mostly young punks. As usual, I was wrestling dirty and those Frenchmen left their seats and stood

around the ring, some trying to reach my legs, and finally, at the blow-off, when I beat Moquin for the second fall, they went out of their minds with rage.

"I was struck by several Coca-Cola bottles. They struck me with chairs, fists, and I had a terrible time reaching the dressing room, and even then, they tried to break the dressing-room door down. I grabbed two quart bottles that the fighters used and I waited for them to come through that door. It's a good thing they didn't because I would have been held for murder.

"The arena looked like a shambles that night after my match. There were no policemen; only ushers with uniforms whom the crowd paid no attention to. Why should the ushers try to save me when they only got a buck a night? They broke one hundred chairs, more or less. Many spectators were hurt from the bottles bouncing across the ring. Some hit the ringposts and smashed in a hundred pieces. After that riot, they served the fans their Coca-Cola in paper cups. That Ottawa crowd were the worst bunch of morons that I ever wrestled for. They finally had to build the ring twice as high as the average ring to keep the crowd away from the wrestlers. They also built a high runway, but that didn't keep them from throwing chairs and bottles. When you wrestled a Frenchman in Ottawa, your life wasn't worth a plugged nickel."

Thrown objects are perhaps the most common danger, and Reb was used for target practice more than once. *"I was out in Dearborn, Michigan, and was wrestling Joe Savoldi, former Notre Dame fullback,"* he wrote. *"I was giving Joe an unmerciful lacing when a big Italian rushed down and hurled a steel stool that caught me between the eyes and split my nose and both eyebrows open. I bled like a stuck pig and they led me to the dressing room. The cop on duty grabbed the offender and pushed him into the dressing room with me.*

"'There he is, Russ! He's all yours — I haven't seen a thing.'

"Whereupon, I wiped the blood from my face and hit the big walrus right in the mouth and knocked out three of his teeth. Then I threw him out of the dressing room before I lost my head completely. They rushed me over to the Ford Hospital and sewed me up with ten stitches."

An incredible array of objects has been thrown at, shot at, and dropped on villains over the years. In Milwaukee, some idiot threw an iron armrest at Gus Sonnenberg. After Ernie Dusek won the first fall from Gino Garibaldi in a New Jersey arena, he was on his way back to the dressing room when a man in the balcony threw a whole chair — not just the armrest — and hit him in the head. When it was announced that Dusek had been knocked out and suffered severe wounds, the crowd cheered. *"Fan Uses Chair to Bust Burper,"* said a New York City headline.

Al Costello was hit by a fire extinguisher. A seven-pound water pump just missed Larry Hamilton in Newark. In Los Angeles, a whiskey bottle aimed at Don Leo Jonathan hit a second-row fan instead, causing a deep scalp laceration. In Madison Square Garden one night in 1957, the tally included a juicy apple that hit ring announcer Al Mitchell over the right eye, a second apple, rolled-up cigarette packages, matches, cookies, coins, a lighted cigarette, a piece of a chair, and a potato. When The Sheik went through bowing-toward-Mecca routine before a match in Boston, he was bombarded with tomatoes, a pear, flashbulbs, hatpins, batteries, beer cans, soap, onions, and eggs.

The situation got so bad in Boston that promoter Abe Ford (who has since been ousted by the territorial boss, Vince McMahon) installed a seven-foot-high Plexiglas barrier around the ring with one passageway in and out. He borrowed the Plexiglas idea from ice hockey, and it at least takes away the good throwing angles from all but the balcony fans.

"*Toru Tanaka, Mr. Fuji, Gorilla Monsoon and somebody else were in the ring,*" recalled Ford, "*and before you know it, there were three or four Puerto Ricans in the ring with 'em. It was just lucky that they saw 'em first. They start hittin' 'em with judo chops and they got out, but some night, there was going to be a killin' there, and I had to put that barrier up then.*

"*I've never seen anything like it when you go to the Garden. They get up in the balcony and throw rocks and bottles. We caught one kid with a whole bag of great big potatoes! Where we used to hire just a few guards, I had to get thirty men — cops, extra ushers. Nobody cares, I guess, but every time some little kid around the ring gets hit on the head, they rush him to the hospital and say, 'Well, how did it happen?'*"

"*They were shooting staples one time,*" recalled my father, "*and one pierced Bobby Becker in the thigh and went right up to the hilt, sharp ends first. They were shooting at me and hit him by mistake, see. And the blood was running down his leg and he couldn't see what it was, and after wrestling for another twenty minutes or so, he went into the dressing room and the staple was in there, right in that muscle, so you know it irritated. He had a sore leg for quite a long time from that staple.*"

Dory Dixon, who often works in Mexico, tells of homemade Mexican fireballs: paper cups rolled up tightly around rocks, doused in lighter fluid, lighted and thrown. Sammy Stein, playing the part of a broken-down boxer in the film *Fat City*, told on the set of his days wrestling as a lightweight in a Mexican bullring. The fans loved to take an active part. "*We're in the bullring with thousands of Mexicans watching and they're all throwing wax matches at the heat* [villains]. *They strike 'em and they throw 'em and they stick to you. Ohhhh.*"

If anyone doubts that human beings are beasts masquerading under a thin, fragile membrane of civilization, he should study wrestling fans. Blood excites them, blood convinces them that the drama unfolding in the ring is spontaneous and unrehearsed. The fan-magazine publishers know this very well and, often, their covers and their article titles are awash in gore:

"*Blood-Thirsty Taro Myaki*"
"*They Found Me on the Floor Lying in My Own Blood*"
"*Bloodbath of the Year!!!*"
"*Bobby Heenan's Bloody Obsession!*"
"*The Sheik's Bloody Scorecard*"
"*Blackjack's Boast: I'll Kick Out Bruiser's Brains!*"
"*Terry Funk vs. Harley Race: A Bloody War Neither Can Win!*"
"*A Saga Written in Blood!*"
"*How a Memory Triggered a Bloody Riot!*"
"*Bob Sweetan, The Bloody Canadian Bruiser*"
"*Bloody Chain Match in Tennessee*"

And my favorite, "*Where There's Blood, There's Blassie.*"

The Bela Lugosi Award for 1972 went to the September issue of *The Wrestler*, which had the words "bloody" (twice), "bloodbath" and "gory" in cover headlines, with matching color photographs.

On a recent airplane trip, a friend of mine, Roy Blount, Jr., one of *Sports Illustrated's* best writers, sat next to a wiry woman in her seventies, an enthusiastic Christian and gardener. "*She loves wrestling and Roller Derby,*" he said, "*and attends regularly in Dallas.*

"*She told me,* 'You know they have the dirty wrestlers that don't fight nice. Sport is the name of the game and sport don't mean you go to kill the other person. But they use karate, they go at the good ones' throats. It wasn't meant in a sport that you use these death blows and all!'

"*She was getting more and more indignant. Earlier, she had told me about the night when, after having been unable to walk for eighteen months,* 'I dreamed my bed was full of fiery coals, like a barbecue pit, and I woke up standing up on the other end of it,' *which caused her, she said, to rouse the whole apartment where she was staying at the time, crying,* 'Praise the Lord!'

"*Now she was getting almost as emotional just thinking about the dirty wrestlers. I was afraid she was going to jump up in her seat in the plane and start calling down the Lord's wrath on them.*

"Aren't they just putting on in a lot of those matches?" *I asked her.*

"*She gave me a hard look.* "Didn't you ever see how they *bleed*?' *she said."*

Many ardent fans think pretty much the same way:

A boy in Boston: "*You know, it's hard to believe in something like wrestling when you're growing up, and then, when you go home, your older brother teases you for wasting your money on a fraud. But I've watched a lot of matches, and I know it's not really fake, although there are some moments when they're resting. I've thought about it a lot, but I can believe in it now. It's real blood.*"

A housewife in Eugene, Ore.: "*The blood last night on Dutch's face was real. Guys aren't going to hurt each other in the ring if it isn't real.*"

A Houston woman: "*I have a dress at the house I keep in a drawer all by itself. Cowboy Ellis, about six or seven years ago, he was hit against the post and cut three gashes in his head. I grabbed him when he rolled out of the ring. I got blood from the neckline of my dress to the hem. I thought he would bleed to death in my arms.*"

An arena guard in Washington, D.C.: "*It's the blood that gets 'em. The crowd always draws closer when there's blood. And when you have two on one in the ring and blood — you're almost bound to have trouble. Sometimes they come up and just hit me in the back for no reason.*"

The whole phenomenon was summed up best by Marilyn F. Kalata, writing in the Harvard *Crimson* after being frightened at the matches in Boston: "*However phony the wrestlers may be, the crowd is for real.*"

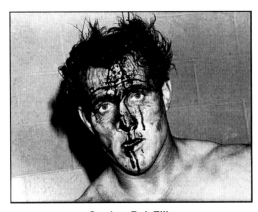

Cowboy Bob Ellis

Chapter 8
Backstage with the Boys

As a professional wrestler adds mileage to his automobile and his body, the bumps he takes make longer-lasting lumps and his waist and his ears get thicker. If he is lucky, diligent and talented, maybe his wallet will get thicker, too. This is nothing new. Acrobatic Antonino Rocca was said to have made close to $180,000 in 1959 and, still further back, Gorgeous George said he raked in $160,000 in 1951. Today, Pedro Morales, a champion crowd-pleaser in the East, claims that he earns $150,000 a year. When Dory Funk, Jr., was king of the National Wrestling Alliance, he made between $250,000 and $350,000 a year, depending on whose envious guess you believed. Fabulous Moolah and Ernie Ladd each claim they earn more than $100,000 a year.

For the Verne Gagnes, Jack Briscos, Bobo Brazils, and other top dogs, it is obviously a lucrative business if they are willing to pay the price in jet lag and time spent away from their families. Johnny Valentine, one of the country's better heels, once wrestled on a Wednesday night in Tokyo and had a commitment to be in Houston for the main event on Friday night.

"There was some mix-up on planes," said promoter Paul Boesch. *"After all, it was a long ways away. I had a policeman meeting him at the airport. He drove him in and, on the way, Valentine put on his shoes and tights. He came in the back door of the Coliseum. I had already announced to the people that there was a possibility that he might not make it, but that we were trying. The fellow who was going to take his place, Wahoo McDaniel, had wrestled earlier on the card and was standing there, about to go in.*

"Valentine walked in the back door and I pointed him to the ring, and he just walked down the aisle and up the steps. You talk about coming close to missing something! That's what you call long-distance booking."

Prepaid round-trip airplane tickets are not all that common, however. They only go to the stars, and to them only when they are asked to make a trip to Japan, Honolulu or Australia. Most of the "boys," as the wrestlers refer to themselves, are more concerned with mundane sorts of trips — say, from Houston to Dallas-Fort Worth for Tuesday-night matches, then to San Antonio on Wednesday, Corpus Christi on Thursday, and back to Houston on Friday. Their payoffs aren't nearly as impressive, either, although Boesch says that even men who regularly lose preliminary bouts — human stepping-stones like Pedro Godoy or Joe Turco — earn $15,000 to $20,000 yearly. About the most my dad grossed in any one year was $25,000. His biggest one-night payoff was $800 in San Francisco (he met Gino Garibaldi in a ninety-minute match in the Civic Auditorium with Joe Louis refereeing; a photograph of Garibaldi stomping on my old man's head made the cover of *The National Police Gazette*). He quit in 1959.

"Boy, you could sure piss away money in travel because you pay it all yourself," said Pop. *"No expense account. Once in a great while, somebody would send you an airplane ticket, like to Honolulu and back. Every once in a while, when I'd*

be down in South Carolina or something like that, and they'd need me up in New York, I wouldn't go unless my way was paid.

"I made a sort of pledge to myself that I had to earn a certain amount of money and, if I ever went below that quota, anytime,

I'd quit. I went to Tulsa and, because of my expenses, travel and all that stuff, I went under my quota and I decided that was it. I always swore that I'd quit, and I quit. I just got disgusted with it. Payoffs were getting worse and I figured I could do just as well getting a job.

"I had a lot of fun and made money — a nice living and I didn't want for anything. But, boy, I went through automobiles like crazy! Three new automobiles in thirteen months once."

Vic Christy

Life on the road is often dull, sitting in a car for hundreds of miles counting the billboards, eating in truck slop-stops, living in hotels, waiting in dressing rooms that do not exactly resemble backstage at the Palace. Like every kind of pro athlete, the wrestler brightens up his life with jokes, or swerves, played on his buddies or on total strangers, and like the business he's in, the swerves are often crude. Wit in a dressing room comes nowhere close to a luncheon at the old Round Table in the Algonquin Hotel. There is very little Noel Coward repartee. The most famous swerve artist in wrestling history is probably Vic Christy, one of two zany brothers from the San Fernando Valley in California.

Christy once went from wrestling in Honolulu to wrestling in and around Buffalo. Driving in his convertible to one of his first matches, he saw a carful of the boys ahead of him on the highway. It had been snowing, but the roads had been cleared and it was a nice, bright day, although frigid as a Richard Nixon press conference. Christy put his top down, took off his coat, and whizzed by the other car, waving and showing off his beautiful tan and his bright, new aloha shirt, wide open at the collar. The driver of the other car sped up and stayed right on Christy's tail for miles — swerve for swerve, so to speak — while Christy tried to shake him so he could put his top back up. Finally he pulled over, laughing; his tan had turned to blue. *"It kind of backfired, didn't it?"* he said sheepishly.

I was driving back to Los Angeles from Bakersfield one night with my father when up next to us on the highway came Christy, sitting on the passenger side of his car. He was doing seventy miles an hour and he was apparently steering with his left hand low on the wheel and one of his long legs reaching the gas pedal. He rolled down the window with his right hand. *"Where you going to eat?"* he called out.

"We're going to eat over at so-and-so," yelled my dad, laughing.

Christy turned to his invisible companion and gestured and away the car zoomed doing eighty-five or ninety.

Vic and his brother Ted were driving to San Diego and pulled their car over to the side and parked it sideways on a steep slope. They opened both doors. Ted sprawled across the hood and Vic sprawled on the ground. Then, as each passerby stopped to give first aid or check the accident scene, they yelled, *"Can't we take a sunbath without being bothered by everybody!"*

Lord Blears tells the story of going to or from an arena with Christy and a carful of other wrestlers. As they passed a "civilian" car, Christy in the back seat pretended to strangle a wrestler in the front seat, to the horror of passing motorists. Their performance must have been convincing because the cops were notified, and later the car was stopped by a roadblock and the wrestlers had to get out with their hands up, looking every bit like a squad of Mafia hit men.

Christy was no better-behaved in a hotel. He would get the timing down pat on the opening and closing of elevator doors. Then he'd get in back with a bunch of women conventioneers, ride down to the second floor, say, *"Out, please,"* and time it so that just his head was out when the door closed. As the doors hit his neck and sprang open, he would do an expert flop and lay on the hallway floor as the doors closed again. Then he'd jump up, race down the stairs to the lobby, and watch the women emerge, screeching that there was a man gravely injured up on the second floor.

A group of wrestlers were gathered around a Las Vegas swimming pool and Christy was, of course, shoving guys in, ducking people in the water, and generally making a nuisance of himself. He left briefly and came back dressed in a suit. He ran over and shoved Nick Lutze into the water.

"You dirty son-of-a-bitch," yelled Lutze as he climbed out, *"you've pushed your last guy in!"*

With that, he grabbed Christy and threw him into the pool fully clothed. *"You dumbbell,"* Christy said when he came up giggling and sputtering. *"I'm wearing your suit."*

His tricks in the dressing rooms were on no higher plane. He stuffed paper into the toes of Strangler Lewis' shoes and Strangler couldn't understand why they had suddenly become so uncomfortable. Or, he would test the strength of a wrestler's neck by having him stand with his back to a wall or a door and let Christy try to pull his head forward if he could. He would strain and pull and then suddenly let go, letting the victim's head fly backward and hit the wall with a thonk.

Probably the nuttiest series of televised dressing-room interviews were conducted by Dave Levin (after his wrestling days) for TV station KTLA in Los Angeles, Channel 5. It seemed that every wrestler would save his craziest specialty for Dave. For instance, Sky-Hi Lee would chew up razor blades and swallow carpet tacks the way other people swallow popcorn. On one show, Levin had an extension cord hanging down with a lighted light bulb, to prove to the viewers that it was real and not some frosted candy concoction. Lee unscrewed it, smashed it in a sink, and ate the fragments. He wrestled that night with the glass in him.

Levin, wrestler Sandor Szabo, and KTLA's remote crew had a little swerve fixed up for guests on the show. After an interview, they would pretend they were still on the air, even to the point of having the camera's red light still on. Levin would say something like, *"Hey, so-and-so, come back a second. We've got to kill two more minutes,"* and then the rib would start. After Abe Kashey had been on, extolling the virtues of his new gymnasium, Szabo came on in the extracurricular period and accused Kashey of peeking into the women's dressing room of the gym through holes he'd drilled in the wall. After Lord Blears' second, Captain Leslie Holmes, talked up his real-estate project, Szabo came on and told how he had heard that the foundations of the houses were sinking.

"We had Steve Stanlee come in one time," said Levin. *"We were off the air, but he didn't know that. And in walks Szabo with just a towel on him, see. And he stands there chatting with us.*

"I said, 'Wasn't that a good match that Steve had tonight?'

Dave Levin, right, known as the "Brooklyn Butcher Boy," posed for this publicity photo with Jack Dempsey, left, at the latter's Broadway restaurant in 1936, just after Levin won the wrestling championship from Ali Baba.

"'Oh, that was a great match,' *said Szabo.* 'I liked it when he picked the guy up and —' *And he raised his arms to pantomime a body slam.*

"And the towel fell on the floor and there stood Szabo, stark naked in the bright TV lights. Stanlee thought it was going out into all the living rooms in Los Angeles. He turned white and said, 'Oh, Jesus!'

"Then the guy in the truck pulled a double swerve. He said, 'Where's Szabo? Put Szabo on.'

"So Szabo got on and the guy in the truck said, 'Hey, Sandor, I didn't know what you were going to do. I had my wife and a couple of girls in the truck here with me!'

"We had such a lot of fun with those guys."

But there are more serious occupational hazards in wrestling than jokers like Christy and Szabo.

Most common of these is the cauliflower ear, that puffed-up sensory organ sticking out from the head that constitutes a membership card in the wrestling fraternity. Red and sore as a carbuncle at first, then stiff and unbendable and truly resembling a cauliflower except in color, this deformity has inspired more sportswriters to flights of fancy and humor than all the slate-gray skies over football stadiums put together. Take this 1938 example from Boston's Austen Lake: "... *incurred by the breaking of the fibre tissue, allowing the blood to flood into the member until it swells like a red exit light and, before healing into a hard fungus-knot of coagulated blood, is sensitive to the touch."* A wrestler from Harvard or Yale might explain that it is caused by a superficial hematoma (collection of blood) between the skin and the fibro cartilaginous skeleton of the ear.

"If you get the ear drained after it's injured, you can prevent that cauliflower look," said Dory Funk, Sr. *"What happens is that when the ear is crushed or twisted, the cartilage breaks. Liquid fills the space where the break occurs and causes it to puff up.*

"If it isn't drained, tissue grows across the swelling and it becomes a lump. After you get it drained, the doctor puts a sort of plaster-of-Paris cast around the ear to keep it from swelling again.

"We [he and his sons] *have enough pride in our appearance to lay off a few days to let the ear heal. I had to have my ear drained seven times one year."*

Some wrestlers don't *want* to be cured. They want to carry around the badge of their profession, and some have been known to go so far as to have a friend kick them in the side of the head. Most of the time, though, it's considered a necessary evil. Wilbur Snyder got his from Sockeye McDonald — in this case, Sockear — when he was just starting out in 1955. He still remembers the pain:

"He was wearing long black wool tights," said Snyder. *"After he had started one of my ears bleeding with a few smashes with his fist, he began dragging those long legs across it whenever we were on the canvas. Man, did that hurt!"*

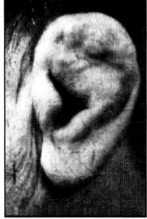

Perhaps the most famous cauliflower ear amongst pro wrestlers and fans is Mike Mazurki's.

Jesse Kuhaulua, a 358-pound Sumo wrestler in Japan, but an American citizen, went through a rugged initiation. *"It isn't so rough as it used to be, but attitude is everything,"* he said. *"When they ask if you're tired, you always say no, you want more. When I started, I told the boss my ear was hurt and I wanted two days off. He said,* 'That's no excuse,' *and he made all the other wrestlers hit me on the ear."*

"I got my cauliflower ear from my brother Paddy in a gymnasium in London," recalled Steve Casey. *"He put a tight head scissors on me. Of course, when you wrestle your brother, you always fight so hard. You never say no, never cry uncle — we never did to each other, anyway. He had those legs around my head and he twisted it one way and the other. When he let me go, my one ear came out like a balloon.*

"Next day, we worked out again. I never stopped and had it fixed. I used to tie it up at night and put a bandage around my head. I used to put hot milk on bread — dip the bread in milk — and put it up against my ear and then put this cloth around my head."

For many years, the most feared occupational hazard was the eye affliction known as trachoma, one of the oldest diseases known to man and one of the world's most common causes of blindness. The microorganisms that carry it can be spread by handkerchiefs, towels, pillows, and such, or by personal contact, which is how wrestlers get it. The disease travels down a rivulet of sweat as easily as a barge floats down the Mississippi. Strangler Lewis went blind from trachoma, and many other men, including Gus Sonnenberg and George Linnehan, had to go through the painful cure, now made unnecessary by modern drugs.

"In wrestling, naturally, the perspiration spreads it," said Linnehan. *"Sooner or later, some of it's going in your eyes and that's what happened to me. We used to put drops in, but at the wrong time. We would put them in right after we were through and then we'd take our showers and it would all wash out, instead of waiting until we went to bed so the medicine would go in our eyes and stay in there for the night. No germ could live through it a whole night.*

"I contacted it, I think, in 1940. I went to a wonderful doctor in Omaha who was very, very good. He had done an awful lot for different ones that had got it. There were quite a few at that time. It was a bluestone that they scraped it with, you know. Unbelievable, the burn. Unbelievable. They rolled your lid to do it. They put drops in and you wouldn't feel it then, but about an hour later, ooh, it really stung."

Another danger comes from dirty mats, although this is not the problem it used to be in Sonnenberg's day.

"Wrestling is a pretty dirty business," he said in an interview with Westbrook Pegler. *"I have to work on foul mats that haven't been cleaned or aired in years. You know what goes on in a ring. Did it ever occur to you that, after two or three years of regular use, a wrestling mat is not a pleasant mattress to roll around on? I have to meet all kinds of men. A man might pick up anything — skin diseases, eye infections, blood diseases."*

Mat burns become perfect entries into the body for streptococcus germs and other nasty bacteria. Dave Levin's strep infection came from a *rope* burn, a seemingly inconsequential injury that kept him in a hospital for three months. It came from a rough ring rope not covered with any velvet-like material. He was delirious, almost died, and had to have numerous transfusions from other wrestlers. He got out of the hospital, but that was only the beginning of his troubles.

"Then my foot healed in what they call a 'dropped foot," he said. *"This was before penicillin. The left ankle is where they had localized the poison and drained it; lots of draining. Only it was dropped stiff! I had to wear a high-heeled shoe while I was walking, although my legs were the same length. I went and had another operation and went back to wrestling. The ankle wouldn't bend. It was fine, I never had any trouble, but because there was no give in it, any twists I'd get there would grind away in the hip, which I never realized.*

"Consequently, I was wearing the cartilage off in the hip. It was, evidently, getting worse all the time and I thought it was just a little touch of arthritis I was getting. Eventually, I was hobbling around on a cane, my leg was so bad."

At age 49, Levin had to have his left hip taken out. His body rejected an artificial hip and, finally, the doctors decided to leave him with no hip at all. Today, he has to wear a special shoe and still limps noticeably, not because the right leg is longer than the left, but because his left *"sponges up because there's no bone there."* And it all started with a rope burn that he hardly even noticed at first.

Levin doesn't feel sorry for himself and insists he would do it all over again rather than not be in professional wrestling. Like pro-football linemen, wrestlers have a code of conduct that calls for the stoic acceptance of injury and pain. In Corpus Christi one night, Johnny Valentine finished out a match with two fractured fingers, the bone sticking out of one. Levin himself remembers how giant Primo Camera handled his little hurts.

"I drove Primo to the matches in Long Beach one night," said Levin, *"and that particular evening he wrestled Wee Willie Davis, who was just as big as he was. So Willie Davis got Camera down flat on the mat and pounded his mouth. Poor Primo had no place to dodge. Zango! He just hit him, cold-blood, right in the mouth. He was a bloody mess.*

"On the way home, he asked me to stop in a bar. He wanted to get a shot of whiskey to cauterize it. So we walked into this bar and there were several people sitting around. They were all looking up at this guy. I could see them in the mirror. He orders a whiskey, I had a beer. And he put that whiskey on the cut

and … did you ever see that movie, Dr. Jekyll and Mr. Hyde*, where that face changes in front of you?*

"He roared like a lion all over the place and I wanted to crawl out, I'll tell you. Those people, half of them were standing up, ready to go, because they didn't know if this guy was going to go crazy or what."

Death, as well as serious injury, is a menace in the ring each year, often striking in the form of heart failure during or just after a match. In 1972, it was Luther Lindsay dying shortly after a bout in Charlotte, and Ray Gunkel dying in the Savannah dressing room before medical help could arrive. In 1971, Alberto Torres died in an Omaha hospital from injuries suffered in a nearby town. The year before it was Iron Mike DiBiase, who keeled over backward from a blow in the Lubbock, Tex., ring and never got up, although wrestler Harley Race, watching from the back of the arena, ran to ringside and tried to rouse him with artificial respiration.

The death-roll is a long one. Cowboy Jack Russell died in the ring in Nashville. Stan Stasiak (the original) died of blood poisoning after being cut in a match in Worcester, Mass., in 1936. Chick Garibaldi, Buddy O'Brien, Jim Wright, Gordon McKinley, Luis Hernandez, Joe Shimkus — the list goes on.

Wrestler's 'Fake' Tumble Is Fatal

NEW YORK, May 31.—(UP)—A week ago Joe Shimkus, a wrestler, was thrown out of a Richmond, Va., ring by the referee, who claimed he was "faking."

Shimkus had collapsed after wrestling for 17 minutes with Walter Podolak.

Several days ago he entered the Polyclinic hoospital.

Today Shimkus died. An autopsy will be held tomorrow.

News article about May 25, 1934 match in Richmond, Va.

"In Joe Shimkus's case, I was due to wrestle him in Hempstead, New York, for Jess McMahon, Vince's father," said Paul Boesch. *"I remember it so well because he had wrestled in Richmond, Virginia, the night before, and he went through the ropes and hit his head or something and actually died right then and there. Somebody substituted for him in Hempstead and I can't even remember who it was, but I remember that the announcer got up and said:*

"'Ladies and gentlemen, in this corner, substituting for Joe Shimkus' — *and some guy, some loudmouth cynic, started hollering,* 'Ahh, fake, fake!'

"And the announcer said, 'If you'll permit me to continue. Joe Shimkus died in the ring in Richmond, Virginia, last night.'"

In Washington, D.C., Jack Donovan had Mike Romano in a wristlock, then switched it into a head scissors. Romano kicked a couple of times, and then lay still. Donovan pinned him. People started to yell *"fake"* and *"phony,"* but Romano never arose. *"He was lying there while everybody was hollering 'phony' and yelling that he was faking his injuries,"* recalled George Zaharias. *"When they carried Mike out, he was dead. You just know that Mike didn't rehearse that one."*

Few things annoy wrestlers and promoters more than the frequent accusations that their sport is rigged, rehearsed, phony, or fixed, although, after all these years, they should have become immune. The attacks and "exposes" have been numerous: *Collier's* in 1949, *Sport* and *The National Police Gazette* in 1950, the respected Sunday TV show *Omnibus* in 1954, the United Feature Syndicate in 1960. New York columnist Dan Parker pounded away in the thirties, and his confederate, Jimmy Cannon, positively foamed at the typewriter when expounding on wrestling, once calling it *"the most incompetent pantomime ever performed"* and *"the silly furies of stupid acrobats"* and adding, *"It is an insult to the human family even to suspect that anyone would give a night of a lifetime to watch this."*

Perhaps most damaging was the expose in the *Saturday Evening Post* in 1954, written with a sense of humor by ex-wrestler Herman Hickman. The article made

Hickman a pariah among many of the wrestlers, but gained a lot of attention and was reprinted in at least one anthology. In one episode Hickman described, he was wrestling Jim Londos in Memphis for the heavyweight championship. Tennessee was Hickman's home state, so the crowd was anxious to see him upset The Golden Greek. He claimed in the article that the whole thing was planned, and that just when he had Londos ready for the pin, he was to miss a flying tackle, sail through the ropes, and land outside the ring in somebody's lap, then lie there unconscious for the count of twenty. Everything went nicely according to the plot, he said, until he found himself *"flat on my back in the infield on a lighted cigar butt."* He stayed put until he heard the ref reach twenty, and then rolled over just as somebody dumped a bucket of ice water on him.

It was Hickman's contention that there had been very few "shooting matches" (legitimate contests) even back in the handlebar-mustache days of William Muldoon and Frank Gotch, or maybe even back to the ancient Greeks. Such statements coming not from a typically skeptical journalist, but from an ex-wrestler, had the ring of truth. From time to time, other ex-wrestlers have bitten the hand that used to feed them, and the fraternity has accused them of being merely dissident losers, or claiming that the events cited were merely isolated incidents.

An example of the latter might have been Nick Condos versus Jack Hurley in Omaha. Hurley was very sick with the flu the night of the matches and the promoter was worried. He had no other man to put on in the main event. Condos offered to carry Hurley through the match. *"Whenever I start to charge him, all he's got to do is clench a fist and threaten me,"* Condos told the promoter. *"We'll make it look good and I won't lay a hand on him."*

So that is exactly what they did. *"I'd go for Jack and he'd double up his fist and brandish it, and I'd back off, cringing, protesting to the referee,* 'Foul, foul, make him open that fist.' *Two, three minutes of that and the crowd was going wild. They'd never seen such a coward.*

"I turned to holler back at the crowd and I heard a kind of 'plop' behind me. I looked around. Poor Jack had passed out cold.'

There was nothing Condos could do but flop on Hurley, pin him, and win the match. The fans, understandably, were ready to tear the arena down until Condos got the bright idea of challenging anybody in the crowd to try to stay thirty minutes in the ring with him and win $50. A skinny fellow was the only one to take up the challenge, so the promoter provided him with trunks and into the ring he went.

"The skinny guy was behind me before I got set," said Condos. *"He put on a cross-buttocks hold and a scissors on one leg and took me to the mat.*

"I thought, 'Well, I'll be jiggered! This isn't going to be so bad.'"

And it wasn't, until Condos decided he had better escape and win so the promoter wouldn't lose the $50. But the more he wiggled, the tighter the volunteer applied his hold until Condos' leg was so numb he thought he'd never walk again.

After it was over and the stranger had pocketed his money, Condos asked him where he had learned that hold.

"Well," said the skinny one, *"I run a hog farm out here in the country a piece. That's the holt I use to ketch the hogs for slaughter."*

To answer the charges of fakery, wrestlers and promoters have a series of standard replies.

The Injury-and-Death Defense: They point to Ray Gunkel's death and Dave Levin's missing hip and say, *"How could it be fake if things like that happen?"*

"I've broken nearly every bone in my body," claimed Mike Mazurki, the wrestler-turned-actor who now runs a restaurant by MacArthur Park in L.A., *"If that was all faked, I took a lot of punishment for nothing."*

The Masked Man of France, angrily replying to a book entitled *Confessions of a Wrestler,* said, *"See that bridgework? Fifteen hundred American dollars. Does pantomime knock out teeth?"*

Ray Stevens testified, *"Everything people see is for real. And so are the injuries."*

The I-Don't-Know-About-the-Other-Guys-but-I'm-Clean Defense: Antonino Rocca said, *"I do not know about anybody else. I always try 100 percent."*

Gene (Big Daddy) Libscomb said, *"People always ask me about fixes. I tell them I just do the best I know. Not once has anyone told me how a match should come out. About the other guys, I don't know. What's more, I don't ask."*

The Get-in-the-Ring-With-Me Defense: Said announcer Dick Lane, *"I'd like to take the biggest skeptic I know and put him in the ring with the worst wrestler I know. These guys didn't get those cauliflower ears from sleeping on hard pillows."*

At a party in Boston once, baseball star Jimmy Foxx called Steve Casey a faker. Casey claimed he grabbed Foxx and snarled, *"You'll have to show me it's fake."* Foxx insisted he hadn't said anything and Casey let him go. (This is a spurious argument, of course. Bobby Biceps could be the toughest fellow on the globe and also be an accomplished faker.)

The No-Wrestlers-in-Jail Defense: Promoter Vince McMahon said, *"They used to ask Ed (Strangler) Lewis, the old champ, whether it was a fake, too. Once the question came up at a lawyer's convention in Chicago where he was speaking. Well, Lewis was very interested in penology and used to study the prison systems of various countries he wrestled in. So he told them,* 'Gentlemen, I've visited many prisons in my time, and I've never met a wrestler in one. But I have met a lot of lawyers there.' (Another bit of illogic. First, it is not illegal to fake a wrestling match. Most athletic commissions require that they be billed as exhibitions, anyway. And Lewis wasn't looking very hard. I know of two wrestlers who have served time for passing bad checks.)

The Never-a-Breath-of-Scandal Defense: *"What most all people overlook about wrestling is that it has a basic appeal that has never changed,"* said McMahon. *"They also overlook the fact that there has never been a breath of scandal in the sport, that it isn't controlled by unsavory characters. All of us arc taxpaying businessmen — including the wrestlers."* (There not only *have* been breaths of scandal, there have been *gusts* and *typhoons,* including the breaking up of trusts, messy lawsuits, and the aforementioned exposés.)

The We-Just-Add-a-Bit-of-Color Defense: This makes more sense. Gorilla Monsoon, a college man, said, *"Every man in this business is a professional who knows the fundamentals and refinements of wrestling. But we also deal in excitement, and the only way to get excitement is to deviate from the rules. If we gave people collegiate, or international, or AAU-type wrestling, the arenas would be empty. We add color."*

Jack Armstrong said, *"Let's face it, we could kill each other at any given time on any given night. A blow to the right place, a foot on the heart too hard, anything. But we realize the other guy's got a family to support and money to make, so we don't go overboard."*

The Top-Guys-Make-the-Most-Money Defense: This is the most sensible one of all, for if wrestling results are prearranged all the time, the promoters would have to be highly skilled diplomats and super-salesmen in order to convince half the egocentric performers on each card to lose. *"That belt is worth $100,000 a year to me,"* Dory Funk, Jr., told the *Charlotte News* when he was champ. *"Now I ask you, why would I throw that away?"*

Dick the Bruiser answered, *"I'm not going to let some unknown beat me. I've worked too hard to build my reputation into real earning power. The promoters know that. They also know that I'll do anything reasonable to give them a good show, to send their fans home satisfied that they've got their money's worth."*

Promoter Abe Ford said, *"It's the real thing. Look, the better a guy does, the more money he makes. Nobody wants to lose."*

It must have tickled the pros to hear Iowa State wrestling coach Harold Nicols admit that his 400-and-some-odd-pound phenom, Chris Taylor, a bronze medalist at the Munich Olympics (who later turned pro), was taking it easy on his collegiate opponents so that the big crowds (3,600 at Wisconsin, 10,268 for the Iowa-Iowa State meet) would go home happy.

"Taylor can pin most of his opponents just about any time he wishes," said Nichols. *"But if he walks out, picks up his opponent, and slams him down in twenty seconds, the fans go home grumbling. So I tell Chris to practice some of his holds during a match and wait before putting on the clincher."*

The last word on the subject comes from wrestler Nick Kozak: *"For those who believe, no explanation is needed. For those who don't, no explanation will do."*

Lou Thesz, the Hungarian shoemaker's son from St. Louis who won and lost the championship of the National Wrestling Alliance twenty or thirty times, it seems.

Addendum 1
Thumbnail Biographies of the Greatest Pro Wrestlers

There are several wrestling halls of fame. The Citizens Savings Athletic Foundation (formerly the Helms Athletic Foundation) has one in Los Angeles which really is just names of amateur greats engraved on a pretty trophy. In January 1973, ground was broken in Stillwater, Okla., for a U.S. Wrestling Federation, hall of fame on the Oklahoma State campus. Again, strictly amateur. Not a peroxide blonde to be seen, unless it's the receptionist. A magazine editor and ex-promoter named Norman Kietzer runs a hall of fame and hands out plaques, but the hall and his Wrestling Writers Association have no home except in the pages of his publications. Promoter Bob Luce has a hall of fame in a small section of the second floor of Chicago's International Amphitheatre, but for the most part, it is just a display of photographs from a defunct magazine, *Wrestling Life*. If the "official" pro-wrestling shrine is ever built — perhaps next to a beer stand in St. Louis's Kiel Auditorium — here are a few candidates for grunt 'n' groan immortality; some of them great wrestlers, some of them great drawing cards, some both:

AFFLIS, DICK (The Bruiser):

The consummate blue-collar heel ("All I want to do is get the job done, give the fans some action, and get out and drink some beer"), he grew up in Indianapolis, finished his college football at the University of Nevada, and played in the line four years for the Green Bay Packers, 1951 through 1954. He and tag-team partner Jerry Graham helped spark one of the worst riots in Madison Square Garden history Nov. 19, 1957. He is often teamed with a man who is supposedly his cousin, Reggie (The Crusher) Lisowski. The Bruiser and The Crusher were main-eventers on the card that grossed about $148,000 in Chicago's Comiskey Park in 1970.

BOTHNER, GEORGE:

Born and reared in New York City. In 1907, he won the professional lightweight title from Tom Riley of England. Like many early-day pros, he barnstormed with a theatrical unit; in his case, it was Barney Gerard's burlesque troupe. He refereed many matches, and Bothner's Gym in Manhattan was for many years a Mecca and meeting-place for wrestlers.

BRISCO, JACK:

Born 1941 in Oklahoma City, reared in Blackwell, Okla. He was twice Big Eight champion at Oklahoma State and was NCAA 191-pound champ in 1965, the same year he turned pro. He won the National Wrestling Alliance (NWA) heavyweight championship on July 20, 1973, from Harley Race in Houston. Brisco had failed in numerous attempts to wrest the belt from Dory Funk Jr., who finally lost it to Race. Younger brother Jerry Brisco is also a wrestler.

BURKE, MILDRED:

Born Mildred Bliss in Coffeyville, Kan., she grew up in Kansas City, Mo., and Glendale, Calif. She started wrestling men in carnivals, switched to men in arenas, and finally found female opponents willing to battle her in public. She won a women's tournament in Columbus, Ohio, and claimed the world's championship, which she held for many years. She finally lost the title to June Byers in Atlanta in 1954, but Burke claims the match was not over when it was stopped and that the championship was stolen from her. Today, she is a grandmother, working for a Los Angeles soft-water company and running a wrestling school in North Hollywood.

BURNS, MARTIN (Farmer):

Born 1861 in Springfield Township, Cedar County, Iowa. He got his nickname when he wrestled in overalls against Evan (Strangler) Lewis and Jack Carkeek at the Olympic Theatre in Chicago, 1889. He toured the country with numerous shows, taking on all comers, then won the U.S. title from Evan Lewis in 1895, losing it two years later to Tom Jenkins. He claimed to have wrestled in more than 6,000 matches and won "all except seven," even though he weighed only 158 pounds in his prime. Burns helped start many men in the business, including Frank Gotch and Rudy Dusek. He died in the '30s.

CASEY, STEVE:

Born 1908, one of the handsome, square-jawed Casey clan that was famous for its wrestlers and oarsmen. Reared in Sneem, County Kerry, Ireland. His brothers Jim and Tom followed him to the U.S. and also had successful ring careers. He won one version of the heavyweight championship from Lou Thesz in the Boston Garden, 1938, but was stripped of the title later that year when he was out of the country. Stripped, that is, by one of the rival factions. In the ring, he lost his title and won it back several times before losing it for good in 1945 to Frank Sexton in the Boston Arena. Casey, still trim and tough, is retired and living with his family and his hunting dogs in Cohasset, Mass.

DUSEK, RUDY:

Born Rudy Hason in Nebraska, he grew up to lead three of his brothers into pro wrestling villainy as The Dirty Duseks or The Riot Squad. *"Never a dull match with a Dusek"* was their slogan. Farmer Burns was one of Rudy's first teachers, at a Midwest YMCA. He turned pro in 1921, but didn't get into the big money until he wrestled Joe Stecher in St. Louis in 1926. Dusek once held Jim Londos to a two-hour draw and went more than four hours to a draw in Tulsa versus Joe Malcewicz. While Emil, Ernie and Joe carried on the eye-gouging, Rudy became a successful promoter in the East, rivaling and sometimes joining Toots Mondt and Jack Pfefer. He died in 1972 at age 70.

FUNK, DORY, JR.:

His wrestling father, Dory, Sr., came from Indiana, but Dory, Jr., grew up in Texas and played tackle for West Texas State before joining his dad's business in 1963. For ten years, they and Dory, Jr.'s, younger brother, Terry, wrestled out of the Flying Mare Ranch in Umbarger, Tex., near Amarillo. Dory, Jr., won the National Wrestling Alliance title from Gene Kiniski in Tampa, Fla., 1969, and lost it to Handsome Harley Race in Kansas City, Kan., 1973, shortly before his father died of a heart attack at the ranch.

GAGNE, VERNE:

Born and reared in Minnesota, he played football for the University of Minnesota and El Toro Marines. A great amateur wrestler, he was Big Ten champion four times in one weight classification or another, NCAA 191-pound champ in 1948, NCAA heavyweight champ in 1949, and an alternate on the 1948 Olympic team. He opted for pro wrestling rather than pro football and has become a millionaire from his bouts, his promotions, his own weight-control concentrate, and other interests. At first, he was a junior heavyweight in the pros, holding the title in that division, but in 1959, he beat Edouard Carpentier, claiming the heavyweight title, and led the splinter group that became the American Wrestling Assocation (AWA). (Carpentier had beaten NWA champ Lou Thesz on a disqualification; the AWA claimed Thesz was constantly fouling out on purpose because the belt could not change waists on a disqualification.) Gagne has held the AWA title most of the time since, specializing in the sleeper hold.

GEORGE, GORGEOUS:

Born George Wagner in Nebraska in 1915 and grew up in Houston with a group of tough kids, many of whom became pro wrestlers. He was just one of the boys; good, but nothing sensational, until he took up The Human Orchid guise about 1943. A few years later, he dyed his hair blond and was ready to become one of the early stars of television in the late '40s and early '50s. He had his name legally changed to Gorgeous George in 1950. He earned fabulous amounts of money and drew a fabulous amount of publicity, but divorce and drink robbed him of his savings and his Beaumont, Calif., turkey ranch. He died Dec. 26, 1963. Friends had to chip in money for his flamboyant funeral.

GOTCH, FRANK:

Born on a farm near Humboldt, Iowa, in 1878, he was a lifelong resident of Humboldt. He met and was defeated by Farmer Burns in 1899, then toured with Burns. Gotch was defeated by Tom Jenkins in Cleveland, 1903, but took the title from Jenkins a year later in Bellingham, Wash. In a Greco-Roman match in Madison Square Garden in 1905, Jenkins took the title back, subsequently losing it to George Hackenschmidt. Gotch took it from Hack in Chicago in 1908 and defended the title against Hack in another big Chicago match in 1911. The Iowa champion retired in 1913 and died of uremic poisoning four years later.

HACKENSCHMIDT, GEORGE:

Nicknamed The Russian Lion, he was born in Eastern Europe in 1878 and was a celebrated strong man and athlete before becoming a pro wrestler around the turn of the century. In his prime, he was five-nine, 225 pounds. He became a big attraction in London under the promotional guidance of C.B. Cochran, in one big match, beating Ahmed Madrali, one of wrestling's innumerable Terrible Turks. He also won two international tournaments in 1901 and defeated title claimer Tom Jenkins in Madison Square Garden in 1905. After his famous title loss to Frank Gotch in Chicago's Dexter Park Pavilion in 1908, he claimed Gotch had slathered himself in oil and was impossible to hold. He lost his rematch with Gotch in Chicago's Comiskey Park in 1911. Hackenschmidt died in England on Feb. 19, 1968, at age 90.

JENKINS, TOM:

Born in Bedford, Ohio, in 1872, he lost most of the sight in his right eye in a childhood accident. He left a Cleveland steel mill to turn pro in 1892 and defeated the famous Farmer Burns in 1897 before the home folks. He wrestled Burns' protege, Frank Gotch, six times altogether, losing the title in Washington state and winning it back again in New York (see Gotch). George Hackenschmidt took the championship away from him for good in 1905 in Madison Square Garden. Jenkins was the wrestling coach at the U.S. Military Academy, West Point, N.Y., 1921-1935. He died in 1957 at age 84.

KOWALSKI, WLADEK (Killer):

One of the great villains, the tall, powerful Kowalski is a quiet, gentlemanly, religious man outside the ring. The son of a Detroit factory worker, he grew up in Windsor, Ontario, across the river from the car city. Mean inside the ropes, and famous for his purple tights with lightning bolts decorating the sides, he has bloodied more heroes than practically any other heel alive. Promoters make a big deal out of the Montreal match in 1964 in which Killer leaped off the ropes, landed on Yukon Eric's cauliflowered right ear and tore it off. Ooooh.

LEVIN, DAVE:

Born and reared in Brooklyn, he went into the wrestling business via the Graphic Grapplers, similar to the Golden Gloves. Promoter Jack Pfefer changed his name from George Wenzel to Levin. The handsome hero won the heavyweight championship in 1936 in Newark, N.J. Substituting for Hans Schnabel, he won when Ali Baba was disqualified for a low kick (Baba and his backers did not accept the decision). Levin lost his version of the title a few months later to Dean Detton in Philadelphia, but in the interim, he defended the title *"twice as many times as Joe Louis did in his whole boxing career."* Levin retired in the early '50s and became a successful locker-room interviewer on Los Angeles TV. Today, walking with a decided limp caused by old wrestling injuries and subsequent complications, Levin manages a liquor store in L.A. and owns an apartment house in Santa Monica.

LEWIS, ED (Strangler):

His real name was Robert Friedrich, but he borrowed his ring pseudonym from an earlier pro, Evan (Strangler) Lewis. Probably the greatest wrestler in pro history, this native of Nekoosa, Wis., won and lost the heavyweight championship (or some version of it) five times. His victories: 1920 over Joe Stecher, 1922 over Stanislaus Zbyszko, 1928 over Stecher again, 1931 over Ed Don George, 1932 over Dick Shikat. He also won and lost several fortunes over his long career, and several wives. He won an international tournament at the Manhattan Opera House in 1915 and was still donning his trunks on occasion more than thirty years later. He died at age 76 in Muskogee, Okla., Aug. 7, 1966, after having been blind, poor and religious the last few years of his life.

LONDOS, JIM:

His real name is Christopher Theophelus. Born in Greece and reared in the San Francisco area, he borrowed his ring name from the author Jack London. The Golden Greek turned pro around 1917 and once wrestled in the backwaters as a light heavyweight. He became one of the great crowd-drawing heroes in wrestling history, nearly always finishing his opponents with an airplane spin and a body slam. In 1930, he beat Dick Shikat for the disputed heavyweight title and consolidated his claim with a 1934 victory over Jim Browning in Philadelphia. He lost his title to Danno O'Mahoney in Boston in 1935. Londos had a long-running feud with Strangler Lewis, losing to Lewis fourteen straight times, then beating him before a big crowd in Chicago's Wrigley Field in 1934. At age 53, he wrestled Primo Camera before another big house in Chicago. Today, he is retired and living near San Diego.

LONGSON, WILD BILL:

A 240-pound native of Salt Lake City, he earned his infamy by being the heavy in a long series of matches with Lou Thesz. He won the National Wrestling Alliance championship in 1942 over Sandor Szabo in St. Louis, in 1943 over Bobby Managoff in St. Louis, and in 1947 over Thesz in the same city. He lost it for good in 1948 to Thesz in Indianapolis. Man Mountain Dean broke Longson's back in 1939, but he came back and had a lucrative return-bout victory over the behemoth Dean.

MALCEWICZ, JOE:

Nicknamed The Utica Panther after his hometown in upstate New York. He became well known after beating Earl Caddock, who was barnstorming his way east for a match against Joe Stecher in New York City. He fought and did well against some of the greatest, including Strangler Lewis, Stecher, and Toots Mondt, then retired in 1937 to spend all his time promoting in the San Francisco area. He died in 1964 while gardening at his home.

MCGUIRK, LEROY:

Born 1912 in Broken Bow, Okla., and grew up in Tulsa. At Oklahoma A&M (now Oklahoma State), he won the NCAA 155-pound class in 1931 and was second in the 174-pound class the next year. He was king of the light-heavyweight division for many years, having taken the title from Hugh Nichols in Tulsa, but his career ended in 1950 when an automobile accident in Arkansas left him blind. Today, he is the promoter in Tulsa and controls a wrestling territory that includes parts of Oklahoma, Arkansas, Missouri, Mississippi and Louisiana.

MONDT, JOSEPH (Toots):

A wily and tough wrestler out of Greeley, Colo., he became an even wilier and tougher promoter, mostly in New York City. He joined with Billy Sandow and Strangler Lewis in the early '20s to form the "gold-dust trio," which controlled the wrestling business in much of the country. He later was involved in all sorts of combines with and against such promoters as Jack Pfefer, Rudy Dusek, Jack Curley and Ray Fabiani. He ran the East with Vince McMahon right up until a few years ago when he retired in St. Louis. Those who saw him in action in his prime, in the ring, or in outside brawls with other wrestlers, say he was in the same league with Lewis and Joe Malcewicz.

MOOLAH, FABULOUS:

Formerly Slave Girl Moolah, her real maiden name was Lillian Ellison. She was born and reared in South Carolina and still lives there, on a large spread near Columbia. Once a stooge for a wrestler named Elephant Boy, she turned to wrestling herself, making her U.S. debut in Boston in 1954. In 1956, she entered a tournament in Baltimore to determine the women's champion and beat June Byers two straight falls in the final. She has clung to the belt ever since and also runs a stable of women wrestlers.

MORALES, PEDRO:

The Puerto Rican darling of New York City's large Latin population, his matches against various despicable heels pack Madison Square Garden once a month. The area has had phony Puerto Ricans in the past, so Morales makes sure to speak at least a few words of Spanish in each TV interview so the viewers can catch his authentic accent. Born in 1943 on the Puerto Rican island of Culebra, he came to the U.S. in 1958, took the World Wide Wrestling Federation (WWWF) belt from Ivan Koloff in 1971, and held it about two years, even in a big match versus fellow good-guy Latin, Bruno Sammartino, in Shea Stadium. Morales finally lost it to Stan Stasiak, who lost it to Sammartino.

MULDOON, WILLIAM:

Born in 1845 in Belfast, N.Y., and reared there, the son of Irish-born parents. He started wrestling in New York City saloons after the "Civil War," soon became the champion of the New York Police Department. He won the Greco-Roman title from Thiebaud Bauer in 1880 and quit the police a year later to give wrestling his full attention. His series of battles against Clarence Whistler were gigantic bores, one of them going eight hours to a draw; it must have been as exciting as watching two sleepy elephants lean against each other. Muldoon, known as The Solid Man of Sport, was a longtime member of the New York Athletic Commission and ran a health resort. He died in 1933.

ROCCA, ANTONINO:

An Italian who grew up in Argentina, Rocca has shrouded his own past with conflicting and ridiculously exaggerated claims of athletic triumphs. What is certain is that he was a superb athlete-showman and one of the greatest drawing cards ever, right up there with Gorgeous George, Jim Londos and Bruno Sammartino. His specialty was leaping around the ring and drop-kicking his opponents silly, leading promoter Toots Mondt to crack, "*Rocca has done more for legs than Betty Grable.*" Rocca first came to the U.S. in 1948, wrestling and leaping for promoter Morris Sigel in Texas and drawing great crowds. Then Kola Kwariani, a Russian wrestler, whispered in his ear that he could make a lot more money working for Toots Mondt in Madison Square Garden. Rocca skipped. And he had innumerable wins and big houses in New York. He once claimed to have never lost, but he had, at least three times to Lou Thesz in Texas, once to LeRoy McGuirk, and even once in the Garden, to Verne Gagne. Rocca retired before the reign of Bruno Sammartino in the '60s.

ROGERS, NATURE BOY BUDDY:

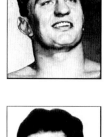

A strutting, peroxide-blond villain, Rogers' real name is Herman Rhode and he comes from Camden, N.J. He turned pro in 1943 and enjoyed a long, lucrative career. He defeated New Zealander Pat O'Connor for the National Wrestling Alliance title in Chicago's Comiskey Park in 1961 and lost it in early 1963 to Lou Thesz in Toronto. Nature Boy was recognized that same year as champion of the World Wide Wrestling Federation, based in New York. Bruno Sammartino took that title away in May of 1963. Rogers retired in 1967.

SAMMARTINO, BRUNO:

Born 1935 in Pizzoferrato, Italy, he moved with his family to Pittsburgh when he was still a teen-ager. With the help of weight lifting, he built a massive 265-pound physique and became one of the top drawing cards in wrestling history, especially in Boston, New York, and his hometown of Pittsburgh. It took him less than a minute to take the World Wide Wrestling Federation title from Buddy Rogers in 1963. He defended the title successfully for eight years before losing it to Ivan Koloff in Madison Square Garden. Later, he won it back from Stan Stasiak. Today, he is a millionaire, or close to it, and wrestles only when he's in the mood.

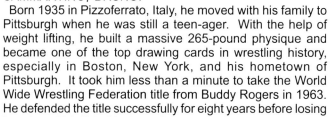

STECHER, JOE:

Born April 5, 1896, on a farm outside Dodge, Neb., this German-Bohemian wrestler specialized in the scissors, claiming he had built up the strength in his legs by squeezing sacks of grain. He weighed 220 pounds in his prime. He won and lost the heavyweight championship three times, beating Charley Cutler in Omaha, 1915; losing to Earl Caddock in Omaha, 1917; beating Caddock in New York City, 1920; losing to Strangler Lewis in New York, 1920; beating Stanislaus Zbyszko in St. Louis, 1925, and losing to Lewis in St. Louis, 1928. His late brother Tony founded the Minneapolis Wrestling Club. Joe died in early 1974 at the age of 80 after thirty years in a Veteran's Hospital.

STEELE, RAY:

Born 1900 in Lincoln, Neb., his real name was Pete Sauer and he was a member of a well-known athletic family in that state (a state that also produced the Stecher brothers, the Dusek brothers, and John Pesek and son). Ray started his career as a strong man and wrestler for the Russell Brothers Carnival, later became one of wrestling's early masked men. He wrestled dozens, maybe hundreds, of matches against the Greek hero, Jim Londos, and lost a famous match against Strangler Lewis in 1933 in New York City. Steele died in 1949 while on a hunting trip in Montana.

THESZ, LOU:

Born April 26, 1916, the son of a Hungarian shoemaker and wrestler. Thesz grew up in St. Louis and had many of his greatest victories (and crowds) there. Between 1937 and 1966, he won and lost the heavyweight championship six times, starting with a victory over Everette Marshall in St. Louis and ending with a loss to ex-football player Gene Kiniski in Tampa, Fla. In-between, there were numerous epic matches versus Wild Bill Longson, Whipper Watson, Baron Michele Leone, Dick Hutton and Buddy Rogers, among others. In 1973, close to 60, Thesz came out of retirement for the umpteenth time and said, "*I feel like I'm 22 years old.*"

ZBYSZKO, STANISLAUS:

His real name was even more of a Polish jawbreaker, Stanislaus Cyganiewicz. His brother Wladek was also a prominent wrestler. He succeeded George Hackenschmidt as the big draw in London, then went to the U.S. in 1909, losing to Frank Gotch the following year. In 1922, way past his prime, he beat Strangler Lewis for the title in New York City, but lost it back to Lewis in Wichita that same year. In 1925, he took the title from Wayne Munn in Philadelphia and lost it the same year to Joe Stecher in St. Louis. One of Zbyszko's great victories came in the courtroom in 1930, when an appellate judge awarded him $25,000 from the *New York American*, which had printed an article on evolution and used Stan's photograph in close proximity to the photo of a hideous gorilla. (There was a rumor that the gorilla sued, too, and settled out of court.) He retired in 1935, but tried a brief comeback in 1939. He died in 1967 in Missouri at age 88.

Addendum 2
Holds You Probably Never Saw in the Olympics

Headlocks, hammerlocks, step-over toeholds, half Nelsons, full Nelsons, flying mares — these are conventional weapons in a wrestler's repertoire. However, the pros, inventive and colorful performers that they are, have made some improvements, if not in the holds themselves, then at least in the nomenclature. The selections below are listed in alphabetical order by wrestler:

• Chief Big Heart: TOMAHAWK CHOP.

Who says the Japanese developed karate?

• Lord Blears: OXFORD LEG STRANGLE.

• Bobo Brazil: COCO BUTT.

Also known as THE KO KO KLOP and THE COFFEE BEAN. In this subtle and intricate maneuver, Brazil, who is from Michigan, not Rio, grabs his opponent's head with both hands and butts him with his own cranium, which is apparently as hard as concrete. Cowboy Bill Watts once wore a boxing head guard against Brazil. One night at the Olympic Auditorium in Los Angeles, George (Crybaby) Cannon let Brazil get a goat-like run at him and butt him in the stomach three times. He was knocked backward, but not down, and then, triumphantly pointing to the target area, crowed to the customers, *"Solid rock! Solid rock!"*

• June Byers: BYERS BRIDGE.

• Lord Leslie Carlton (Tug Carlson): SOUTHERN CROSS.

• Jim and Steve Casey: KILLARNEY FLIP.

• Killer Karl Cox: BRAINBUSTER.

• The Crusher (Reggie Lisowski): CRUSHER BOLO PUNCH.

• Bud Curtis: COCOANUT CRUSHER.

• Danny Dusek (Sid Nabors): FILIPINO GUERRILLA HOLD.

Nabors, a pseudo Dusek brother, was a World War II prisoner of the Japanese in the Philippines.

• Don Eagle: INDIAN DEATH LOCK.

• Ike Eakins: MOUNTAIN DROP.

• Billy Edwards: KNUCKLE HEADLOCK.

• Cowboy Bob Ellis: BULLDOG HEADLOCK.

Ellis gets his opponent in a conventional side headlock, then runs partway across the ring, drops to the mat, and smashes the victim's head to the canvas. After which, presumably, he hogties and brands him.

• Dory Funk, Sr.: SPINNING TOEHOLD.

This has been passed on to his son, Dory, Jr. Quite a legacy.

• Verne Gagne: SLEEPER.

• Timothy Geohagen: IRISH WINDMILL and IRISH LULLABY.

The latter, as perhaps you guessed, is a variation of the sleeper.

• Ed Don George: WOLVERINE SLAM.

• George was an outstanding wrestler at the University of Michigan, where the teams are nicknamed Wolverines. He was a Big Ten and National AAU champion and went to the final of the 1928 Olympics before losing to a Swede.

Gorgeous George (George Wagner): FLYING SIDE HEADLOCK.

• King Curtis Iaukea: BIG SPLASH.

Iaukea, a grossly fat native of Hawaii, runs and does a bellyflop on his supine opponent. He once was a tackle for the University of California (leading the Pacific Coast Conference in offsides) and the British Columbia Lions. His recommended way to decide football games is to put eleven tents on the field. One guy from each team — by positions — enters each tent. Whichever team has the most men walk out wins. League administrators have not adopted the idea.

• Hard-Boiled Haggerty (Don Stansauk): SHILLELAGH SWING.

A long, well-telegraphed, roundhouse right. He was the third wrestler to use the Haggerty nom de mat, following Pat McClary and Louis Reynheer, both of whom were also heels.

• Herman Hickman: BELLY BOUNCE.

The Big Splash in an earlier incarnation.

• Dan Hodge: BANANA SPLIT.

• Brother Frank Jares: UTAH HANGMAN.

• Sergei Kalmikoff: RUSSIAN BEAR HUG.

• The Kentucky Butcher: CLEAVER CHOP.

• Duke Keomuka: STOMACH CLAW.

This Hawaiian heel would clamp his hand on an opponent's stomach and supposedly produce convulsions and cramping of the abdominal muscles. Promoter Paul Boesch and wrestler Larry Chene came up with the Larry Chene Protective Shirt, which had a front padding of foam rubber, but referees in Dallas ruled it illegal.

• Lord Athol Layton: ENGLISH OCTOPUS.

Layton is from Australia, but perhaps the octopuses there aren't as fierce as those from the seas around Great Britain.

• The Leduc Brothers: LUMBERJACK BEARHUG.

• Chief Little Wolf (Benny Tenario): INDIAN DEATH LOCK.

Sorry, Chief, but Don Eagle stole your hold later. These eastern forest Indians just have no respect.

• The Spoiler (Don Jardine): IRON CLAW.

• Stan (Crusher) Stasiak: HEART CRUSHER.

An earlier Stan Stasiak, one of the great villains, died of blood poisoning in 1936 after being cut in a bout in Worcester, Mass.

• Ray Stevens: BOMBS AWAY.

• Chief Jay Strongbow: SLEEPER.

Heel Jim Valiant once pretended to befriend the chief and managed to get him to divulge the secret of the hold, then the rat used it against him. "Valiant" is obviously a misnomer.

• Professor Toru Tanaka: JAPANESE COBRA.

No matter that the cobra is a snake more associated with India than Japan, Tanaka is sneaky enough to swipe anything.

• Lou Thesz: KANGAROO KICK and AIRPLANE SPIN.

The legendary Golden Greek, Jim Londos, was also a great exponent of The Airplane Spin and used it to clinch almost all of his New York City triumphs.

• Chief Thunderbird: WOODPECKER.

A thunderbird is mythical, like a unicorn. The chief, for some reason, modeled his favorite maneuver after a real, far less glamorous bird.

• Ray Urbano: FILIPINO FLIP.

• Johnny Valentine: FLYING ELBOW SMASH and ATOMIC SKULLCRUSHER.

• Fritz Von Erich (Jack Adkisson): IRON CLAW.

So powerful is this grip that Von Erich, an ex-SMU football player, has to hold his wrist with his left hand to keep it under a semblance of control. He clamps the right hand/claw over his opponent's face.

• Cowboy Bill Watts: OKLAHOMA STAMPEDE.

• Oni Wiki Wiki: SURF CURL.

• Tony Marino: COBRA TWIST.

• Farmer Marlin: MULE KICK.

• Mil Mascaras: FLYING BODY PRESS.

Also the specialty of Pedro Morales, the Puerto Rican hero. The idea is to get your opponent dazed and staggering around in the middle of the ring. Climb to the top rope and leap at him like Superman taking off from a window ledge. Hit him chest-first and pin him.

• Wahoo McDaniel: TOMAHAWK CHOP. Again.

• Leo (The Lion) Newman: DIAMOND-DRILL NECK TWIST.

• Danno O'Mahoney: IRISH WHIP.

• Tony Parisi: SICILIAN SLEDGE.

Not to be confused with the Sicilian wedge, which is a piece of pizza.

• Bill Parks: SUNSET FLIP.

• Johnny Powers: POWERLOCK.

"When I first broke into the pro ranks I had a manager, Bobby Davis, who taught me the figure-four leglock," said Powers, a big hero in Cleveland. *"I took it from there and invented a much more punishing hold. Your opponent can break out of a figure-four, but I bet 10-to-1 he can't get out of The Powerlock."*

• Les Roberts: KOALA-BEAR HUG.

• Nature Boy Buddy Rogers: ATOMIC SPLIT.

• The Russians: RUSSIAN HAMMER.

• Whiskers Savage: LOG-ROLLING "HOLT."

• Baron Michele Scicluna: MALTESE HANGMAN.

• The Sheik: CAMEL CLUTCH.

• Wilbur Snyder: COBRA HOLD.

Addendum 3
Wrestlers vs. Boxers

Fight night in my youth was something special, a time when my mother left Pop and me alone in the kitchen with the dirty dinner dishes and the radio, listening to *The Gillette Cavalcade of Sports.* My old man always stood with one foot up on a chair close to the speaker, working a toothpick in his mouth and paying strict attention as Joe Louis battered Billy Conn or some other opponent of the '40s and the machine-gun blow-by-breathless-blow descriptions by the announcer ruined my digestion but tickled my imagination. Pop is a boxing fan to this day but always insists that as a method of self-defense it is a poor second to his sport, wrestling. A boxer might beat a wrestler occasionally by getting in a quick knockout punch, he says, but most of the time a wrestler would grab an arm or dive for a leg and it would be all over in a hurry. He is undoubtedly right. Wrestler/promoter Verne Gagne once had a pretty good boxer in his stable named Ronnie Marsh. *"He had thirty wins out of thirty-one or thirty-two fights when I had him,"* said Gagne, *"and he wanted to see how long he'd last. It was down in the gym with some of the guys and the trainer standing around. So I pinned him five times, or made him give up, within a minute and a half. There was no contest to it."*

Here are some other wrestler-against-boxer incidents:

WILLIAM MULDOON versus JOHN L. SULLIVAN, 1887:

Boxing and wrestling historian Nat Fleischer wrote that this confrontation between Irish-American heroes took place in a baseball park in Gloucester, Mass., and that a crowd of about 2,000 saw Muldoon slam Sullivan to the ground (or canvas). Then, said Fleischer, *"the crowd rushed in and stopped the combat."*

The excellent sports editor Stanley Woodward wrote, *"The two never met in formal physical combat, but Muldoon became respected … because he was the only man who ever was able to make John L. train."* I think that while Muldoon certainly could have whipped Sullivan, this was just a training-camp dido — two lusty Irishmen horsing around, if it really happened at all. And I can't believe the crowd would have broken it up if it had been any kind of formal match.

FARMER BURNS versus BILLY PAPKE, 1910:

Sports Illustrated said this battle in Reno took place in 1921, but propaganda from Burns's wrestling school in the Midwest said it happened in 1910, which fits in better with when Papke was in his prime as one of the country's best middleweights (Burns also was considerably less than a heavyweight, competing at about 158 pounds in the nineties). Burns was in Nevada helping Jim Jeffries train for a fight and Papke dropped by to visit the camp. Burns' story was that Papke started razzing him and wrestlers in general. The result was that Burns bet $1,000 that Papke couldn't beat him (and Burns was more than 50 at the time). They met in a boxing ring and Burns pinned him in eighteen seconds.

STRANGLER LEWIS versus JACK DEMPSEY, 1922:

This one never got past the ballyhoo stage. Mostly, it consisted of Lewis's manager, Billy Sandow, issuing challenges to Dempsey via the sports pages of newspapers, including the *Nashville Banner* of March 16. Said Sandow, *"I mean business. Let him deposit a check for five thousand dollars, as I have done on the behalf of Lewis, and the match will most assuredly be staged. Our money is up and we stand ready to deposit another five thousand dollars when Kearns* [Dempsey's manager] *puts up the money for Dempsey. And my personal wager of five thousand dollars still stands that Lewis can beat Dempsey inside of twenty minutes in any ring in the world."*

Said Lewis, *"… Once I got hold, he would not have a chance because he does not know how to break wrestling holds, and I am stronger than he is. Of course, there is one chance in a thousand that he might hit me with a punch hard enough to knock me out before I could get hold of him, but that is only one chance."*

TOOTS MONDT versus LOUIS ASPIN, 1923:

Mondt humiliated his boxing opponent in the first round in San Francisco, then in the second, literally hogtied him, bowed to the crowd, and departed.

WILD BILL LONGSON versus JACK DEMPSEY, 1931:

On September 15 in Salt Lake City, Dempsey knocked out Longson in the first round. It is listed in the record book as an exhibition. Both wore gloves, so it really wasn't wrestler versus boxer. It was a handicapped-by-gloves wrestler versus boxer.

RAY STEELE versus KINGFISH LEVINSKY, 1935:

A quickie in St. Louis. Levinsky hit Steele twice, according to spectator George Zaharias, then Steele got the boxer off his feet and pinned him. Elapsed time: less than a minute.

A SERIES OF WRESTLERS versus JACK DEMPSEY, 1940:

Dempsey was active as a wrestling referee this year and often, it seems, had trouble making the villains behave. Three times such run-ins resulted in challenges and subsequent boxing matches in which the wrestlers handicapped themselves by putting on gloves. Dempsey KO'd Cowboy Luttrall in the second round in Atlanta, Bull Curry in the second round in Detroit, and Ellis Bashara in the second round in Charlotte.

LOU THESZ versus ROCKY MARCIANO, 1950:

Another one that never got past the challenging stage. Most of the evidence indicates that Thesz would have loved to meet Marciano inside the ropes and that Rocky and his managers wisely stayed away. Rocky, of course, claimed he would win. Thesz said, *"Any of a dozen wrestlers could lick Marciano. I say this while acknowledging Rocky is a great champion."*

Rudy Dusek said, *"There's no question about it. Thesz would win. I once fought a free-for-all with a good fighter in Memphis, Tennessee. I threw him, twisted his arm, dislocated his shoulder, and tore his arm muscles. It was over in one minute and fifty-two seconds. Although I'm fifty, I'd be glad to take on Marciano."*

NATURE BOY BUDDY ROGERS versus JERSEY JOE WALCOTT, 1956:

Rogers pinned the ex-heavyweight champion of the world.

Dempsey Knocks Out Bull Curry In Second Round

(By Associated Press)

DETROIT, July 15. — Former Heavyweight Boxing Champion Jack Dempsey knocked out Bull Curry, Hartford, Conn., wrestler in the second round of a scheduled six-round exhibition bout here tonight, that was anything but a pugilistic show.

The knockout blow—at 1:05 of the round—was a vicious right to the wrestler's stomach and was the only one Dempsey was able to land.

From the time the bell sounded for the first round Curry turned the affair into a wrestling match. He got the ex-champion in a headlock and Referee Sam Hennessy finally pried the two apart.

Thirty seconds before the round ended Curry grabbed Dempsey by the legs and both fighters went hurtling through the ropes into the lap of Chairman John Hettche of the state boxing commission.

Jack Dempsey
vs. Bull Durry
Detroit, Michigan
July 15, 1940

Addendum 4
Wrestling Football Players
(or vice versa)

ADKISSON, JACK (ring name: Fritz Von Erich):
 Defensive tackle, Southern Methodist, 1948-49. Played at 225 pounds, 6-foot-3 inches for Coach Matty Bell until he lost his grant-in-aid because he got married. Mustangs won Southwest Conference championship in 1948, led by the great Doak Walker. Adkisson also was a discus thrower and held the school record for a long time.

AFFLIS, WILLIAM FRITZ (ring name: Dick the Bruiser):
 Guard, Nevada. Green Bay Packers, 1951-52-53-54.

BASHARA, ELLIS:
 Guard, Oklahoma, All-Big Six in 1933. Played at 5-foot-10 inches, 180 pounds. Ex-Oklahoma Coach Ben Owens said Bashara "was as good a guard as we ever had here." Picked for all-time Sooner team by fans in 1933.

BELL, KAY:
 Tackle, Washington State, 1934-35-36. Chicago Bears, 1937. Columbus Bullies, 1940-41. New York Giants, 1942. Washington State had a 15-9-3 record during his three years on the varsity.

DIBIASE, MIKE:
 Guard and tackle, Nebraska, 1946-48-49.

FUNK, DORY, JR.:
 Tackle, West Texas State, 1959-60-61-62. He was a starting tackle in 1962 when the Buffaloes beat Ohio University 15-14 in the Sun Bowl.

FUNK, TERRY:
 Lineman, West Texas State, 1963-64-65.

GAGNE, VERNE:
 End, Minnesota, 1943-48-49. The Minnesota native lettered as a freshman in 1943, then played for the El Toro Marines with fine players such as Elroy Hirsch and Paul Governali. He missed the 1947 season because of scholastic problems. Played in the 1949 College All-Star Game in Chicago.

GEIGEL, BOB:
 Tackle, Iowa, 1946-47-48-49. Played for Coach Eddie Anderson. Went 60 minutes versus Minnesota, Purdue, Northwestern and Notre Dame. Three-year letterman. Made finals of Olympic wrestling trials in 1948.

HICKMAN, HERMAN:
 Guard, Tennessee, 1929-30-31. All-America 1931. Brooklyn Dodgers, 1932-33-34. Head football coach at Yale. College football expert for Sports Illustrated. Elected to College Football Hall of Fame in 1959.

IAUKEA, CURTIS (ring name: King Curtis):
 Tackle, California, 1956-57. British Columbia Lions, 1958-59-60. Did not play senior year at Cal, when the Golden Bears went to the Rose Bowl. Though Curtis claims otherwise, Canadian Football League records show him with British Columbia only in 1957.

JOHNSON, WALTER:
 Fullback, Los Angeles State. Defensive tackle, Cleveland Browns, 1965 through 1969, 1970-71. Went to high school in Cincinnati.

KARRAS, ALEX:
 Tackle, Iowa, 1956-57. Consensus All-America in 1957 and made at least one All-America team in 1956, too. Detroit Lions, 1958 through 1962, 1964 through 1970. Suspended in 1963 for gambling. Won Outland Award in 1957 for being the nation's outstanding interior lineman, as selected by the Football Writers Association. Never lettered in wrestling at Iowa.

KEMMERER, CHARLES (ring name: Babe Sharkey):
 Tackle, Temple, 1932-33-34. Started at times but did not play in the first Sugar Bowl, New Year's Day, 1935.

KINISKI, GENE:
 Arizona. Edmonton Eskimos in Canadian Football League, 1949-50.

KRUSKAMP, HARDY:
 Blocking back, Ohio State, mid-1920s.

KUUSISTO, WILLIAM:
 Guard, Minnesota, last season 1940. Green Bay Packers, 1941 through 1946.

LADD, ERNIE:
 Tackle, Grambling. San Diego Chargers, 1961 through 1965. Houston Oilers, 1966-67. Kansas City Chiefs, 1967-68. Fifteenth-round draft choice of San Diego in 1961.

LEE, WILLIAM:
 Tackle, Alabama, 1932-33-34. All-America in 1934. Brooklyn Dodgers, 1935-36-37. Green Bay Packers, 1937 through 1942, 1946. He was captain of the Crimson Tide team that beat Stanford in the 1935 Rose Bowl.

LEVY, LEONARD (Butch):
 Guard, Minnesota. Cleveland Rams, 1945. Los Angeles Rams, 1946. Los Angeles Dons, 1947-48.

LIPSCOMB, EUGENE (Big Daddy):
 No college. Tackle, Los Angeles Rams, 1953-54-55. Baltimore Colts, 1956 through 1960. Pittsburgh Steelers, 1961-62.

LOLOTAI, ALBERT (ring name: Alo Leilani):
 Guard, Weber Junior College, 1941-42. Washington Redskins, 1945. Los Angeles Dons, 1946-47-48-49.

MACALUSO, LEN (Legs):
 Fullback, Colgate, 1928-29-30. Scored 145 points in one season, place-kicked a 35-yard field goal in 1930, scored 29 points in one game (versus Syracuse).

MCCLAIN, MAYES:
 Fullback, Haskell Institute and Iowa, 1926-27-28. Guard, Portsmouth Spartans, 1930-31. In 1926, playing football for Haskell, he scored 253 points on 38 touchdowns, 19 extra points and two field goals in 11 games. The following year he transferred to Iowa, where in 1928 he made 432 yards on 116 carries.

MCDANIEL, ED (Wahoo):
 End and defensive halfback, Oklahoma, 1956-57-58. Guard, Houston Oilers, 1960. Denver Broncos, 1961-62-63. New York Jets, 1964-65. Miami Dolphins, 1966-67-68.

MCMILLEN, JIM:
 Guard, Illinois. Chicago Bears, 1924 through 1931, 1935. Opened holes for the immortal running back Red Grange.

MILLER, BILL:
 Tackle, Ohio State, last season 1950. He played on the Buckeye team that beat Cal 17-14 in the 1950 Rose Bowl. Big Ten discus champion and member of the wrestling team.

MOSCA, ANGELO:
 Notre Dame. A star lineman in the Canadian Football League for many years. Hamilton, 1958-59. Ottawa, 1960-61. Montreal, 1962. Hamilton, 1963 through 1972. Nominated 1970 for the league's outstanding lineman award but did not win it.

MUNN, WAYNE (Big):
 Tackle, Nebraska, 1918-19-20. Kansas City Cowboys, 1925.

NAGURSKI, BRONKO:
 Tackle, Minnesota, 1927-28-29. All-America in 1929. Fullback, Chicago Bears, 1930 through 1937, 1943. Elected to the Pro Football Hall of Fame in 1963 with the very first "class."

NOMELLINI, LEO:
 Tackle, Minnesota, last season 1949. San Francisco 49ers, 1950 through 1963. First draft choice of San Francisco after making All-America in 1948 and 1949. Elected to the Pro Football Hall of Fame in 1969.

PAIDOUSIS, MIKE:
 Tackle, Tennessee, 1944-45-46. A starter until a returning World War II veteran replaced him on the 1946 team that went to the Orange Bowl.

PESEK, JACK:
 End and punter, Nebraska, mid-1940s. He set two Cornhusker punting records.

PRITCHARD, RON:
 Linebacker, Arizona State, 1966-67-68. Houston Oilers, 1969-70-71. Cincinnati Bengals, 1972. Led ASU in tackles for three seasons, then was Houston's first draft pick in 1969.

SAVOLDI, JOE:
 Back, Notre Dame, 1928-29-30. Chicago Bears, 1930. Sportswriter John Kieran said of his performance against Penn in 1930, *"Jumping Joe Savoldi was gaining more ground with tacklers clinging to him than Penn backs were gaining when running in the clear."* Left school in 1930 because he got married. Received 110 votes for the all-time Fighting Irish team in a 1962 poll, but George Gipp beat him out.

SHURTLEFF, BERT:
 Back, Brown, early 1920s. Providence Steamrollers, 1925-26. Boston Braves, 1929. Buffalo Bisons, 1929.

SONNENBERG, GUS:
 Guard, Dartmouth, 1919-20; University of Detroit, 1922. Columbus Tigers, 1923. Pottsville Maroons, 1924. Detroit Panthers, 1925-26. Providence Steamrollers, 1927-28-30.

SPELLMAN, JOHN:
 Tackle, Brown, class of '24. Providence Steamrollers, 1925 and 1931. Boston Braves, 1929 and 1932. Olympic light-heavyweight wrestling champion in 1924.

SNYDER, WILBUR:
 End and tackle, Utah, 1948-49. Quit after junior year to turn pro. On L.A. Rams' training-camp roster in 1952. Edmonton Eskimos, 1952-53.

STANSAUK, DONALD (ring name: Hard-Boiled Haggerty):
 Tackle, Denver. Green Bay Packers, 1950-51.

STEIN, SAMMY:

End, Staten Island Stapletons, 1929-30. New York Giants, 1931. Brooklyn Dodgers, 1932.

STITH, CAREL:

Tackle, Nebraska, 1965-66. Houston Oilers, 1967-68-69. All-Big Eight for Cornhuskers in 1966.

STRODE, WOODY:

End, UCLA, last season 1939. Los Angeles Rams, 1946. Also Calgary Stampeders. Better known as an actor than a wrestler or football player.

WHITE, ARTHUR (Tarzan):

Guard, Alabama, 1934-35-36. New York Giants, 1937-38-39, 1945. Chicago Cardinals, 1940-41. International News Service named him an All-America in 1936.

(above) **Gene Kiniski, Wlbur Snyder, Warren Bockwinkel & Joe Blanchard**
(below right) **Ed (Wahoo) McDaniel**

Addendum 5
Ring Aliases

Pseudonyms are not a phenomenon peculiar to wrestling. In boxing, Joe Louis' real name was Joe Louis Barrow, Jersey Joe Walcott was really Arnold Cream, Sugar Ray Robinson was Walker Smith, and Jack Sharkey was Joseph Zukauskas. On stage and screen, hardly anyone, it seems, uses his real name. Witness John Wayne (Marion Morrison), Rock Hunter (Roy Fitzgerald), and the late Bobby Darin (Robert Cassotto). Below is a small sampling of wrestling aliases; some understandable, some weird, some used over an entire career, some used just a short time in one territory:

RING NAME	REAL NAME
Abdullah Farouk	Ernie Roth
Abdullah the Butcher	Larry Shreeve
Ad Santel	Adolph Ernst
Al Costello	Giacoma Costa
Ali Baba	Arteen (Harry) Ekizian
Alo Leilani	Al Lolotai
Antonino Rocca	Antonino Biasetton
Baba the Giant	Shohei Baba
Babe Sharkey	Charles (Dutch) Kemmerer
Barbara Nichols	Joyce Fowler Becker
Beast, The	Yvan Cormier
Bill Lewis	Bill Whitfield
Black Bart	John Paul Black
Black Venus	Waver Pearl Bryant
Blackjack Mulligan	Bob Windham
Blimp, The	Martin Levy
Bobby Becker	John Emerling
Bobby Managoff	Bobby Manoogian
Boris K. Fabian	Bob (Reb) Russell
Buddy Fuller	Edward Welch
Buddy Rogers	Herman Rhode
Chester Hayes	Chester Chonowski
Chief Jay Strongbow	Joe Scarpa
Chief Little Wolf	Benny Tenario
Chief Sunni War Cloud	Sonny Chorre
Chief Thunderbird	Baptiste Paull
Crusher, The	Reggie Lisowski
Danny Dusek	Sid Nabors
Dave Findley	David Crockett
Dave Levin	George Wenzel

Dennis James	Demi James Sposa
Dick Lane	Dick Johnson
Dick the Bruiser	William Franklin Afflis
Doc Zoko	Pedro Godoy
Don Eagle	Carl Donald Bell
Don Fargo	Don Kalt
Dusek Brothers	Hason Brothers
Ed (Strangler) Lewis	Robert H. Friedrich
Elmer the Great	George Wagner
Fabulous Moolah	Lillian Ellison
Frank Kennedy	Frank Gotch
French Angel, The	Maurice Tillet
Fritz Von Erich	Jack Adkisson
Geeto Mongol	Newton Tattrie
Gene Stanlee	Eugene Stanley Zygowicz
George Holmes	Jackie Wilkins
George Koverly	Gojko Kovacovich
George Winchell	John Schweigert
George Zaharias	Theodore Vetoyanis
Gino Garibaldi	Sam Curcuru
Golden Superman	Walter Podolak
Gorgeous George	George Wagner
Gorilla Monsoon	Gino (Bob) Morella
Grand Wizard, The	Ernie Roth
Great Malenko, The	Larry Simon
Great Scott, The	John Schweigert
Great Togo, The	Taro Ito
Hans Schmidt	Guy Larose
Hans Schnabel	Jake Moehler
Happy Humphrey	William J. Cobb
Hard-Boiled Haggerty	Pat McClary-Louis Reynheer-Don Stansauk
Haystack Calhoun	William Dee Calhoun
Heather Feather	Peggy Jones
Hillbilly Spunky	Frank Robinson
Humid Kala Pasha	Joe Rickard
Ivan Bulba	Johnny Shaw
Ivan Rasputin	Hyman Fish man
J. Wellington Radcliff	Ernie Roth
Jack Curley (promoter)	Jacob Schmul (or Schuel)
Jackie Fargo	Henry Faggart
Jean Ferre	Andre Roussimoff
Jesse James	Jimmy James
Jim Dillon	James Morrison
Jim Londos	Christopher Theophelus
Joe Bommerito	Guiseppe Mazza
ohnny Cotto	Juan Cotto Rivers
Johnny Long	Billy Strong
Johnny Valentine	John Wisniski

June Byers	DeAlva Sibley
Jungle Boy	Lou Vertucci
King Curtis	Curtis Iaukea
Little Louie	Louis Waterhouse
Lord Carlton	"Tug" Carlson
Lucky Simunovich	Simunovich Zivko
Luther Lindsay	Luther Jacob Goodall
Mad Murdock	Bert Shurtleff
Man Mountain Dean	Frank Leavitt
Mike Riker	Mike York
Mildred Burke	Mildred Bliss
Missouri Mauler, The	Larry Hamilton
Pat O'Shocker	William Hayes Shaw
Paul Jones	Andy Lutse
Polish Angel, The	Wladislaw Talun
Ray Schwartz	John Emerling
Ray Shire	Ray Stevens
Ray Steele	Pete Sauer
Red Bastien	Rolland Bastien
Ricki Starr	Bernard Herman
Rikidozan	Mitsuhara Momota
Rose Roman	Rose Hesseltine
Salvatore Balbo	Johnny Iavanna
Scuffling Hillbillies, The	Chuck Conley & Rip Collins
Sheik, The	Edward Farhat
Sir Clement Beresford	Steve Beresford
Smasher Sloan	Donald Whittler
Stan Lisowski	Stan Holek
Stan Neilson	Stan Holek
Stanislaus Zbyszko	Stanislaus Cyganiewicz
Super Swedish Angel	Tor Johnson
Swedish Angel	Phil Olaffson
Sweet Daddy Watts	J.T. Holloway
Terry McGinnis	Max Martin
Thing, The	Frank Jares
Tiger Joe Marsh	Joe Marusich
Tim Woods	George Woodini
Tito Infanti	Danny Frian
Tom Packs	Anthanasios N. Pakiotis
Toru Tanaka	Charles Kalani, Jr.
Waldo Von Erich	Walter Sieber
Wally Dusek	Charles Santen
Whipper Watson	William Potts
Whiskers Savage	Eddie Civil
Wild Red Berry	Ralph Berry
Yukon Eric	Eric Holmbeck

Addendum 6
Masked Marauders of the Mat, A Collection of Devils, Demons, Phantoms, Xs, and One Pussycat

Masked men in wrestling date back at least to 1915, when The Masked Marvel created quite a sensation at the Manhattan Opera House, until Strangler Lewis beat him and sent him back to Pennsylvania. There was even a masked pro tennis player once (Eddie Alloo donned a hood during the pro championships in Cleveland), but wrestling has a monopoly on this particular form of show biz.

MASKED WRESTLERS	IDENTITIES
?, The	Angelo Poffo
Assassins, The	Joe Hamilton and Tom Renesto
Avenger, The	Reggie Parks
Avenger, The	Ricky Hunter
Battman	Tony Marino
Ben Justice	Gerald May
Black Baron, The	Bruce Swayze
Black Demon, The	Tony Nero
Black Devil, The	Tony Lanza
Black Secret, The	Mike Paidousis
Blue Demons, The	Frank Martinez and Tamayo Soto
	Frank Martinez and Al Greene
Blue Infernos, The	Gypsy Joe and Frank Martinez
Blue Terrors, The	Jack Spencer & Pepe Lopez
Bounty Hunter, The	Killer Tim Brooks
Caped Crusader, The	Tony Marino
Champion, The	Tarzan Tyler
Claw, The	Tom Anderson
Clawman, The	Ike Eakins
Convict, The	Stan Frazier
Count Barticelli	Geoff Conliff
Crimson Knight #2, The	Gene Kiniski
Crimson Knight, The	Dr. Bill Miller
Dark Secret, The	Joe Pazandak
Destroyer, The	Stan Pulaski, Dick Beyer
Dr. Blood	Dale Lewis
Dr. Death	Paul Lincoln
Dr. Scarlet	Bill Watts
Dr. X	Jim Osborne, Dick Beyer, Bill Miller
El Diablo	Dutch Hefner
El Lobo	Luke Graham
El Medico	Caesereo Manriquez

El Olympico	Joey Corea
Executioner, The	Donn Lewin, Guy Mitchell
Fantomas	Ramòn del Rio Morales
Gladiator, The	Ricky Hunter
Golden Gladiator, The	Ronnie Hill
Golden Terror, The	Bobby Stewart, Frank Jares
Good Doctor, The	Dick Dunn
Gorilla, The	Tony Lanza
Grappler, The	Johnny Walker
Great Bolo and Bolo, The	Al Lovelock and Pepper Martin
	Tom Renesto and Joe Hamilton
Great Goliath, The	Moose Evans
Green Hornet, The	Jim (Goon) Henry
Green Shadow, The	Eddie Malone
Hangman, The	Gene Lebell
Hooded Terror, The	Cowboy Don Lee, Tony Lanza
Infernos, The	Frankie Cain and Rocky Smith
	Rocky Smith and Curtis Smith
Intercollegiate Dark Secret	George Bollas
Interns, The	Bill Bowman and Joe Turner
	Billy Garrett and Jim Starr
	Tom Andrews and Jim Starr
Invader, The	Dick Murdoch
Iron Russians, The	Lou Newman and Hans Schnabel
Kamikaze	Modesto Aledo, Guy Robin, Jean Menard
Kendo Nagasaki	Peter Thornley
Madam X	Mae Weston
Marauder #1, The	Gene Kiniski
Marauder #2, The	Larry Hulin
Mask, The	Pepper Martin
Masked Bat, The	Bob O'Shocker
Masked Cougar, The	Ted Cox
Masked Hornet	Joe McCarthy
Masked Marvel	Bulldog Bill Garmon, Ray Steele,
	Mort Henderson, Rebel Bob Russell,
	Dory Funk, Sr.
Masked Marvels	Billy Garrett and Jim Starr
Masked Outlaw	Dory Funk, Sr., Dory Funk, Jr.
Masked Terror, The	Jay (The Alaskan) York, Pedro Godoy
Medics, The	Billy Garrett and Dick Dunn
	Billy Garrett and Jim Starr
	Donald Lortie and Tony Gonzales
	Luis Hernandez and Tony Gonzales
Mephisto and Dante	Louie Papineau and Red Donnan
	Frankie Cain and Bobby Hart
Mephistos, The	Corsica Joe and Jim Dalton
Mighty Hercules, The	Larry Hulin
Mighty Loco	Don Leo Jonathan

Mighty Yankees	Moose Evans and Bob Stanlee
	Eddie Sullivan and Frank Morrell
	Charlie Fulton and Frank Morrell
Mil Mascaras	Aaron Rodriguez
Mr. M	Dr. Bill Miller
Mr. Pro	Pepe Lopez
Mr. Wrestling #2	Johnny Walker
Mr. Wrestling	Tim Woods, Gordon Nelson
Mr. X	Doug Scoggins, Hans Mortier
Mummy, The	Benji Ramirez
Pantheress, The	Lina Magnani
Preacher, The	Clyde Steeves
Professional, The	Doug Gilbert (Lindzy)
Purple Flash, The	Henry Piers, Mae Weston, Wild Bill Longson
Purple Phantom, The	Black Jack Dillon
Purple Terror, The	Judo Jack Terry
Red Demons	Billy Boy Hines and Jimmy (Bad Boy) Hines
Red Devil, The	Eddie Blanks
Red Menace, The	Pedro Godoy
Red Phantom, The	Tom Rice
Red Scorpion, The	Nick Roberts
Red Shadow, The	Pedro Godoy, Pat Fraley, Dick Dunn
Russians, The	Pedro Godoy and Juan Sebastian
Santo, El	Rodolfo Guzmán Huerta
Santo, La	Maria Pisa
Scarlet Pimpernel, The	Ben Sherman
Shadow, The	Marv Westenberg, Clyde Steeves
Sicodelico, El	Pabo Rodriguez
Solitario, El	Roberto González Cruz
Sombra, The	Vic Holbrook
Spoiler II, The	Smasher Sloan
Spoiler, The	Don Jardine
Spook, The	Chester Hayes
Student, The	George Steele
Super Gladiator	Ricky Hunter
Super Infernos	Curtis Smith and Doug Gilbert (Lindzy)
Tarzan Zorro	Hans Mortier
Taurus	Dennis Hall
Torbellino Blanco	Mariano Yugueros
Toro, El	Bibber McCoy
Unknown Gladiator, The	Johnny James
White Angel, The	Francisco Farina
White Venus, The	Peggy Patterson
Wrestling Pro	Leon Baxter
Zebra Kid, The	George Bollas, Lenny Montana
Zodiac	Bob Orton
Zorro	Gino Garibaldi

Addendum 7
A Chronology of
Pro Wrestling in America

1897: Tom Jenkins takes the United States title away from Iowa's Martin (Farmer) Burns in two straight falls in Cleveland's central Armory. Burns had won it two years earlier from Evan (Strangler) Lewis.

1898: European strongman George Hackenschmidt wins the world Greco-Roman championship in Vienna. This type of wrestling does not allow tripping or holds below the waist.

1899: Burly Frank Gotch of Iowa has his first professional match, in the Russell Opera House in Humboldt, Iowa, winning three straight falls with strangle holds … Farmer Burns takes Gotch under his wing, promises to make him a champion.

1901: Gotch tours Alaska under the name Frank Kennedy and comes home with a sack full of gold … George Hackenschmidt wins two so-called world-championship tournaments in Europe, one in Vienna, one in Paris.

1903: In Cleveland, heavyweight champion Tom Jenkins easily defends his U.S. title against Gotch.

1904: Gotch wins the U.S. heavyweight championship from Jenkins in Bellingham, Wash., ending Jenkins's six-year reign.

1905: Gotch defends the title against Jenkins in the latter's own backyard, Cleveland … Jenkins beats Gotch in a Greco-Roman match in Madison Square Garden … Hackenschmidt beats Jenkins in the Garden in a match billed as being for the world championship.

1906: Gotch takes the U.S. title back from Jenkins in Kansas City, Mo … In New Orleans, Fred Beell, the woodchopper from Marshfield, Wis., wins the U.S. title when Gotch strikes his head against a ringpost … Gotch wins their rematch in Kansas City in straight falls.

1908: Frank Gotch defeats George Hackenschmidt in Chicago's Dexter Park Pavilion and brings the world title into American hands. The *New York Times* of April 4, 1908, says that Gotch "*side-stepped, roughed his man's features with his knuckles, butted him under the chin, and generally worsted Hackenschmidt until the foreigner was at a loss how to proceed.*" Hackenschmidt later was to charge that Gotch's body was "*literally soaked in oil*" and that the Iowan "*dug his nails into my face, tried to pull my ear off, and poked his thumb into my eye.*"

1909: Europe's Stanislaus Zbyszko has his first match in the United States.

1910: Gotch beats Zbyszko in Chicago, continuing his mastery over Europeans and breaking Zbyszko's claimed chain of 945 straight victories.

1911: Gotch defeats Hackenschmidt in their Chicago rematch in the White Sox ballpark. Hack goes in the ring despite an injured knee and the Iowan takes two straight falls.

1912: Dr. B.F. Roller takes the U.S. title from Charley Cutler … Ad Ernst Santel takes the light-heavyweight title from William Demetral in Oklahoma … Joe Stecher follows his brother Tony into the pro ranks.

1913: Gotch retires ... Henry Ordeman defeats Jess Westegaard in the start of a tournament to determine a successor.

1914: Charley Cutler defeats Henry Ordeman for the heavyweight crown.

1915: Dr. B. F. Roller loses the U.S. title to Strangler Lewis, who, by the way, is no relation to Evan (Strangler) Lewis (Strangler's real name is Robert Friedrich) ... The Masked Marvel (Mort Henderson) spices up an international tournament in the Manhattan Opera House, but the tourney is won by Ed (Strangler) Lewis ... Joe Stecher takes the world title away from Charley Cutler.

1916: Lewis and scissors-king Stecher battle five-and-a-half hours to a draw in Omaha. ... Jim Londos, born in Greece, but reared in the San Francisco area, turns pro.

1917: Lewis draws with Ad Santel before 15,000 fans in the San Francisco Civic Auditorium ... Lewis beats Stecher in Madison Square Garden in three hours and eight minutes, but Joe had already lost his title in Omaha to Earl Caddock ... Gotch dies of uremic poisoning at age 41.

1920: Caddock, of the Army, loses the title back to Stecher, of the Navy, in a battle of the services in Madison Square Garden ... Strangler Lewis takes the world title from Stecher at the Seventy-first Regiment Armory, New York City, in a Jack Curley-promoted match watched by more than 8,000 fans ... Martin (Farmer) Burns beats middleweight boxer Billy Papke in Reno in one of the first boxer-versus-wrestler confrontations.

1921: Zbyszko takes the heavyweight title from Lewis ... Rudy Dusek becomes the first of the infamous Nebraska Duseks to enter pro wrestling ... Tom Jenkins becomes the first wrestling coach at the U.S. Military Academy, West Point, N.Y.

1922: Zbyszko loses his title back to Lewis in Wichita, Kan.

1923: Hans Steinke arrives in the United States.

1925: Lewis loses his title to ex-Nebraska football player Wayne (Big) Munn at the Convention Hall, Kansas City, Mo ... Zbyszko takes the title from Munn in Philadelphia ... Lewis beats Munn on Memorial Day at Michigan City, Ind., before 20,792 fans. ... At the old Federal League ballpark in St. Louis, Zbyszko loses the title to Joe Stecher.

1928: Gus Sonnenberg, ex-football star at Dartmouth and Detroit, has his first professional match, in Providence, R.I. … In a match that takes almost two-and-a-half hours, Lewis takes the title from Stecher in St. Louis's Coliseum. It is Strangler's fourth time as champion of the world ... George Zaharias turns pro ... Clarence Eklund beats Ad Santel in Melbourne, Australia. Both had been claiming the light-heavy title. Says Eklund, "*Santel learned more in that match about wrestling at 175 pounds in fifteen minutes than he had learned in fifteen years of talking of wrestling at that weight.*"

1929: Sonnenberg takes the title from Lewis in Boston ... About 25,000 fans see Sonnenberg successfully defend against Lewis in Boston's Fenway Park ... Everett Marshall turns pro ... Dick Shikat from Germany beats Jim Londos in Philadelphia and claims that he is the champion ... Hugh Nichols wins tournament in Cincinnati to determine the light-heavyweight champion.

1930: Londos, The Golden Greek, wins one version of the title back from Germany's Shikat in a rain-soaked match in Philadelphia. ... Ed Don George, ex-college wrestling star from Michigan, in his first year as a pro, beats Sonnenberg in Los Angeles for another version of the title. From now into the 1970s, the championship picture in pro wrestling will almost always be blurry ... Eddie Quinn starts promoting in the Boston area. Later he will become the czar of wrestling in Montreal.

1931: Lewis wins the title from George in Los Angeles' Wrigley Field before 12,000 fans ... Lewis is robbed of his championship on a phony disqualification in Canada. The new champ is Henri DeGlane ... George takes the title from DeGlane in Boston ... Dean Detton and Earl McCready, three times National Collegiate champion from Oklahoma A&M, turn pro.

1932: Strangler Lewis beats Dick Shikat at the Garden Bowl, Long Island, and becomes a heavyweight king once again ... Paul Boesch, Terry McGinnis and Mayes McClain turn pro.

1933: William Muldoon, famous wrestler of the 1800s (wrestling's equivalent of John L. Sullivan) and a powerful figure in New York State athletics, dies ... Lewis loses his title to Jim Browning in New York City ... Lewis loses again to Browning before 12,000 people in a Mexico City bullring ... Strangler defeats Ray Steele in a famous Madison Square Garden bout ... Rebel Bob Russell turns pro, and Bronko Nagurski makes his pro debut in promoter Tony Stecher's first show in Minneapolis ... Ex-American champ Fred Beell, now working as a bank guard, is killed in a holdup.

1934: Jim Londos beats Browning for one version of the heavyweight title, in New York City ... Londos pins the paunchy Lewis in Chicago's Wrigley Field after 49 minutes, with a crowd of 35,265 paying anywhere from $86,000 to $108,000, depending on which report you believe ... Londos and Man Mountain Dean draw 34,000 people for a big outdoor show in Los Angeles. ... Jim Crockett starts promoting in Charlotte, N.C. ... LeRoy McGuirk beats Hugh Nichols for the light-heavy belt.

1935: Steve (Crusher) Casey is the first of Ireland's mighty Casey clan to arrive in the U.S. ... Mildred Burke starts her long wrestling career by going out on the carnival circuit under the promotion of Billy Wolfe, who later will become her husband and the sultan of women grapplers ... About 12,000 fans in St. Louis see Ray Steele beat boxer Kingfish Levinsky in less than a minute ... Irish Danno O'Mahoney makes his U.S. debut, beating Ernie Dusek in Boston Garden. He later beats Londos in Fenway Park ... Stanislaus Zbyszko announces his retirement ... Whiskers Savage wrestles for the first time in Houston, where he is to become the town's greatest all-time drawing card ... O'Mahoney beats Ed Don George in Boston and becomes champion ... Joe Malcewicz starts promoting in San Francisco.

1936: Dick Shikat beats O'Mahoney in Madison Square Garden for the title and supposedly breaks up a wrestling "trust." ... Shikat loses the title in Detroit to Ali Baba, who is supposedly a Turk, but is really an Armenian-American named Harry Ekizian ... Dave Levin, substituting for Hans Schnabel in Newark, N.J., takes the title from Baba on a disqualification. The State Athletic Commission reverses the decision, but Jack Pfefer, Levin's boss, continues to claim the title for his man ... Mike Romano collapses in a Washington, D.C., ring and dies before an ambulance arrives. ... In L.A., 20,000 spectators watch Levin defend his title against West Coast favorite Vincent Lopez ... Levin loses his title in Philadelphia to equally clean-cut Dean Detton ... Ali Baba loses his version to Everett Marshall in Columbus, Ohio ... Sammy Menacker and Angelo Martinelli turn pro.

1937: Promoter Jack Curley dies. ... Clara Mortensen claims women's world title in Chattanooga ... Steve Casey beats Danno O'Mahoney in Fenway Park, Boston, taking the expatriate Irish title if nothing else ... Lou Thesz takes the title from

Everett Marshall in St. Louis. ... The first mud match is staged in Seattle between Bhu Pinder and Gus Sonnenberg.

1938: Steve Casey beats Thesz for the championship in Boston Garden. Later in the year, when Casey is out of the country, a group of promoters recognize Marshall as the champ ... George Zaharias, the Crying Greek from Cripple Creek, marries golf star Babe Didrikson.

1939: "Carnation Lou" Daro retires as the Los Angeles promoter after a squabble with the State Assembly ... Wild Bill Longson suffers a broken back in a bout against Man Mountain Dean ... Thesz takes the title from Marshall in St. Louis, then loses it to football star Bronko Nagurski in Houston ... Zbyszko has a comeback match in Detroit versus Frederick Von Schacht ... Steve Casey loses his version of the title to The Shadow (Marv Westenberg), one of the few times on record that a masked man has held any sort of important title. Casey soon wins it back ... Two ex-college football players, Babe Sharkey and All-America Arthur (Tarzan) White, turn pro.

1940: Ray Steele takes the title from Nagurski in St. Louis ... Hans Steinke retires ... Woody Strode turns pro.

1941: Nagurski takes the title back from Steele in Minneapolis, then loses it in St. Louis to Sandor Szabo, a handsome import from Hungary ... George Zaharias retires.

1942: The title bounces from Szabo to Bill Longson to Yvon Robert to Bobby Managoff (the brother of singer Kay Armen) ... Cal Eaton promotes his first show in Los Angeles' Olympic Auditorium.

1943: Old Greco-Roman champion Ernie Roeber dies at age 82 ... The California State Athletic Commission approves a limited number of women's matches a year ... Longson takes the title from Managoff in St. Louis ... Probably this year George Wagner is first called Gorgeous George, in Oregon ... Buddy Rogers turns pro.

1944: Gus Sonnenberg dies in a Naval hospital near Washington, D.C ... Veteran wrestler Paul Jones starts promoting in Atlanta ... Thesz, Longson, Ellis Bashara, Dave Levin, and others take part in a joint benefit performance with the Houston Symphony Orchestra and sell more than a million dollars worth of war bonds.

1945: Olympic Auditorium in Los Angeles starts weekly wrestling telecasts with Dick Lane at the microphone. He will still be broadcasting wrestling 28 years later.

1946: Ex-heavyweight boxing champion Primo Camera makes his New York City wrestling debut in a match versus Bobby Bruns at St. Nicholas Arena ... Shirley Temple's brother, George, turns pro.

1947: Ring around the rosy. The heavyweight championship goes from Longson to Whipper Billy Watson to Lou Thesz to Longson ... Bobo Brazil and Dory Funk, Sr. start their pro careers, and papa Gino Garibaldi breaks in his son Leo.

1948: The National Wrestling Alliance (NWA) is formed and recognizes Orville Brown as its champ ... Jeffries' Barn, a rustic little arena in Burbank, Calif., closes ... Thesz takes the title from Longson in Indianapolis ... Antonino Rocca, a bouncy Italian who has lived most of his life in Argentina, makes his U.S. debut in Houston, beating Lord Blears. ... Thesz and Rocca wrestle 90 minutes to a draw in Texas, then Thesz beats the newcomer twice ... Lord Athol Layton turns pro.

1949: NWA officials award Thesz its title after Orville Brown is injured in an auto accident just before a scheduled Thesz-Brown championship match in St. Louis ... Wrestling returns to Madison Square Garden after an 11-year absence; the promoters are Bill Johnston and Toots Mondt ... LeRoy McGuirk beats Rocca in Dallas. Three nights later Thesz beats Rocca in Houston. Later on, the Argentine acrobat, never known as a disciple of the truth, will have a severe memory lapse and claim he has never been beaten ... Ray Steele dies at age 49 while on a hunting trip in Montana.

1950: Jim Londos versus Primo Camera in Chicago Stadium draws a $54,000 house ... Don Eagle beats Frank Sexton in Cleveland for one version of the title (the one that used to be Steve Casey's) ... Verne Gagne, not long out of the University of Minnesota, wins a light-heavyweight tournament in Tulsa ... Sam Muchnick of St. Louis is elected president of the NWA, succeeding Pinkie George ... Rikidozan quits Sumo wrestling in Japan. Later he will become the father of U.S.-style pro wrestling in his country.

1951: LeRoy McGuirk is blinded in a car crash ... Pat O'Connor arrives in the U.S. from New Zealand ... Bill Miller turns pro.

1952: Thesz beats Baron Michele Leone in Gilmore Stadium, Hollywood, drawing a $103,000 house ... George Linnehan retires from the ring ... Johnny Rougeau turns pro.

1953: Verne Gagne beats Rocca in Madison Square Garden ... Dick Hutton and Bearcat Wright turn pro.

1954: Ex-wrestler Karl Pojello dies in France. Thirteen hours later, his old friend Maurice Tillet, The French Angel, dies of a heart attack ... Bobby Becker dies of leukemia in New York City ... Mildred Burke leads a pioneering tour of Japan, after which a Japanese women's wrestling organization is started ... Baron Michele Scicluna and Wilbur Snyder turn pro.

1955: Antonino Rocca and Miguel Perez join in a lucrative tag-team partnership.

1956: Ex-heavyweight boxing champion Joe Louis becomes a pro wrestler for a short time. He is an uninspired performer but wins consistently ... Whipper Watson takes the title from Thesz in Toronto, loses it back to Lou in St. Louis ... Fabulous Moolah, formerly Slave Girl Moolah, wins a Baltimore tournament to decide the women's championship of the world ... Ex-L.A. promoter Lou Daro dies.

1957: Ex-champ Tom Jenkins, wrestling coach at West Point for many years, dies ... Edouard Carpentier beats Thesz for the title in Chicago, but there is a dispute over the outcome and both end up claiming the championship. ... In Toronto, Cowboy Dick Hutton beats Thesz for the NWA-recognized belt ... New pros: Penny Banner, Karen Kellogg.

1958: Ex-wrestler Herman Hickman, once an All-America lineman at Tennessee and head football coach at Yale, dies in Washington, D.C., following an ulcer operation. He is not mourned by most in the mat fraternity because he once wrote an "expose "of the business for *The Saturday Evening Post*. ... Pedro Morales turns pro.

1959: Brother Frank Jares retires from the ring and another Pittsburgher, Bruno Sammartino, turns pro. ... In Omaha, Verne Gagne beats Edouard Carpentier for one of the heavyweight crowns. ... Pat O'Connor, an Irishman from New Zealand, takes the NWA title from Hutton in St. Louis.

1960: El Medico, the popular masked hero from Mexico, dies of cancer ... The American Wrestling Association (AWA) is formed and bills itself as the "major league of professional wrestling." ... Cowboy Bill Watts turns pro.

1961: In Chicago's Comiskey Park, 38,000 (or 41,383) fans see Nature Boy Buddy Rogers wrest the NWA belt from O'Connor ... Promoter Billy Wolfe dies ... Roy Shire starts promoting in San Francisco.

1963: Japanese star Rikidozan dies ... Thesz wins the heavyweight title for the sixth time, beating Buddy Rogers in Toronto ... Dory Funk, Jr., just finished with his last football season at West Texas State, beats Jack Dalton in his first pro match ... Bruno Sammartino beats Rogers in Madison Square Garden for the championship of something called the World Wide Wrestling Federation, a creation of promoters Toots Mondt and Vince McMahon ... Gorgeous George dies of a heart attack ... City Auditorium in Houston is torn down.

1964: Joe Malcewicz, longtime promoter in San Francisco and once a great wrestler (nicknamed The Utica Panther), dies at his home while gardening ... Ernie Ladd turns pro.

1965: Yukon Eric commits suicide ... Abe (King Kong) Kashey dies in California at age 61 ... Jimmy Valiant turns pro.

1966: Thesz loses the NWA title to ex-football player Gene Kiniski in Kiel Auditorium, St. Louis ... Strangler Lewis dies in Veteran's Hospital, Muskogee, Okla., at age 76. ... L.A. Promoter Cal Eaton dies; his stepson Mike LeBell takes over ... Houston Promoter Morris Sigel dies. Paul Boesch takes the reins.

1967: Primo Camera dies of a liver ailment in his hometown of Sequals, Italy ... "Frank Gotch Week" celebrated in Humboldt, Iowa, the ex-champion's home town ... Stanislaus Zbyszko dies in Missouri at age 88 ... Buddy Rogers retires ... Whiskers Savage dies.

1968: George Hackenschmidt dies in England at age 90.

1969: Dory Funk, Jr., wins the NWA title from Kiniski in Tampa, Fla ... Longtime Chicago Promoter Fred Kohler dies in Sun City, Ariz., at age 66 ... Toots Mondt retires from promoting and moves to St. Louis, leaving Vince McMahon as the big wheel in the East.

1970: More than 30,000 fans turn out at Comiskey Park in Chicago to see Verne Gagne defend his American Wrestling Association crown versus Baron Von Raschke.

1971: Ivan Koloff wins the WWWF title from Sammartino in Madison Square Garden, but loses it right away to Puerto Rican favorite Pedro Morales ... Old-time wrestler Hans Steinke dies of lung cancer in Chicago at age 78. ... Whipper Watson retires.

1972: The New York State Athletic Commission drops its ban on women wrestlers ... Ray Gunkel dies in a Georgia dressing room following a bout. His widow starts an opposition promotion in Atlanta, battling old-timer Paul Jones. She is teamed up with Tom Renesto, formerly one of The Assassins ... British star Billy Robinson arrives in the U.S.

1973: The finicky New York State Athletic Commission, after having outlawed masked wrestlers for years, makes an exception for the Mexican hero, Mil Mascaras. ... Harley Race takes the NWA title from Dory Funk, Jr., in Kansas City, Kan., then loses it in Houston to Jack Brisco. ... Death takes Dory Funk, Sr., Philadelphia promoter Ray Fabiani, Charlotte promoter Jim Crockett, ex-wrestler/football player Bill Kuusisto, Nick Condos and Wild Red Berry.

Addendum 8
Heavyweight Title Succession at a Glance

1897	Tom Jenkins over Martin (Farmer) Burns—Armory—Cleveland
1901	George Hackenschmidt wins two international tournaments in Europe Vienna, Paris
1902	Dan McLeod over Tom Jenkins
1903	Jenkins over McLeod—Worcester, Mass.
1904	Frank Gotch over Jenkins—Bellingham, Wash.
1905	Jenkins over Gotch—Madison Square Garden—New York City
1905	Hackenschmidt over Jenkins—Madison Square Garden —New York City
1908	Gotch over Hackenschmidt—Dexter Park Pavilion—Chicago
1913	Gotch retires, picks two men to battle for his crown
1913	Henry Ordeman over Jess Westegaard—Omaha
1914	Charley Cutler over Ordeman—Minneapolis
1915	Joe Stecher over Cutler—Omaha
1917	Earl Caddock over Stecher—Omaha
1920	Stecher over Caddock—Madison Square Garden—New York City
1920	Ed (Strangler) Lewis over Stecher—71st Regiment Armory —New York City
1922	Stanislaus Zbyszko over Lewis 22nd Regiment Armory —New York City
1922	Lewis over Zbyszko—Wichita Municipal Forum—Wichita
1925	Wayne Munn over Lewis—Convention Hall—Kansas City
1925	Zbyszko over Munn—Philadelphia
1925	Stecher over Zbyszko—Federal League ballpark—St. Louis
1928	Lewis over Stecher—Coliseum—St. Louis
1929	Gus Sonnenberg over Lewis—Boston Garden—Boston
1931	Ed Don George over Sonnenberg—Boston Garden—Boston
1931	Lewis over George—Wrigley Field—Los Angeles
1931	Henri DeGlane over Lewis by disqualification—Montreal
1931	George over DeGlane—Boston
(1929)	Dick Shikat over Jim Londos; claims title —Philadelphia
(1930)	Londos over Shikat—Philadelphia
(1932)	Lewis over Shikat—Garden Bowl—Long Island City
1933	Jim Browning over Lewis—Madison Square Garden—New York City
1934	Londos over Browning—Garden Bowl—Long Island City
1935	Danno O'Mahoney over Londos—Fenway Park—Boston
1935	O'Mahoney over Ed Don George, who had been claiming title since 1931 win over DeGlane—Boston

1936   Dick Shikat over O'Mahoney—Madison Square Garden
                                                  —New York City
1936   Ali Baba over Shikat—Olympia—Detroit
1936   Dave Levin over Baba on disqualification; State Commission overrules;
                both claim title—Meadowbrook Bowl—Newark, N.J.
1936   Dean Detton over Levin—Philadelphia Arena—Philadelphia
1936   Everett Marshall over Baba; nine guys claiming title, including Detton,
                who lost it to Bronko Nagurski, who lost it to Lou Thesz—
                                          Haft's Acre—Columbus, Oh.
1937   Lou Thesz over Marshall—Kiel Auditorium—St. Louis
1938   Steve Casey over Thesz—Boston Garden—Boston
1938   Group of promoters recognize Marshall as champ when Casey is out of
the country*

   Casey, naturally, did not accept the decision. He lost the title to Marv
   Westenberg, who lost it to Gus Sonnenberg, who lost it back to Casey.
   Steve lost it for good to Frank Sexton in the Boston Arena in 1945. Sexton
   lost it for good to Don Eagle in 1950, but the title never had much national
   acceptance after it was taken away from Casey and handed to Marshall.

1939   Thesz over Marshall—Kiel Auditorium—St. Louis
1939   Bronko Nagurski over Thesz—Coliseum—Houston
1940   Ray Steele over Nagurski—Kiel Auditorium—St. Louis
1941   Nagurski over Steele—Minneapolis Auditorium—Minneapolis
        Sandor Szabo over Nagurski—Kiel Auditorium—St. Louis
        Bill Longson over Szabo—Kiel Auditorium—St. Louis
1942   Yvon Robert over Longson—Forum—Montreal
1942   Bobby Managoff over Robert—City Auditorium—Houston
1943   Longson over Managoff—Kiel Auditorium—St. Louis
1947   Whipper Watson over Longson—Kiel Auditorium—St. Louis
1947   Thesz over Watson—Kiel Auditorium—St. Louis
1947   Longson over Thesz—Kiel Auditorium—St. Louis
1948   Thesz over Longson—Coliseum—Indianapolis
1949   National Wrestling Alliance recognizes Thesz after Orville Brown
                                is hurt in auto accident
1956   Watson over Thesz—Maple Leaf Gardens—Toronto
1956   Thesz over Watson—Kiel Auditorium—St. Louis
1957   Dick Hutton over Thesz—Maple Leaf Gardens—Toronto
1959   Pat O'Connor over Hutton—Kiel Auditorium—St. Louis
1961   Buddy Rogers over O'Connor—Comiskey Park—Chicago
1963   Thesz over Rogers—Maple Leaf Gardens—Toronto

   That same year, the World Wide Wrestling Federation, the baby of
   Toots Mondt and Vince McMahon, recognized Buddy Rogers as its
   champion. That title, not recognized outside the East, has since passed
   to Bruno Sammartino, Ivan Koloff, Pedro Morales, Stan Stasiak and
   Sammartino again.

1966   Gene Kiniski over Thesz—Kiel Auditorium—St. Louis
1969   Dory Funk, Jr., over Kiniski—Ft. Homer Hesterly Armory—Tampa
1973   Harley Race over Funk—Memorial Hall—Kansas City, Kan.
1973   Jack Brisco over Race—Coliseum—Houston

Addendum 9
Big Gates and Crowds

1908—Frank Gotch vs. George Hackenschmidt
        Dexter Park Pavilion, Chicago—10,000—$60,000
1911—Frank Gotch vs. George Hackenschmidt
        Comiskey Park, Chicago—35,000—$87,053
1917—Ad Santel vs. Strangler Lewis
        Civic Auditorium, San Francisco—15,000
1925—Joe Stecher vs. Stanislaus Zbyszko
        St. Louis—15,471—$51,670
1925—Strangler Lewis vs. Wayne Munn
        Michigan City, Ind.—20,792—$64,162
1929—Strangler Lewis vs. Gus Sonnenberg
        Fenway Park, Boston—about 25,000—$72,000
1929—Gus Sonnenberg vs. Ed Don George
        Boston Garden—$62,000
1930—Gus Sonnenberg vs. Everett Marshall
        Wrigley Field, Los Angeles—17,580—$69,745
1930—Jim Londos vs. Ferenc Holuban
        New York City—19,715—$48,205
1930—Jim Londos vs. Jim McMillen
        Madison Square Garden, New York City—22,200—$59,496
1931—Jim Londos vs. Jim McMillen
        Madison Square Garden, New York City—$60,216
1931—Jim Londos vs. Ray Steele
        Yankee Stadium, New York City—35,000—$70,000
1931—Henri DeGlane vs. Gus Sonnenberg
        Braves Fields, Boston—32,000
1934—Jim Londos vs. Man Mountain Dean
        Los Angeles—39,000, $38,000
1934—Jim Londos vs. Strangler Lewis
        Wrigley Field, Chicago—35,265—$86,000 or $96,000
1934   Jim Londos vs. Ed Don George
        Fenway Park, Boston—30,000—$60,110
1934   Jim Londos vs. Jim Browning
        Garden Bowl, Long Island City, N.Y.—about 20,000
1934   Jim Londos vs. Joe Savoldi
        Chicago Stadium—20,200—$32,000
1935   Jim Londos vs. Danno O'Mahoney
        Fenway Park, Boston—about 30,000
1936   Dave Levin vs. Vincent Lopez
        Wrigley Field, Los Angeles—20,000
1939   Mildred Burke vs. Lupe Acosta
        Monterey, Mexico—14,000—$20,000
1941   Mildred Burke vs. Elvira Snodgrass

Louisville, Ky.—18,000—$25,000
1947 Primo Camera vs. Jules Strongbow
Cleveland Arena—$21,000
1947 Primo Camera vs. Fred von Schact
Chicago Stadium—$20,000
1947 Primo Camera vs. Babe Sharkey
Boston Garden—$19,000
1948 Primo Camera vs. Yvon Robert
Forum, Montreal—about 14,000—$38,000
1949 Antonino Rocca vs. Gene Stanlee
Madison Square Garden, New York City—17,854—$51,639
1949 Antonino Rocca vs. Gene Stanlee
Newark Armory—$28,000
1949 Gorgeous George vs. Yvon Robert
Forum, Montreal—$24,000
1950 Primo Camera vs. Jim Londos
Wrigley Field, Chicago—$54,000
1950 Antonino Rocca vs. Gene Stanlee
Madison Square Garden, New York City—about 53,000
1952 Lou Thesz vs. Baron Michele Leone
Gilmore Field, Los Angeles—25,246—$103,277
1953 Verne Gagne vs. The Mighty Atlas
Madison Square Garden, New York City—15,851—$51,265
1955 Lou Thesz vs. Leo Nomellini
Cow Palace, Daly City, Calif.—$70,000
1957 Ricki Starr vs. Dick the Bruiser
Madison Square Garden, New York City—19,995—$62,565
1957 Rocca-Perez vs. Fargo-Stevens
Madison Square Garden, New York City—20,125—$63,753
1959 Rocca-Perez vs. Graham Brothers
Madison Square Garden, New York City—21,240—$63,896
1960 Antonino Rocca vs. The Mighty Zuma
Madison Square Garden, New York City—21,950—$64,680
1961 Buddy Rogers vs. Primo Carnera
Madison Square Garden, New York City—20,400—$62,562
1961 Buddy Rogers vs. Pat O'Connor
Comiskey Park, Chicago—38,622—$128,071
1970 Verne Gagne vs. Baron von Raschke, Vachons vs. Crusher-Bruiser
Comiskey Park, Chicago—about 30,000—$148,000
1971 Bruno Sammartino vs. Ivan Koloff
Madison Square Garden,—New York City—21,106—$85,544
1971 Pedro Morales vs. Stan Stasiak
Madison Square Garden,—New York City—22,070—$104,456
1972 Fred Blassie vs. John Tolos
Los Angeles Coliseum—25,847—$142,150
1972 Fritz Von Erich vs. Dory Funk, Jr.
Texas Stadium, Arlington, Tex.—26,339—about $85,000
1972 The Sheik vs. Jacques Rougeau
Jarry Park, Montreal—26,000+
1972 Pedro Morales vs. Bruno Sammartino
Shea Stadium, New York City—22,508—$140,923
1972 Verne Gagne vs. Ivan Koloff, Crusher-Bruiser vs. The Blackjacks
Soldier Field, Chicago—12,000—$101,000

An Interview with the Author

This interview with Joe Jares was conducted by Scott Teal in December 2013. Supplemental follow-up questions were asked in July 2015.

When did you first discover professional wrestling, and were you a fan?

Somewhere in the late 1940s or early 1950s, we were the first family on our block in West Los Angeles to have a TV set — a big Admiral with a postage-stamp-size screen. Programming only at night. The neighborhood kids would gather on our living-room rug and gaze at the test pattern until the first children's show came on at about six.

Wrestling soon became huge on TV. It was on seven days a week in L.A. — from Hollywood Legion Stadium (later a bowling alley), from Ocean Park Arena (later a bowling alley), from Olympic Auditorium (a rotting downtown hulk today), from the East and Midwest via Kinescope. No coaxial cable in those dark ages. At the same time, my pop went from being a packing-house butcher, amateur weightlifting champion, and amateur wrestler to pro grappling. And I was a fan like almost everyone else, although Pacific Coast League baseball and college sports interested me more.

What was your father's involvement in the book?

He sat down for a long taped interview for the *Sports Illustrated* article, "My Father the Thing," that preceded the book. And he supplied a raft of photographs, which the *SI* art department used to great effect. And, of course, he was involved because I had lived and traveled with him.

Did your father ever ask what your intent was, or what the thrust of the book would be?

No.

Was he okay with the stories you told, i.e. any exposé of the business?

He did not utter one word of complaint, but I sensed that he was uneasy with any "secrets" revealed. The code in those years called for insistence that the game was not phony. I was sensitive to this when writing and generally revealed the true business only when needed for a good anecdote.

Did you have any negative feedback from wrestlers who felt some of the things you wrote might be exposing the business?

Two things I recall. The son of a wrestler — it might have been Don Leo Jonathan, but I'm fuzzy on that — wrote a critical note. And Vince McMahon Sr. never would grant me an interview for the book, I believe because of things revealed in the *SI* piece.

Pop's code was to not expose the "business." I understood that. As a kid, when I was asked (frequently) if wrestling was fake, I'd answer, *"Is your dad a crook?"* When I decided to write the article, and then WHTGG, the business had been exposed a number of times in national magazines and newspapers. I decided to be as careful as I could, playing it somewhat naively, revealing secrets only when necessary to complete an entertaining anecdote. Pop never scolded me. He cooperated by giving me umpteen photographs (SI's art department did a fantastic job on the layout). I don't think he was comfortable with some of the revelations, but he kept quiet. He had to like being splashed all over a national magazine. It was groundbreaking only in that it was better written than all or most of the exposes. *SI*, years later, named WHTGG one of the "Top 100 Best Sports Books of All Time." That tickled me, but let's face it. I had written the best book on pro wrestling, meaning I was the world's tallest midget.

Did your father talk to you openly about the wrestling business when you were young?

Whatever Happened to Gorgeous George?

BY JOE JARES (1974)

AN AFFECTIONATE DEPICTION of pro wrestling in the 1940s, '50s and '60s, when the sport had a more benign, vaudevillian flavor. Jares does a terrific riff on the masked men, ersatz Indian chiefs, "leaping lords" and other baddies who routinely smuggled "foreign objects" in their trunks.

Absolutely. He was open about it, and cynical about other sports. *"The only thing on the level is mountain climbing,"* he would say. He actually didn't have to spell it out for me. George and Bobby Becker would be with our family for shashlik and borscht at a friend's home in the afternoon, and I would watch the Beckers beat up on my old man that night on TV. I remember asking George to make some sort of gesture just for me from the Olympic ring. He showed me some gesture he'd use. It turns out he made that gesture all the time anyway; he was just "swerving" me a bit.

Did you interview your father during the book-writing process?

No. I was living in Riverdale, NY, and he was in L.A. The interview had taken place for the *SI* piece.

Not too long ago, I heard from Phil Moeller, the son of Hans Schnabel, who was close pals with my dad. We always knew him as "Jake," and I knew his true surname was Moeller. I told Phil there weren't any stories about his dad in my book, but I did have a card on him in my wrestling file. The information on the card came from a 1966 interview I did with my dad.

> Jake lived at 261 Genoa Drive in Simi Valley, CA. Always wore tights. He had one leg that was deformed. He was born with one leg up his back. He was never supposed to walk on it and he lifted weights and he used it ... he wore pads on the side of it. They're all from upper New York. Farm country up through there.
>
> He was rugged. What arms he had. He started professional. Otto started the whole family off; he ain't the oldest brother, but he's the oldest wrestling brother. Bill is the oldest. He goes by Moeller now as a guard; that's government. Had tattoos. Had thicker fingers than Primo Carnera.

Do you remember any of the wrestlers using the word "kayfabe" when you were around?

No. Never heard that. The wrestling lingo I did hear included "swerve" (prank), "potatoes" (as in punches that really hurt), "the business," "shoot" (wrestle for real), "the boys" (the wrestlers), "babyface" (clean wrestler), "heel" (dirty wrestler), "finish" (climactic moment of a match).

Did you ever do anything in the business, like timekeeper, ring announcer, etc.?

Writing about it, that's about it. I did count houses (roughly), so my old man could guess if the promoter was stiffing him. And, I held wallets for the boys (they would wrap their watches around the wallets). And one night in Gadsden, Alabama, I guarded the entrance to the men's room while Pop washed up (there were no showers!).

Did you ever worry that being a part of the inner circle would jaundice your view of the story you were trying to tell?

Not at all. I knew I didn't want to expose the business any more than necessary, but that brought no guilt feelings.

Exactly how long did you tour with your dad?

Apart from occasional treks to, say, Bakersfield or San Bernardino within his home L.A. territory, just the two months in the summer of 1956 — headquartered in Nashville, trips to Birmingham, Kingsport, Chattanooga, etc.

Were you allowed in the dressing room during the matches?

Always. And entertaining places they were. I remember my old man loved to have the lisping Dusek brothers sing "Sioux City Sue," which they would willingly and loudly do. And it was in the Ocean Park Arena dressing room, or just outside, where Gorgeous George gave me a gilded Georgie pin and made me swear never to call it a bobby pin.

Do you have any stories of your time on the road with your dad that you left out of the book that you would like to tell now?

No, Scott, I pretty much poured it all out.

What did your family think about your project?

I didn't hear much about it from them. The book was dedicated to my mother, but she had eye problems and couldn't read it. Sometime later, when she suffered from macular degeneration, I enrolled her in the Braille Institute to get free books on tape. Luckily, Paul Boesch in Houston had read it for Braille, and I was able to order it for her ears.

Was there anything your dad asked you not to print?

Yes, a family scandal from his boyhood in Pittsburgh. I will obey him to this day.

Did the focus of the book change from what you originally planned?

No. When I joined *Sports Illustrated* in the 1960s, two or three of the editors took me upstairs to an executive dining room for a get-acquainted luncheon. I told some wrestling stories and one of them said, *"That sounds like a bonus piece."* (*SI* in those days called the major feature at the rear of an issue a "bonus piece.") I realized that a collection of anecdotes from the wrestling business would not only make a good magazine takeout, but also a book.

What were your thoughts going into the project? Did you think wrestlers, who were "television stars," were making big money, or did you already realize that many of them were making only enough to eke out a living? If the latter, were you shocked to learn that?

We lived in a two-bedroom, one-bathroom house in L.A. I knew *we* weren't rich. Pop made a better — and certainly more interesting — living than as a butcher, and he did well when he was the champ in the Nashville territory, but it was easy for me to see that most of the boys were just getting along, wearing out their welcome in one territory and hoping that a promoter elsewhere would want their services. I went to a relatively expensive private school, USC, but I had a full-tuition journalism scholarship.

Did you send a manuscript to anybody in the wrestling business for feedback or opinions before you went to press?

I did not.

WHTGG was one of the first books that took readers behind the scenes of the world of pro wrestling. After publication, what kind of response did you get from both wrestlers and fans?

I don't remember any feedback from wrestlers or fans, but the media loved the book. It got good reviews all over the country. My friend Paul Boesch told me that I had spent too many words on Mildred Burke in the women's chapter, and he was correct. I let her go on and on about she got gypped in a title match.

The fact that my earlier *Sports Illustrated* piece was so well-received was what led to me deciding to write the book. My piece on Gorgeous George for *Sports Illustrated* was ridiculously cut down to *George was Villainous, Gutsy and Gorgeous*, whereas it should have been another bonus piece. It suddenly dawned on me, *"Bingo!"* Two chapters of a book were already written. Chapter two of the book was the GG piece restored to its original form. I had so much energy in those days. I could work all day reporting and writing for *SI* and still write on private projects at night and on weekends. Later, I wrote a mystery novel I wasn't able to sell, but I loved doing it anyway.

What kind of response did you get from your dad when he read the book?

I don't recall that he said or wrote anything. Weird, eh? We were a loving father and son, and the fact that he would have loved to have me be part of a father-son tag team was there, but unstated. He wanted me to be Leo Garibaldi to his Gino Garibaldi. He had a son who was an A-student, and he was happy about that, but bigger biceps would have been better.

He often prodded me to work out with the weights in our garage. He sent me to the Los Angeles Athletic Club to learn how to wrestle from his dear friend, Tommy Peratis, the coach there. Pop had been a champion weight-lifter there, and a winning grappler. But I would travel downtown and just play basketball — within sight of Tommy training somebody else. That was a mistake on my part. Even if I didn't want to get into rasslin', it would have been a golden opportunity to learn self-defense from a master. Pop would rather I had cauliflower ears instead of a Phi Beta Kappa key, but he didn't push it too hard and let me develop in my own way.

Do you know if any other wrestler or promoters ever read the book?

Boesch was the only one I know of. But I'd bet that many did read it and passed it around. Probably feeling amused and injured at the same time.

Have you stayed in touch with any of the wrestlers you knew back in the day?

No. The son of Hans Schnabel (nee Jake Moeller) is researching his dad's career and, once in a while, comes across something about my dad. That's it for wrestling contacts. Schnabel, the Becker brothers, Butch Madray, Bud Curtis, Vic Holbrook, Tommy Peratis (coach at LAAC) are all deceased, I believe.

Did you go on a book-signing tour after the book was published?

I was traveling a lot for *Sports Illustrated*, so the Prentice-Hall publicity department used that to get me on radio stations and TV stations in a few places — Philadelphia and L.A. were two. I never saw the book in a bookstore, despite the reviews. In later years, I did find it in used-book stores. In Santa Barbara, California, my wife found a copy that I signed to someone named Nancy. It didn't hurt my feelings. I bought it for $20.

What were some of the things you did related to the book after publication?

Other than radio-TV appearances, not much. My agent handled the sale of paperback rights, and I was busy with the next book and work for *Sports Illustrated*. Not to mention trying to help rear two daughters.

Was there ever any interest from a movie studio in regards to producing a movie based on the book?

That's a whole tangled web. Paramount has the rights and has been sitting on them for years. I had bad advice and did not put a time limit on the option. A number of producers have come calling over the years, but I have to tell them to go see Paramount. Maybe, someday, my lawyer daughter or lawyer son-in-law can pry loose the rights.

After your dad got out of wrestling, did you ever go back to the wrestling matches again?

I remember that Pop and I did just once. I don't remember the occasion, but we went "backstage" at the venerable Olympic Auditorium. More like "in the catacombs" than "backstage." Crude, old, cramped. Mr. Moto was the matchmaker, I think, and he and Pop had been pals going back maybe to Honolulu days in the early 1950s. I remember Mil Mascaras kept his mask on in the locker room, and a sweaty, peroxide-blond heel bitching about what some security guard had done or not done.

And for a column in the L.A. *Daily News* many years later, I interviewed Vince McMahon Jr. at the L.A. Sports Arena (I think after a general, few-days-before-a-big-card press conference). After my last question, he said, *"It's a pleasure to talk to someone who knows so much about our business."* I didn't mention my background, the book, or the fact that his father had refused to give me an interview.

Tell me what you can about your dad regarding his life after wrestling, leading up to his death.

I don't remember the year, but Pop got a lousy payoff somewhere in the Midwest, was thoroughly disgusted, got in his car, and drove home — hanging up his jock, so to speak. He got a job as a packing-house butcher in San Fernando, California. Specifically, all night long he would be a beef breaker. The carcasses would roll in on hooks and he would take a power saw and break it down into various cuts. Doing it well can make a lot of money for the owners; doing it poorly can cost the owners money.

He hurt himself on the job. I don't remember the details. He got disability and retired. He and my mom sold their house in the Palms section of West L.A., where I grew up, and bought a little place in Valencia, just north of the San Fernando Valley. My brother and his wife lived nearby. They enjoyed daily lunches at a senior-services center, where their table was the most popular because of his kidding and storytelling. He would joke, *"I never tell a story the same way twice."*

Wrestlers often use stage names. Is "Jares" your real last name?

Yes. The surname is Czech (Bohemian). It's pronounced Yaresh in the Czech Republic. When I was in Prague a few years ago, I found about 89 Jareses in the telephone directory, and 15 Josefs, but no Jareses in my grandfather's hometown, Vodnany. There was one Jares in the resort town in Southern Bohemia where we stayed (Cesky Krumlov). My old man, Pesek, the Duseks — all Bohunks. I'm English, Irish, and Scottish on the other side. My maternal grandparents both were born in South Carolina.

Have you read other books written about pro wrestling?

I finished reading Lou Thesz' *Hooker* not too long ago. As I read, so many images popped into my feeble mind as I enjoyed Lou's stories: Bobby Managoff sitting in our apartment in Honolulu (between Waikiki and the Ala Wai Canal), medallion of veal imperiale at Luchow in New York City, Joe Malcewicz ("The Utica Panther") in the San Francisco booking office (he was too sharp to fall for any of our stupid gags), Vic Christy zooming past us in his car returning to L.A. from Bakersfield (nobody was in the driver's seat and Vic pretended to read a newspaper in the passenger seat), Sammy Menacker describing finish after finish in a dressing room in some little Tennessee arena, Leo Nomellini with his big paws, drinking Scandinavian beer with Thesz in Scandia, a now-defunct Scandinavian restaurant, before he went on with Tom Harmon before the Southern California Sports Broadcasters, and on and on.

What occupations have you been involved with?

Just journalism. I was a professional at age 17, working as sports editor of a small daily newspaper, the *Culver City Star-News* and *Venice Vanguard*.

Tell me about what you did with your life after you finished the book.

After 16 years writing for *Sports Illustrated,* I was a freelancer for a year, then a writer and editor for the L.A. *Daily News* for 20 years. WHTGG had been my fourth book. I wrote or co-wrote five more. The most impressive of those is *Conquest: A Cavalcade of USC Football* (with USC head coach John Robinson) (1981). It's a big, beautiful coffee-table book designed by the late Dave Boss, a talented art director for NFL Properties. I wrote a book with George Toley (*The Golden Age of College Tennis*, 2009), who had won ten NCAA championships coaching the USC men's tennis team. I also wrote *Basketball, the American Game* (1971), *The Athlete's Body* (with John Robinson) (1981), *Clyde: The Walt Frazier Story* (with Walt Frazier) (1970), and *White House Sportsmen* (with Edmund Lindop) (1964).

When I returned to California from New York in 1974, I taught 20 classes in reporting and sports reporting at USC and served as president of the USC Journalism Alumni Association. My wife worked as a reporter for *People* magazine, then taught English as a second language. My daughters were excellent students, attending Columbia and UC Berkeley. Hayley became a lawyer in L.A., Julie became a writer and editor in San Francisco.

After 20 years at the *Los Angeles Daily News*, I retired at age 65, but continued for several years to write for *USC Report*, a tabloid newspaper for Trojan fans. Since that paper ceased publication several years ago, I have gone from creating media to consuming it — movies, TV, books, plays, magazines, newspapers. Because of health problems — limiting my physical activities, but not as yet life-threatening — my wife and I don't travel much. My "bucket list," which included walking on the Great Wall of China and seeing at least one performance at the Sydney Opera House, will not be completed. Our two grandchildren live only 20 minutes away, so life is good.

Tell a little bit about your travels.

Covering tennis got me to London five times, and also to Caracas and Bogota. *SI* and *Daily News* assignments got me to most major American cities, and more than few hamlets. No trip was as colorful as some of my treks with Pop that magical summer in the South. I remember driving through the Smoky Mountains in the middle of the night and stopping at a tiny joint for sausage sandwiches; we didn't go for the white lightning stored under the counter … or dining sumptuously at Charlie Nickens' Pit Barbecue in Nashville … just soaking up the atmosphere in dowdy locker rooms.

The highlight of my life recently, apart from enjoying my children and grandchildren, was being inducted into the USC Athletic Hall of Fame. A new class is picked every two or three years, and it always includes one media person. Sixteen of my Kappa Alpha fraternity brothers preceded me into the mythical hall. That includes Olympic gold-medal winners, NCAA champions, first-team All-Americas, and world-record holders. I am the first KA to sneak in without a varsity letter (I did, however, letter in freshman basketball.) Two NFL coaches were inducted on the night I was, as well. The best part of it all, though, was having my kids, grandchildren, and brother and sister-in-law at my table. It was great to see my sprouting 13-year-old (at the time) grandson in a tux and my 16-year-old granddaughter looking so pretty and grown up.

The republishing of my wrestling book, though, is going to rate right up there with the USC honor.

Thank you for taking the time to do this interview, Joe, and for allowing us to re-publish your great book.

It's my pleasure. I'm very excited to see it back in print.

Original book jacket design

The material presented from this point on is supplemental material not found in the original publication.

On the road
with Frank Jares

Frank Jares—West Coast Hercules

By "WIB" SCHARZBERGER

WHEN we were at Los Angeles at the Olympics in 1932, we met most of the weight lifters in that section. Termine, Aroff, Kingsbury, Tom Tyler, former national heavyweight lifting champion, but for years a cowboy star in the movies, Noah Young, another great lifter who made good in the movies, appearing in Harold Lloyd comedies, Willoughby, Ceretanni, and others. We didn't meet Frank Jares about whom we are writing. If we had, I doubt if we would have been impressed, for then he weighed about 145 pounds and was quite an ordinary young American.

We liked the climate in Los Angeles, we envied the people who reside there, the marvelous living conditions which they enjoyed. But we felt that everyone could not live there. Someone had to stay in Pennsylvania to continue with our physical training work. But we never forgot the fine opportunity that men in Los Angeles have to be strength stars. The weather is hot there during the day. It is cool enough for overcoats and blankets at night. Ideal training conditions. With such perfect surroundings it does seem a wonder that there aren't more great lifters in California. Lack of competition must be the answer. Sam Termine has long been the best of the California lifters. At the Olympics as a middleweight, he made a beautiful try with 242 two hands snatch, an almost unheard of lift at that day. He repeatedly cleaned over three hundred. But Sam found himself working on a goat ranch sixty miles from Los Angeles, and this almost total absence of training greatly handicapped his lifting progress. He never fails to make well over seven hundred total in spite of his lack of training.

And now another great strength star has risen in California. Frank Jares is the man. His picture appeared in S. & H. months ago. It was nice, but Jares weighed 175 pounds the day he posed for that picture. In the great physical study, which appears with this article, he weighs 210 pounds. Training during the last year accounted for these thirty-five additional pounds of shapely, powerful manhood.

The principal reason for the great improvement is found in the following short paragraph from Frank Jares' recent letter. "A year ago I read an article that you wrote, which convinced me that dumbell training was very important. Since that time I have gained thirty-five pounds and improved my body strength and my ability with the three Olympic lifts, so

you can see what dumbell training has done for me. Hoping York puts out more training courses as simple and good as those of the past."

You will remember the stories of Jack

FRANK JARES, 210 pounds. He gained 35 pounds this last year with York dumbell training and lifting.

Russel, Ed Zebrowski and others. Strength stars, leading lifters, who had not increased in weight for several years. Yet a special session with dumbells brought their weight up by a considerable margin, greatly improved their physiques and lifting ability.

Dumbells have played a major part in the development of the hundreds of new strength stars we have today. Five years have gone by since this magazine had its inception. From the beginning we wrote enthusiastically about the results dumbell training would bring. At first we were censored from many angles by those who had been led to believe, by other writers in the field, that dumbell training was not good. It was said that dumbells would make a man muscle bound while hundreds of pounds of weights would not. This was truly ridiculous to come from leading bar bell instructors. Why in the world should a pair of twenty to forty pound dumbells in one's training cause one to be slow while hundreds of pounds of weights in the shape of dead lifts and deep knee bends would not?

Dropping water wears away the stone. Constant writing and convincing stories of what others had done proved that dumbells were perhaps the most important single piece of training equipment. I say perhaps, for heavy weights are needed to develop the larger muscle groups of the body too. The ideal training equipment consists of a heavy bar bell for two hands pressing . . . rowing motion, dead lifting, deep knee bending and practice of the Three Olympic lifts in particular. But dumbells for the arms, to exercise the muscles from the countless angles in which they are designed to work. And dumbells for the legs, too, which require the Iron Boot. If the feet could work as do the hands in holding the dumbell as the various movements are practiced, Iron Boots would not be necessary. For Iron Boot training is nothing but dumbell training for the legs.

Once again the sensational results that scores of thousands of men are receiving with the Iron Boots has proven the great advantage of this form of training. Much work, much convincing proof led up to the present position that dumbells offer in the physical training world today. There were always dumbells, light ones, one to five pounds, nearly useless. But dumbell training such as we offer it to the world is the same method that men like Sandow used to develop the greatest physique of all time and Arthur Saxon used to build the greatest strength of all time. Remember that Saxon said, the best movements are done with heavy dumbells.

Many articles were written, such as, "The Egyptians don't use dumbells, so what?" Last month 1530 dumbell sets

(Continued on Page 49)

Page 37

Reprint of page 37 of the November 1937 issue of *Strength & Health*

About a half hour of weight lifting three times a week is the limit of his training. Not much, when one considers that champion athletes often spend hours of training on a single day to reach the top in their chosen sport. He's truly a product of heavy exercise. Mostly of attempts with high poundages in the three Olympic lifts. He would have a more attractive physique, with greater separation or definition of the muscles, if he trained more and used dumbells and training accessories. His time is usually up when he is through with the three lifts with perhaps a few exercises that build proficiency in their execution. Nevertheless hit hurried training has built great strength and a powerful physique that many men can well envy.

The case of Mike Dietz is that of an ordinary young man who is making good in a big way in weight lifting circles. There is nothing in his heredity or mode of living that has given him an advantage. His mother and father are each about five feet six inches in height, normal in build. His father is foreman in a wholesale tobacco warehouse. As already told he had no preliminary training. His success is good proof that most any undeveloped man, with the right training methods and sufficient ambition is sure to succeed in a physical way.

Lifting is one sport that the busy man of any age can enjoy. Any other sport takes a lot of time. Team sports are impossible for the ambitious business man. Even tennis or golf requires most of the afternoon and a partner. But a weight lifter can rush to his training quarters and go through his lifts any time that he can spare in the afternoon, evening or late at night. And minute for minute, effort for effort he'll obtain several times as much physical benefit, recreation and actual pleasure as in the practice of any other physical pastime.

FRANK JARES—WEST COAST HERCULES

(Continued from Page 37)

were shipped from our building. No wonder stars of strength and development are being produced much more rapidly now than ever before. The York team paved the way. I wish you could see Terlazzo, Bullock, Terpak, Zagurski, Levan, Bachtell, Harrison, to name only a few of the York lifters who have made the name York synonymous with great strength, go through almost countless dumbell movements. Heavy lifting first, develop the large muscle groups, then many movements with dumbells for the arms and shoulders as well as the legs with the Iron Boot, and such physiques as the men mentioned possess are sure to emerge from the mediocrity a man may have to begin with. But this isn't a dumbell article, it's a story about Frank Jares. A glance at the amazing physique pictured in this article which Frank tells us came from heavy lifting and dumbell training causes us to become almost too enthusiastic for such a short article.

Seven years ago when Jares was seventeen years of age he started to train with weights. Prior to that time he found an outlet for his athletic ambitions through competitive speed swimming. He was tall and thin, weighing 145 pounds at his height of around six feet.

When in Los Angeles we met quite a group of bar bell men from the Los Angeles Y. That's where Frank Jares made his start. He improved in his lifts rapidly and in a very short time was offered a place on the Los Angeles Athletic Club lifting team, by Jere Kingsbury, national vice chairman of weight lifting. He competed in meets and exhibitions representing that club for the better part of five years.

During these five years of training, from seventeen to twenty-two years of age, his weight increased from 145 to 175 pounds. At that time he moved to Huntington Park, which made training at the L. A. A. C. impossible. After considerable lost time Frank with a group of friends started a small club called the Huntington Park A. C. 300 pounds of York equipment, including dumbells and the York bar bell courses and the forty-eight dumbell exercises were their sole training equipment. At the present time membership in this club has grown to 52. There are other men whose physiques entitle them to a story in this magazine who have been developed by this group which started small and will become world famous. Pictures of these new stars of strength and development will appear in subsequent issues.

There are few men in the world who possess the beautiful rugged figure that Frank Jares has developed. 210 pounds of beautiful, powerful manhood. He has everything that could be desired in a physical way. Perfect proportions, with huge muscles and great strength. Speed and athletic ability which makes it possible for him to star at a number of athletic sports.

Similar effort and similar training methods will bring similar results to other ambitious fellows. Almost forget to state that Jares is now capable of a lifting total closely approaching eight hundred. If he were more favorably situated with intersectional competition he would be with those at the very height of the Strength world in lifting. Mayor, this year's senior champion, Grimek, last year's senior champion, and Bullock who beat them both in the junior national championships of last year and is on a par with them now. 3-6-97

YOU NEED GOOD LEGS

(Continued from Page 23)

legs, or even walking upon them, is not really exercise. The muscles receive very little movement. The column of bone does most of the supporting. Ligaments, tendons, and attachments as well as the muscles, must hold the body upright, but rather than the strength from exercise, there is a strained weakness to which they are subjected. In time they become flaccid and stretch. The many muscles, nerves, ligaments, tendons, attachments, joints, and bones of the entire lower limbs make a very complicated assembly. When some of these parts get a bit out of shape, there is congestion at the joints, both in nerves and blood vessels. The blood becomes sluggish, there are deposits at the joints and before long there is pain.

The muscles are not unlike leather or rubber: Either of these substances lasts much longer and serves better when used. They do not have the power to renew themselves as does the human body, but they remain resilient, soft, pliable and alive much longer if used than if not used. You must have observed this with any unused strap or with the tires of an automobile stored for long periods at a time. In spite of the fact that these materials can not renew themselves, either will be in better condition when put back in use. The rubber tire or a rubber band will become softer, more pliable and have more spring, unless it has been unused for so long that it breaks.

We have said that the lower limbs are complicated in construction. Truly we are wonderfully and fearfully made. With this great number of complex parts, all designed to exert force from different angles, many

Reprint of page 38 of the November 1937 issue of *Strength & Health*

FRANK JARES in STRENGTH & HEALTH MAGAZINE

September 1935

Frank Jares listed at 186 lbs. Total lifts: 726.

"Frank Jares is coming right along on all his lifts. If he can make 181 lbs., he'll be a dangerous competitor in the light-heavy class.

"I would like to stage a contest with Termine and Jares, light-heavy, and Turbyfill and Aroff, heavy. Will do if Jares can shave down."

Writer: Jere Kingsbury. Among lifters mentioned: Bill Komoff, Sam Ormont.

January 1936

"Recent weightlifting at South Gate, California."

"Frank Jares performed some splendid lifts in the 181 lb. class, 225 snatch and 286 clean & jerk. As a heavyweight, Frank has succeeded with 297½ in final lift, and has jerked 320 overhead." Table showed him at 181 lbs and total lifts of 714½."

February 1936

Competed for Sid Teeples' Gym in South Gate vs. Los Angeles Athletic Club.

"Frank Jares, from South Gate did some really nice lifting, making a total of 720 ½. He just missed 236 by a whisker and took 297 on his third clean & jerk, a weight he has done on several occasions, but just couldn't hit right this time." Lifted at 187 lbs; old friend Bill Komoff at 151 lbs."

June 1936

Contest at LAAC [Los Angeles Athletic Club], March 27, 1936.

Jares won at 186 ½ lbs. Total of 709 ½. Komoff won at 154.

May 1937

Contest in L.A. reported by Jere Kingsbury.

Jares at 199 had total of 737 on the three lifts. Also at event: John Grimek (at 190 he had total of 781), Sam Ormont, Sam Weston, Otto Schultz.

July 1937

Contest at Huntington Park, CA, AC.

Jares at 201 lbs. had total of 761. Also there: Sam Ormont, Otto Schultz. Sid Teeples was announcer and referee.

September 1937

Contest in L.A.

Jares at 201 ½ lbs., total of 753 ½. Sam Termine at 189 had same total.

November 1937

Had feature, "Frank Jares—West Coast Hercules" by "Wib" Scharzberger. Page 37. (see previous page) Photo of a *ripped* muscleman, the elder Jares.

March 1938

Meet at LAAC.

Frank Jares, 203 lbs. Press 231, snatch 231, clean and jerk 302 ½, total 764 ½. Apparently won his weight class. Date of meet: Dec. 10, 1937, when eldest son Joe was barely two months old.

(photo at left) A group of the nation's best at Santa Monica Beach, Cal. This photo taken when Johnny Terpak and Louis Abele were on their western tour. Front row, left to right: Leo Wonder, Bruce Conners, Les Stockton, Johnny Terpak, Fred Currie, Stan Freed and Armand Tanny. Back row, George Blades, Jim Sullivan, Frank Jares, Vic Tanny, Vic Holbrook, Louis Abele, and Gordon McRae. (from *Strength & Health*, September 1941)

October 1938

Pacific Coast Invitational Weightlifting Championships at LAAC.
  Jares, 205 lbs. Press 231, snatch 242, clean & jerk 313 ½, total 786 ½. Apparently won.

June 1939

Meet involving LAAC.
  Jares, heavyweight winner. 242, 242 (???), 319, total 803.

August 1939

At LAAC.   Jares, 203 lbs. 242, 253, 319, total 814.

September 1939

National champ Steve Stanko did 895 total, an American record. Guy from Philadelphia did 875. Then somebody at 805, so Frank Jares, if entered, would have been about third.

May 1940

California Tri-City Weightlifting Meet (L.A., San Diego, Long Beach), Saturday, Feb. 24, 1940.
  In meet were Armand Tanny (2ⁿᵈ to Jares in heavyweight class), John LaLanne, Sam Weston, Sam Ormont. Jares 240, 230, 320, total 790.

June 1940

  Esther Williams and "Gwenn" Verdon had photos in an article called "You Can Learn to Swim."

September 1940

So. Calif. Senior Weightlifting Championships, L.A. YMCA, May 11, 1940.
  Jares 2ⁿᵈ to Armand Tanny. Jares 230, 240, 315, total 785. Tanny had 790.

February 1941

Pacific Coast Invitational Championships for 1940.
  Jares at 208 lbs., won with 242, 253, 319, total 814. Tanny 2ⁿᵈ with 803.

March 1941

Feature on Armand Tanny (misspelled Tanney in the piece).
  "The piece de resistance of the evening's program was a contest between Frank Jares, a big, powerful West Coast Hercules, formerly from Pittsburgh, and the much smaller, younger, and aspiring Armand Tanney." Gym owner Vic Tanny, Armand's older brother, wrote, "At present Armand and Frank Jares are hotly contesting each other pound for pound, and there is a great deal of rivalry and friendly abuse here at my gym. They threaten each other with disastrous defeats and work like Trojans trying to keep ahead. They are, however, the best of friends and are setting quite a pace for the West Coast lifters to follow."

May 1941

  Five-team meet at Tanny's gym in Santa Monica, CA, March 15, 1941.
  Jares 260, 250, 330, total 840. Armand Tanny also had 840, which was California state record.

June 1941

  Vic Tanny wrote a West Coast column. Mentioned Frank Jares' press of 270. "We like Frank Jares' chances of cracking 900 before the year is up. Frank's unofficial total is 870 and is capable of making more. Jares weighs 220 and is unbelievably powerful and hasn't yet reached his peak."

July 1941

Tanny's column had "muscles of note on the coast," including "Frank Jares' neck."

September 1941

Tanny's column: "I received quite a letter from Fred Grace of L.A. disputing, and taking exception to the fact that I referred to Frank Jares' 20-inch neck as a neck [sic]. Well, Freddie my boy, you should try standing on a handkerchief and, with bare hands, squeeze necks with Jares some time. That, in my opinion, would be a famous last trick. This humorous letter so singed Frank that he stepped right out and pressed the 280 that he has been after for the past month." ... Group beach photo had 14 men, including Frank Jares, Vic Tanny, Armand Tanny, Vic Holbrook (later a wrestler, like Jares), Bruce Conners, Les Stockton, Johnny Terpak, Louis Abele. Page 9 of the mag.

November 1941

Photo of Jares on page 40. Caption: "Frank Jares, weighing 220, shows the muscles which won for him the Pacific Coast Amateur Wrestling Championship and many West Coast and California State titles in Weightlifting." On p. 43, a photo of Jares and Vic Holbrook wrestling in the sand, apparently clowning around.

December 1941

Tanny column: "Tony [Terlazzo] defeated Frank Jares in a match contest with a splendid 840 total. Tony made a 260 press, 250 snatch, and 330 clean and jerk. Jares made a 270 press, 250 snatch, and missed all his jerks after having cleaned 330 twice."

August 1942

Third annual AAU State of California Open Weightlifting Championship, May 16, 1942.

One "Jeres" won heavyweight division with 260, 260 (tying state record), 320, total 840.

December 1942

Tanny column mentioned Jares' swimming prowess.

January 1943

Jares a referee at Los Angeles City Championships, Nov. 7, 1942. Bill Kornoff competed.

June 1943

Tanny column briefly mentions Jares vis-à-vis Bert Goodrich [then or later Tanny's brother-in-law and an owner of a gym or gyms].

October 1943

Photo of Jares on p. 10. "For many years, powerfully built Frank Jares, of Los Angeles, has been the leading heavyweight on the West Coast. His rugged physique has been the envy of many a novice body builder. Frank's strength is best proved by his press of 270, his snatch of 260, and a clean and jerk of 330. He is slightly over 6 feet tall."

May 1944

Tanny's column lists Jares among those "lounging" at Muscle Beach in Santa Monica, CA.

Nothing from then through Feb. 1945. Apparently Jares moved into pro wrestling and out of the West Coast weightlifting scene.

LISTEN . . . Maybe you can hear him grunting. It's Frank Jares of Los Angeles Athletic club and he's Pacific coast weight lifting champion in the heavyweight class. Jares defends his crown tonight at LAAC in the coast AAU title meet.

Newspaper ad from the
Long Beach (CA) *Independent*
November 28, 1941

Local Weight Lifter Wins Coast Title

Lawrence Weeks, Long Beach weight-lifter, brought the Pacific Coast light-weight title to this city as the result of tossing a total of 676½ pounds of iron above his head at the championship contests held recently in the Los Angeles Athletic Club gymnasium. Second place in the same division was won by Weeks' training partner, Orval Wertzbauer, who is associated with Adolph Rein's Physical Culture Gym, 20th and American, in Long Beach.

Two brothers. Hal and Bill Porter, creditably represented Long Beach in the heavy- and light-weight divisions, respectively. Frank Jares, L. A. Athletic Club lifter, retained his heavyweight title in the Pacific Coast championships.

Meeks' lifts were 209 pounds in the military press, 209 in the two-hand snatch, and 258½ in the clean and jerk. These are the three official styles of lifts used in Olympic weight-lifting competitions.

Long Beach, California
June 22, 1940

Frank Jares Wins Lifting Contest

Frank Jares, Pacific Coast heavyweight champion, won a three way weight lifting contest from John Terpak, world's middleweight champion, and Armand Tanny, California champion. In an exhibition staged last night in the Fresno YMCA Gymnasium.

Jares hoisted a total of 820 pounds, five more than Terpak and fifteen pounds more than Tanny. He lifted 260 pounds in the two arm press, 240 pounds in the two arm snatch and 320 pounds in the clean and jerk.

Louis Abele, who recently became national heavyweight champion, broke the existing Olympic Games two arm snatch record of 292½ by grabbing 295 pounds.

Henry Stark, claimant to the world's bag punching title since 1895, gave a demonstration at the start of the program. He will conduct bag punching classes all this week in the Y Gymnasium, starting nightly at 7 o'clock.

Motion pictures of the Mr. America contest were shown.

Fresno, California
June 15, 1941

Bill Koznoff, Vic Tanny, Frank Jares and Gordon McRae

Frank poses for a classic, old-
school bodybuilding picture.

The first mention we could find of Frank wrestling was a May 18, 1945 card in San Bernardino (see below), in which one of the entrants for a tournament was a Frank Schnable. A school of thought is, he may have used a fictitious name due to worries about losing his AAU eligibility in weightlifting competitions, but he also may have been encouraged to do so by his close friend Hans "Jake" Schnabel. Frank wrestled in San Bernardino again the following week, but was billed as "Brother Frank."

WRESTLING
Friday Night

Gigantic One Nite Elimination Tournament

7 -- MATCHES -- 7

JACK CLAYBOURNE vs. KOLA STASIAK
BRO. JOHNATHAN vs. ROBERT MADRY
CLIVE THIEDE vs. FRANK SCHNABLE
HARDY KRUSKAMP vs. CZECH ANGEL

SAN BERNARDINO ARENA
137 SOUTH G STREET — RESERVATIONS PHONE 541-69

Seven Bouts for Mat Tournament

Seven wrestling matches have been scheduled at the San Bernardino arena Friday night for the elimination tournament in which eight of the best matmen on the Pacific Coast will compete.

Jack Claybourne, Negro champion of the Pacific Coast, will oppose Kola Stasiak, the husky Russian in the opening tussle. The second bout sends Brother Jonathon, the bearded Salt Lake City grappler, against Robert Madry, a rough and tumble performer.

Cliff Thiede, the St. Louis muscle mangler, will take on plenty of competition when he tackles the unruly Frank Schnable, of Milwaukee and in the opener Hardy Kruskamp meets the Czech Angel. The winners in each of these four matches will meet, leaving two winners for the finals.

Each match has been limited to 20 minutes and the first bout is scheduled at 8:30 p.m.

San Bernardino, California
May 18, 1945

Mat Second May Get Suspension

Frank Schnable a wrestler and second, may face a 60-day suspension because of his action last week in the Brother Jonathon vs. Jack Claybourne match, it was learned yesterday by Promoter Henry Sonenshine.

Acting as a second to Jonathon in last week's match, Schnable is charged with grabbing Claybourne's leg and tripping him so that Jonathon was able to secure the deciding fall.

After the confused referee awarded the match to Jonathon the fans created a near riot but the Salt Lake grappler hurried to his dressing room. Claybourne waited more than five minutes when it became evident that Jonathon would not return.

Promoter Sonenshine said the athletic commission has ruled that a return match must be booked at the club this week. It will be in addition to the regular mat program and Jonathon and Claybourne will meet in a one fall encounter to a finish. There will be no time limit.

The feature match sends Tiny Roebuck against Big Ben Morgan. In another match Hardy Kruskamp meets Brother Frank and the opening tussle is between Johnny Del Rio and Ralph Alberson.

Claybourne Meets Jonathon in Return Wrestling Mix Tonight

Two of the largest men in the wrestling game clash during the feature tussle at the San Bernardino arena tonight when Tiny (Theodore) Roebuck, Oklahoma Indian, opposes Big Ben Morgan, of Missouri. Each wrestler weighs better than 270 pounds.

Big Ben Morgan is a rough and tumble grappler but he is certain to have trouble against the rugged Indian during the scheduled two out of three falls match. Roebuck, a good defensive matman, is exceptionally fast for a big fellow.

RETURN MATCH

The mat program offers four bouts tonight as the result of the return tussle between Jack Claybourne, Negro champion of the Pacific Coast, and Brother Jonathon, of Salt Lake City.

In their match last week Jonathon was given a questionable and decidedly unpopular decision over Claybourne. The rematch at the club tonight was ordered by the state athletic commission, according to Promoter Henry Sonenshine who also added that neither wrestler had been paid for last week's match. They will now meet in a one-fall tussle to a finish.

Hardy Kruskamp of Ohio, has been pitted against Brother Frank, of Salt Lake City, in a two out of three falls, 45 minute scramble. Hardy is making a determined comeback and since winning a recent Los Angeles tournament, has set his goal for the Pacific Coast wrestling championship now held by Miguel Torres, recent victory over Vincent Lopez in a titular match.

The opening bout sends Johnny Del Rio, of Mexico City against a versatile performer in Ralph Albertson, of Portland. They are light-heavyweights. This is a one fall scuffle limited to 30 minutes.

(above) This card, held on May 25, 1945 in San Bernardino, was the first known card on which Frank appeared as Brother Frank.

(right) On November 4, 1945, Frank appeared in a tag team match with a "Brother Myron" as his tag team partner. The clip is from November 30.

(below) Sacramento, California, December 2, 1945 – the first newspaper reference found with Frank actually listed as "Frank Jares."

McClain Will Wrestle Cox Tomorrow Night

Maes McClain will be the opponent for Ted (King Kong) Cox who will return to the local wrestling wars here tomorrow night in the memorial auditorium. Tom Rice and Flash Gordon will meet Tommy O'Toole and Frank Jares in the tag team bout.

Mormon Matmen Meet Martinez

Czech Angel Draws Toughie in Kashey

Although defeated in a rousing match last week Brother Frank and Brother Myron, a pair of husky Mormon wrestlers, will again tackle Tony Martinez, of Mexico City in a handicap match at the San Bernardino club tonight.

The handicap match last week had as its climax a near riot in which the fans threatened the Mormons before they left the ring.

Martinez won the purses of the Mormons to get double pay for his work in the rough and tumble last week and Promoter J. W. Sonenshine declares that Martinez has again declared he will win over his two rugged opponents by getting a fall from each of them within the hour time limit.

Mikaloff falls to Ras Samara

Ras Samara, e b o n y - toned smoothie from Seattle, spotted Russian Ivan Mikaloff the first fall in the main event at the Fair Grounds rassle show Wednesday night before roaring back to take two in a row from the burly Russian to win the match.

Mikaloff, using rowdy tactics, subdued Samara in two minutes and a half for fall No. 1. Samara, using his pet hold, copped the next fall in 18 minutes, repeating in four minutes for the second fall and victory.

• • •

IN THE semi-final, little Abe Coleman, Brooklyn bone-bender, copped one fall from Jack Conley, Denver, in 26½ minutes. The match exceeded the time limit before either grappler could get another fall.

Frank Jares, Stockton, Calif., won the preliminary when Al Galento was disqualified by Ref Joe Zikmund for using foul tactics.

Coast Newcomer Foe of Rowdy Joe Dusek

Frank Jares, the Stockton (Cal.) (Cal.) heavyweight who never before has come to grips with a mat foe in Omaha, will make his first local appearance against Omaha's Joe Dusek in the semiwindup of the Friday night City Auditorium show.

AND STILL CHAMPION

SPOKANE, Wash., July 23.—(U.P)—Texas Babe Sharkey retained his unofficial world's heavyweight wrestling championship last night with a two-fall decision over Challenger Frank Jares, of Salt Lake City. Two-Ton Tony Galento, of Orange, N. J., former heavyweight boxing contender, refereed the match.

(left) Frank makes his first road trip when he goes to the Nebraska territory. Clip is from Lincoln, Nebraska, February 13, 1946.

(middle left) Omaha, February 15, 1946

(bottom left) Frank traveled to Washington State. While there, he wrestled Babe Sharkey, one of the claimants to the "world heavyweight title." Date of the match was July 22, 1946.
  On occasion in Washington, he was billed as "Frank Jarvis."

(below) In an article about George Temple, brother of child film star Shirley Temple, George mentions wrestling Frank in Los Angeles.

The Sport Realm
—By BILL WESTWICK

SHIRLEY'S BROTHER MATMAN.

If there is to be another member of Shirley Temple's family in motion pictures it will be after her brother George has finished his professional wrestling career. George Temple, who hopes to catch some of the fame in mat circles his sister has achieved, as a cinema star, turned up in Ottawa last night and watched some of the bouts at the Auditorium.

Since his discharge from the U.S. Marine Corps, George had been doing quite well as a professional grappler until he ran into a knee injury in a New York bout a month ago. Bothered by the ailment, he went to Montreal for treatment from Bill Head, the Canadiens' trainer, and figures he will be ready to show again any day now.

Tanned and bearing a marked resemblance to his famous sister, Temple figures he might get into the picture game, but first he'd like to make a go of wrestling, which he took up seriously while serving four and a half years with the Marines in the South Pacific.

SPOTTED BY TALENT SCOUT.

While the cinema has attracted more than one member of famous Hollywood families, such as the Pickfords, Cagneys, Fairbanks, Beerys, Chaneys, the Temple family contribution will remain sister Shirley so far as George is concerned. "No, pictures never figured in my plans at all", the 24-year-old matman said last night.

"They didn't figure in Shirley's plans either", he added with a grin. "Although we were born in Los Angeles there never were any plans for Shirley for pictures so far as I know. A talent scout picked her out on the beach one afternoon when she was about three years old, signed her up, sent her to dancing school and she came along from there."

Someone mentioned that "she'd come quite a distance", and George said:

"Yes, quite a long ways from the time I speak of. I'd like to go as far as a wrestler. I always liked the game as a boy at school, but I didn't really give a mat career serious thought until I was in the Marines. You meet a lot of fine athletes, including some good wrestlers, in the Marine Corps, and I did a lot of mat work in my spare time.

"It's quite popular in California and while in the service I decided I'd follow it up when I was discharged. I'm enjoying it a lot, too."

THE PICTURES CAN WAIT.

Someone was bound to ask if his sister followed his matches, and George said:

"I wouldn't say she follows them, but she has come to see me. She turned up for one of my first important matches in Los Angeles. I was wrestling a tough customer by the name of Frank Jares. I got along pretty well against him and won the bout. Shirley was in the ringside, but after she said it was pretty 'gruesome'."

There are good openings in other branches of the motion picture industry apart from the acting end, but they don't interest George.

"Besides Shirley and me there is only another brother in the family. He's in the production end. I'm set on wrestling now. My knee is coming around well, and I'll be going again soon. I might get around to doing some Westerns after a while, but the pictures can wait."

Frank Jares to meet Indian in main bout here Wednesday night

Frank Jares will be pitted against Chief Little Wolf, Indian grappler, in the main tussle on Wednesday night's mat card at the Fair Grounds according to an announcement by Promoter Adam Krieger.

In the semiwindup Krieger brings Al Galento back for a fight against Joe Dusek of Omaha. Both the top bill and semi-windup will be two falls out of three.

Jack Conley has been signed for the opener altho his opponent has not yet been named.

Turns On Torture

Chief Littlewolf Resorts To Pet "Indian Deathlock" To Dispose of Frank Jares.

Chief Littlewolf did more than gain a win over Frank Jares in the main event of Prof. Adam Krieger's mat show at the fairgrounds arena Wednesday night.

The Chief got a torture hold on Jares called the "Indian Death-lock" and Frank is now in an Omaha hospital being treated for torn ligaments in one of his knees.

After the Chief clamped the lock on Jares, forcing the latter to give up, he went to work on the same leg and applied another hold on Jares for the next fall and the match. Jares was helped from the ring and immediately rushed to Omaha for treatment.

Joe Downs Galento.

Joe Dusek tossed Al Galento for two out o' three falls but kept Referee Joe Zikmund on his toes trying to rule out the rough stuff. With one fall apiece, the bone-benders started bouncing off the ropes at each other but Joe tossed Galento over his head and kept him flat for the final fall.

Barefoot Tex Steddums and Jack Conley battled to a draw in the opener. The rough-and-tumble event kept the customers on their feet. Tex wrestles without shoes because, he says, he can grip the mat better.

WRESTLE

Wed., Feb. 27
8:30 P. M.
Arena—Lincoln Fair Grounds

CHIEF LITTLE WOLF

Chief Little Wolf
Indian Champion
vs.
Frank Jares

Joe Dusek
vs.
Al Galento

Jack Conley
vs.
? ?

Joe Zikmund
—Referee

General Admission 80c
Reserved Seats $1.35
Children accompanied
by parents 35c
Tax included

Tickets at **DAVIDSON'S**
1400 O St. 3-5675

Frank is quickly pushed into the main event, as shown on these articles from the Feb. 27, 1946 card in Lincoln, Nebraska.

Wrestling at Hazleton

Four wrestling bouts are scheduled for Holy Trinity Hall in Hazleton tonight. In the topnotch attraction, Emil Dusek meets Tony Martinelli. In other matches Angelo Savoldi vs. Wally Dusek, Jim Wallace vs. Fritz Ziegfried and Frank Jares vs. Abe Yourist.

Swedish Angel, Mormon Meet

Tussle to Feature Arena's Mat Card

The Swedish Angel has been matched with Frank Jares, the unruly Mormon bruiser, in the headline tussle at the San Bernardino arena, tonight.

This two out of three falls match should highlight the mat program despite the assurance that Ed "Strangler" Lewis, who held the national wrestling title five times during the peak of his career will appear on the card. Lewis has been matched against Wee Willie Davis. The Lewis vs. Davis tussle is also a two out of three falls affair but is limited to 45 minutes.

Vincent Lopez, the popular Mexican wrestler who once held the national championship, will oppose Sammy Menacher, a former Army officer.

Tony Andell, Santa Fe employe and a former champion of the S. F.A.C., has been matched with Frank Cutler, from Ohio.

O'Toole, Jares In Tag Match Victory Here

Johnny Sepada and Chief Thunderbird were beaten by Frank Jares and Tom O'Toole at the civic auditorium last night in one of the wildest tag matches staged for the Santa Cruz ring world in a long while.

Jares and O'Toole won the first fall in 19 minutes and 45 seconds; the second fall went to Thunderbird and Sepada in six minutes and 30 seconds, while the final fall was hammered out in six minutes and 40 seconds.

Jares, a substitute in the flurry for Ray Eckert and doing an entertaining job, started the affair against Thunderbird by bashing the big Indian in the nose with a looping fist, followed with a headlock that brought grunts of rage.

Just as Jares was going good, Thunderbird tagged his partner, Sepada, who came into the ring with a cocked fist and sank it into the midsection of Jares, who folded down, gasping for air.

Regaining his second wind quickly, Jares snared Sepada in a full nelson and rammed his out-thrust head into the fist of O'Toole, who was waiting eagerly behind the ropes for such an opportunity.

Although the punch dazed and hurt Sepada it took a repeat blow in the same manner to drop him flat. The second time Sepada went limp in the arms of Jares, who capitalized with a body press for the first fall.

Shortly after, Jares nailed Sepada in the full nelson again and tried the same tactic for another fall. Unfortunately the attempt backfired when O'Toole's speeding fist missed Sepada and landed with a smack in the eye of Jares. Jares staggered back with Sepada throwing punches that felled the newcomer to the mat and he was pinned for the three-second count.

In the last minutes of the bout, things got completely out of hand, with all four groaners in the ring whacking each other about and even swinging at the referee when he popped into range.

While the referee was trying to separate Jares and Sepada, O'Toole stomped on Thunderbird's chin, which was all that was needed for a body press and the winning fall.

In the curtain opener, Mays McLain and Tom Rice took one fall each and battled to the one-hour limit and a draw. Rice won the first fall in 43 minutes and 55 seconds with a finger hold, and McLain won the second fall in eight minutes and 55 seconds with a body press.

The referee's work was sharp, despite a bit of unpreventable confusion in the tag match.

Frank made a cross-country trip to the Northeast where he wrestled in New York and Pennsylvania. By July 1947, he was back in southern California, where he would be featured on wrestling cards through February 1950. In 1948, he made a trip back to the Northeast and spent two months wrestling in Hawaii.

(top) Hazleton, PA: March 6, 1947

(above) San Bernardino, CA: October 17, 1947

(right) Santa Cruz, CA: November 5, 1947

TERRIFIC!

TWO Great Main Events!

GORGEOUS GEORGE
RAVE OF HOLLYWOOD

VS.

HARDY KRUSKAMP
COLORFUL EX-GRIDDER

THE GORGEOUS ONE
AND HIS VALET ARE
THE SENSATION OF THE
WRESTLING WORLD.

DON'T MISS THEM!

BIG VIC HOLBROOK
POPULAR GIANT

VS.

BRO. FRANK JARES
WILD EX-PREACHER

PLENTY OF "CLARET"
FLOWED IN THEIR WILD
TEAM BRAWL LAST
WEEK. NOW VIC
WANTS REVENGE
BY HIMSELF.

PLUS

PAT FRALEY vs. **FLASH GORDON**
EX-COAST CHAMP   UNBEATEN DROP-KICKER

SATURDAY 9:00 P. M.
RYAN'S ARENA
PHONE 2-1323 FOR RESERVATIONS

SPONSORED BY DISABLED AMERICAN VETERANS

REFEREE

Vol. 90 — No. 19   MAY 14, 1949

GREAT SHOWMAN

FRANK JARES

Jares is one of the most popular wrestlers now appearing in Northern California rings. The blonde Panther-terror fails to give fans a great performance. Jares is to be seen in action at San Francisco, Tuesday night, when he teams up with Juan Humberto in a Tag Team match against Gino Garibaldi and Bob Ford.

(left) Fresno, CA: April 4, 1948

(above) Frank featured on the cover of the May 14, 1949 San Francisco arena program.

(below)
  San Bernardino, CA: Aug. 21, 1948

Primo Carnera Gets Mat Verdict Over Wee Willie, Jares at Arena

Primo Carnera, the big, powerful ex-world heavyweight boxing champion, proved his superiority in the wrestling ring last night by downing Wee Willie Davis and Brother Frank Jares in a handicap match that turned into a wild free-for-all.

Before it was over, Davis and Jares were joined in the ring by Hardy Kruskamp, Ted and Vic Christy and Alex Kasaboski. But out of the madhouse, Referee Bobby Coleman (himself the victim of a blow from Jares) raised Carnera's hand in victory.

Primo body pressed Jares into submission in 10 mins., but Frank didn't like it and took a poke at Carnera during the rest period. The second fall went to Primo on disqualification, when both his foes were in the ring together.

The semi-windup went to the speedy Vic Christy who took two of the three falls from Hans Schnabel, both in 5 mins. with a flying scissors off the ropes. Schnabel won his fall with a body press in the rough match.

The opener went 20 mins. to a draw, with Hardy Kruskamp and Terry McGinnis turning in some clean grappling. The second match went to Ted Christy in 18 mins. over Alex Kasaboski. Both were in and out of the ring many times, with Ted using a toe hold to finally win out.

BROWN BOMBER TO THE RESCUE—Gino Garibaldi, U.S. Pacific coast wrestling champ, was well on the way to making an accordion of Frank Jares' face while he dug down, but hard, on the latter during their recent wrestling match at San Francisco, Calif. The victim was saved by the referee, retired heavyweight champion Joe Louis, who decided it was time to put a restraining hand on Gino. Garibaldi won the match—or did you guess?

Torres Flattens Jares at Arena

Rugged Brother Frank Jares took considerable punishment in the feature wrestling match last night, losing two of the three falls at the San Bernardino arena to Enrique Torres.

Torres, claimant to the wrestling championship, appeared none too satisfied over losing the initial fall and started to work on Jares, dealing out considerable head punishment in drop kicks and face locks.

Jares won the first fall with a knee neck cracker in 12 minutes. Torres won the next fall in 3 minutes of rapid fire action with a flying body scissors. The deciding fall was the result of face locks, elbow smashes and drop kicks, Jares being flattened after 18 minutes of rough mauling.

In the tag match, Terry McGinnis paired with George Temple to win over the team of Chester Hayfield and Jim Coffield.

Temple tossed Coffield in 14 minutes, then Hayes flattened Temple with a Boston leg crab hold in nine minutes. Terry clinched the match over Coffield by using elbow smashes and a press in 12 minutes.

Basher McDonald, a Scotch heavyweight, used his favorite hold, the Highland fling to win from Johann Skaaland, of Norway in 19 minutes.

WRESTLING

Sat., Sept. 24th, 8:30 P. M.

ENRIQUE TORRES

Plus Tag-Team and Perlim.

FRANK JARES

Plus Tag-Team and Prelim.

San Bernardino Arena
137 So. G St.　Sat. Nite

(opposite page, top) San Bernardino, Sept. 11, 1948
(opposite page, bottom) San Francisco, May 1949
(top left & above) San Bernardino, Sept. 24, 1949
(bottom left) San Bernardino, Jan. 7, 1950
(below) Van Nuys, Jan. 14, 1950
(bottom) San Bernardino, Feb. 25, 1950

"Saturday Night Is Wrestling Night In The Valley"

• WRESTLING •

SATURDAY, JAN. 14, 8:30 P.M.
MAIN EVENT

Baron Michele Leone vs. Brother Frank Jares

2 OUT OF 3 FALLS—TO A FINISH
NO HOLDS BARRED
Semi-Windup

BOMBER KULKY　vs.　JOHN CRETORIA
2 out of 3 Falls—To a Finish

TWO MORE GREAT MATCHES

Special Added Attraction—Mr. America Will Give Demonstration

JEFFRIES' BARN

Victory at Buena Vista, Burbank.　New Phone STanley 7-2522
FREE PARKING

WRESTLING

SAT., JAN. 7th

The

AMAZING ROCCA

World's Most
Sensational Wrestler

versus

Bro.

FRANK JARES

Wild Mormon From Utah

3 Other Great Bouts

San Bernardino Arena
Sat., Jan. 7th, 8:30 P. M.

Jares Grapples Baron Michele in Grudge Match at Arena Tonight

Frank Jares, the Mormon from Provo, Utah, who insists that Baron Michele is just another Italian who needs a hair cut, will get a chance to trim the Baron tonight, when they meet in a scheduled two out of three match at the San Bernardino arena.

The remark was made during a recent tag team match, in which the Baron carried on his usual rough tactics in the ring, while Jares had a joust with Argentina Rocco.

Jares took a trouncing in his match with Rocco before a packed house, and made his remark about the Baron in the dressing room.

If there is any significance to the remark the Jares vs. Leone tussle should be replete with action, and it should be rough as that is the style of both grapplers.

A tag match offers another feature on the mat card. Karl Davis and Marvin Jones, a couple of rough characters in the muscle mangling pastime, tackle Ernie Piluso, a former junior heavyweight champion and his partner, a promising young Mexican grappler, Lupe Fernandez. This match is for two of three falls, with a 45-minute limit.

Mel Peters, the handsome Portland mauler, has been matched with Jim Sixsay, a clever Hungarian in the opener. They will clash in a bout limited to one fall.

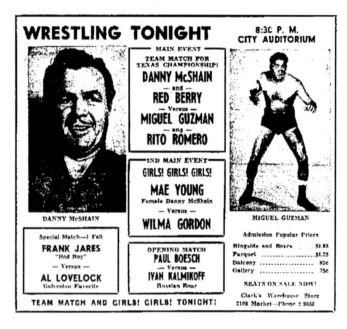

(top) March 1950, Frank wrestled for eight weeks in Texas. Ad is for Galveston, March 16, 1950.

(right middle) Denton, Texas, April 12, 1950

(above) Back to San Bernardino, Aug. 5, 1950

(right) Wrestling in the main event in San Bernardino on July 7, 1951 against NWA world heavyweight champion Lou Thesz.

10:45 Sports Final—
with Charlie Harville
11:00 Wrestling from Hollywood—
Al and John Smith vs Frank
Jares and Danny McShain
12:00 News, Final Edition, signoff

Brother Jares Loses Tooth Last Night

Brother Frank Jares lost a tooth and didn't win a fall last night at Strelich Stadium. Using eye gouges and ear pulls, his partner in the next-thing-to-crime, Ted Christy, won the first fall in 9:50.

The Romeros won the match. Pablo drop-kicked Jares into a state bordering on extinction and took the second ·in 6:26. Then's when Jares dropped that tooth.

After a terrifying series of rights to the jaw and drop kicks, Rito downed Christy in 7:23.

Poor referee Stanley Pinto was in a tizzy most of the time. Dirty works were always going on behind his back. No man would have been quick enough to see all that nefariousness. Honest Lloyd Miller, the announcer, avoid personal injury by staying far away from the slow-cooling principals.

Dr. Lee Grable took the second and third falls in 4:53 and 7:36 with a flying tackle and body press and an octopus hold, while Honest John Cretoria won the first in 10:40 with a half crab.

Tom Runestr bested Vic Christy in 8:46 and 7:06. Christy won the second in 3:44.

JUNGLE BOY, JARES UPSET TAG CHAMPS

Brother Frank Jares punched Pablo Romero's eye, then rendered Carlos Guzman helpless with knee drops, thus gaining with Partner Jungle Boy an upset victory over the tag team champions of San Bernardino Saturday night at the S.B. Arena.

Guzman and Romero last week had captured a tag tourney, and Jares and Jungle Boy had promised revenge. They got it, using all the mean tricks of the trade.

Bushy-haired J u n g l e B o y pinned Pablo in 19:33 minutes by stomping on his throat. Carlos evened it 10 minutes later by tying up Jungle Boy into a pretzel. The decider came 9:47 minutes later.

In the 45-minute semi-windup, Vic Christy disposed of Antone Leone in two falls. Leone, who brags being the homliest wrestler in captivity, lost the first in 22:06 on disqualification. Christy used leg scissors to end it 7:46 later.

In the curtain raiser, Referee Joe Wood called it a draw between Rey Urbano and Ali Bey, when neither the Filipino nor the Turk could manage a fall in the 30-minute limit.

Frank wrestled in North Carolina from January through March 1952.

(top left) Publicity photo

(left) Frank and The Jungle Boy win the tag team titlefrom Pablo Romero and Carlos Guzman in San Bernardino on Aug. 23, 1952. They would drop the belts to Rito and Pablo Romero the following week.

(above top) Sept. 11, 1952 Greensboro, NC TV guide listing for *Wrestling from Hollywood*

(above) Bakersfield, CA, Sept. 17, 1952

Jares Lets Self in for Large Order of Pain

Just gecause Brother Jares, a mean customer, won a wrestling tournament at Strelich Stadium last week, he thinks he's invincible—or so it seems. He's gone so far as to permit himself to be booked with Sandor Szabo, the Champ, tonight. It's his funeral is what followers of the game are saying.

The main event of the evening is for two-out-of-three falls, one-hour limit.

Of lesser duration will be a team-tag between George Becker and Pablo Romero on one side and Tony Morelli and Ted Christy on the other. It will be a two-out-of-three falls, 45-minute affair.

Leo Salvoldi is slated to go against Ray Gideon in the one fall to a finish preliminary.

The bouts will be started come 8:45 p.m.

Sandor Szabo Whips Jares

Brother Frank Jares might not know what the Greek-Roman word "swplex" means but he certainly has first hand knowledge of what a swplex feels like. He's been.

Sandor Szabo did it to him last night at the Strelich Stadium to win the second fall in 4:59. To spectators the swplex looked like a terrible body slam and a body press. Szabo explained the word means: lift 'em up over your head, tear 'em, and then smash 'em down. That's what he did.

Szabo won the third and decisive fall in 4:33 after a beautiful rhubarb during which the referee was scathed. Szabo was counted out and the bout was originally awarded to Jares. But then it was explained to the ref that Jares had been using the ropes for leverage. The ref called Jares back into the ring to discuss the matter. Jares didn't come. The ref awarded the bout to Szabo.

Pablo Romero and George Becker bested Ted Christy and Toni Morelli in a team tag. It was Christy over Romero in 12:50 with a Gilligan twist; Romero and Becker in a 7:46, referee's decision for unnecessary roughness, and Becker over Christy in 5:54 with a knee lift to the chin and a body press.

Ray Gideon took Leo Salvoldi in 22:30 in the preliminary: body press.

(two clips on right) Bakersfield, Oct. 1, 1952
(below) Mesa, Arizona: Dec. 18, 1952

WRESTLING PREVIEW
MESA CIVIC CENTER

Vol. 3, No. 13   OFFICIAL PROGRAM — 10¢   Mesa, Ariz. Thurs., Dec. 18, 1952

BIG 6 MAN TAG TEAM MATCH

ALI BEY   MASKED STRANGER   FRANK JARES

SONNY KURGIS   PIERRE LA BELLE   RAY PIRET

★彡彡彡彡彡彡彡彡彡彡彡彡彡彡彡彡彡彡彡彡彡彡★

POT O' GOLD QUIZ TONIGHT'S GRAND PRIZE $10 IN CASH

★ ADDITIONAL PRIZE: 2 RING SEATS TO NEXT WEEK'S MATCHES ★

TICKETS ON SALE AT JOHNSONS' NEWS STAND, 66 W. MAIN,
and EVERYBODY'S DRUG STORE.
FOR RESERVATIONS PHONE MESA 5858

PROGRAM
PROMOTER
HONEST MONTE LaDUE

6 Man Tag Team Match
2 Out of 3 Falls — 1 Hour

ALI BEY
MASKED STRANGER
FRANK JARES

vs.

SONNY KURGIS
PIERRE LaBELLE
RAY PIRET

ALSO

| Frank JARES | vs. | Ray PIRET |
20 MINUTE MATCH

| MASKED STRANGER | vs. | SONNY KURGIS |
20 MINUTE MATCH

| ALI BEY | vs. | PIERRE LaBELLE |
20 MINUTE MATCH

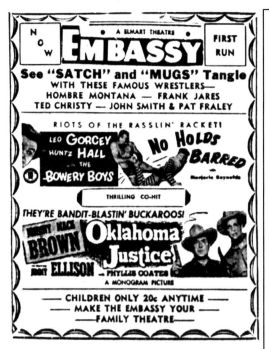

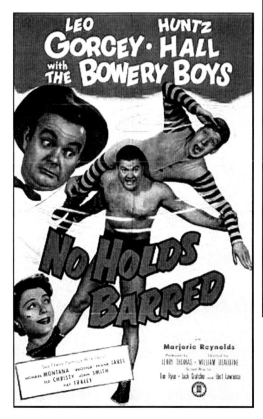

Behind The Movie Sets

WITH

BUDDY MASON

If the main-match wrestlers at your arena should enter the ring and start putting toe-holds on the announcer and referee — do not be surprised! Chances are, they've recently been working in Allied Artists' "Stranglehold" and are still a trifle confused!

Working in a 'Bowery' Boys comedy is, at best, not conducive to rational behavior. But when you have to wrestle with Huntz Hall and read script lines at the same time, you're likely to wind up in the park racing the other squirrels for your share of the nuts.

Memorizing wrestling routines may not be too strange a chore for a potential "fall-guy." Adding lines of dialogue might not overly complicate matters. But when the ad-libbing Huntz and his gag-men change both the action and spoken words just before each scene — the boys are to be excused if they end up putting strangleholds on themselves.

Hombre Montana, Henry Kulky, Frank Jares, Ted Christy and a gentleman who has been around (if you can believe the nation's motel registers), a Mr. John Smith, were all cast members. In respective weak moments, they had signed up as actor-wrestling partners for Huntz Hall. With all the native innocence of men who had never before braved the rigors of "Bowery Boys" comedies, they checked in for their stipulated stints.

In the comparative safety of grunt-and-groan circles, these huskies observe sort of give-and-take courtesies. Perhaps not quite up to Emily Post standards of conduct — but, nevertheless, ethics of rough-hewn behavior. If an opponent gnaws a bit on your ear or playfully tromps on your nose you are permitted certain liberties to put him in his place. A body-slam, followed by a warning tap-routine danced on his mid-section may serve as notice that you expect him to wrestle

(left) Movie ad for *No Holds Barred*, a 1952 comedy featuring the Bowery Boys with apperances by wrestlers Frank Jares, Hombre Montana, Ted Christy, John Smith and Pat Fraley.

BROTHER FRANK JARES

Mitchell, Jares Grapple Tonight

Jim Mitchell, known to the trade as the Black Panther, has been matched with Brother Frank Jares, the unruly Mormon from Utah, in the headliner at the San Bernardino arena tonight.

The Black Panther who specializes in the cranium cracker as his best offensive, will undoubtedly use it frequently to stiffen the unruly Mormon. Jares, a former weight lifting champion, is a veteran grappler and a trickster in the ring.

Another outstanding attraction will be a tag team match. It is also two out of three falls between Chick and Gino Garibaldi meeting a team comprising The Champ and Karl Davis.

The Champ and Karl Davis were held to a draw last week in the tag team brawl against the Becker brothers. It was a riot during the full one hour time limit with each team getting a fall.

In the opener Matt Murphy a strong Irish bruiser, will tackle Leon Carilenko.

EDITORIALS

A Noble Wrestler

Our own newspaper gave the world an interesting story of human nobility the other day, and thereby raised the entertainment of wrestling high in our estimation.

The story appeared on the sports pages, and concerned a gentleman called Brother Frank Jares, who weighs 225 pounds and loves little children. He is a wrestler by trade.

Brother Frank, according to the news story, enjoys nothing more than spending time with youngsters—helping them in "physical culture training." He also is said to be vitally interested in the general field of child welfare.

Of course, the story points out, Brother Frank is so busy wrestling these days he hasn't much spare time to give the kiddies. But we are assured he helps youth whether youth needs help or not, whenever lapses in the wrestling schedule permit.

In the ring, we are told, Brother Frank loses his soft-heartedness immediately and becomes a clawing tiger of a man. In other words, he loves children and hates adults who wrestle with him.

This brief story of Brother Frank's interest and capabilities struck us as so noble—especially for a muscled wrestler—that editorial comment seemed mandatory. We tried to find out if he also gives away money to good causes, or if he has a sideline speciality of carrying elderly ladies and invalids across thoroughfares. Those questions were not answered readily, but we did learn that Brother Frank is, indeed, a prince of a fellow.

So must all wrestlers be. Those who participate in the exhibitions promoted by Mr. William "Big Bill" Lewis in Richmond apparently earn a great deal of money by grunting, groaning, falling, and grimacing all at the right times for audience appeal. If any of them are like Brother Frank, they could help mankind greatly by donating funds and excess energies to various child welfare organizations.

Come to think of it, the wrestling "profession" might represent an untapped mine of talent particularly suited for good work among the young.

Ethel Barrmore Theater, 9:30. "The Duke," Patrick Knowles and K. T. Stevens in a story of a jewelry robbery in which suspicion points to The Duke. A cat used to distract the guard later leads to the real criminals.
Wrestling from Hollywood, 10. Sandor Szabo vs. Mr. Moto (main event) Brother Frank Jares vs. Freddie Blassier (semiwindup).
Nite Owl Theater, 11. "Honeymoon Limited," Neil Hamilton, Irene Harvey.

(top left) San Bernardino, Dec. 1, 1951

(above top) Article from the Petersburg, VA newspaper, Sept. 18, 1953

Frank wrestled in the Carolinas from Sept. 1953 through Feb. 1954.

(above top) July 2, 1953 Salem, OR TV guide listing for *Wrestling from Hollywood*

Bro. Frank Says 'Ref' Shoved Fan

Wrestler Brother Frank modestly gave the referee credit Friday for helping him toss a spectator out of the ring but insisted the fan did not land in a lady's lap.

The wrestler, whose true name is Frank Jares, is being sued for $7250 by Mrs. Virginia McAlma, who was sitting at the ringside when the action occured here Aug. 7, 1952.

Brother Frank testified Friday in Superior Court that he merely gave the spectator a shove. He said the referee also shoved the fan off the mat the same time.

The wrestler was standing outside the ring during a tag match when an unidentified spectactor jumped up on the mat.

The fan landed on the floor at Mrs. McAlma's feet, according to Brother Frank.

The matman's co-defendant, Promoter Harry Rubin, was asked by the housewife's attorney if some wrestlers were known as "villians" and others "heroes" at Municipal Auditorium.

"I'll stipulate Brother Frank is a hero," Defense Atty. James E. Collins offered.

However, Mrs. McAlma's attorney continued his efforts to make Brother Frank a "villain," noting he had been booed and hissed by the crowd that night.

Mrs. McAlma, 723 Elm Ave., asserted she suffered damage to the veins in her right leg when the spectator struck her.

The trial will be resumed Monday in Judge Joseph M. Maltby's court.

Thesz Soon Disposes Of Brother Jares

Lou Thesz, "world" wrestling champion, required only 17 minutes to polish off rough Brother Frank Jares before a packed house last night at Turner's Arena.

Jares lost the first fall in 13 minutes when he was disqualified for strangling. Thesz then applied a body press to take the next fall in four minutes.

In other match baldi drew with Jack Witzig O'Brien and Kin over Tony Marti

(above) Long Beach, CA, May 15, 1954

Frank returned to the Carolinas in October and stayed there for several months.

(top right) Spartanburg, SC, Dec. 4, 1954

(center right) Washington DC, Feb. 9, 1955

(bottom right) Hagerstown, MD, Feb. 14, 1955

Frank made one shot in Madison Square Garden, New York City, on March 21, 1955.

BLYTHEVILLE LEGION ARENA
WRESTLING

Monday, Feb. 6   8:15 p.m.   Adults 50c — Children 15c

Championship Match

This Match Conducted by Nat'l Wrestling Ass'n.
No Time Limit — Best 2 Out of 3 Falls

FRANK JARES
Southern Junior Heavyweight Champion
—Vs.—
JOE WELCH

90-Minute Time Limit
Best 2 out of 3 Falls

Ramon Cernadas
South America
—Vs.—
Herb Larson
Sweden

WRESTLING
JULES STRONGBOW
Guest Announcer
SATURDAY AT 8:30
*See Wrestling History Made
Through Mind Conditioning*

BRO.
FRANK **JARES**
vs
SKI
HI **LEE**

2 Out of 3 Falls — 1 Hour
**Dr. Grable at Ring Side
to Assist Brother Frank**

****
THE WRESTLER
****

VOL. X, NO. 38   Knoxville, Tennessee, Friday, September 14, 1956   Price 10 Cents

JARES TO TAKE ON TONIGHT'S WINNER

GOLIATH
He's Been Here

FRANK JARES
Gets Title Shot

Will Get Shot
At Title Next
Friday Night

Brother Frank Jares will get a shot at the world's junior heavyweight championship next Friday night at Municipal Baseball Stadium.

The Prince Utah, Montana has been promised a title bout next week in Knoxville. He will take on the winner of the Irish Mike Clancy-Al Chesko's Galento bout tonight for the championship.

TONIGHT'S PROGRAM

LEO GARIBALDI
VS.
NICK BOCKWINKLE
2 Out of 3 Falls — 45 Min.

DR. LEE		VIC
GRABLE	vs.	CHRISTY
	1 FALL 30 MIN.	
IRISH PAT		CARLOS
FRALEY	vs.	MORENO
	1 FALL 20 MIN.	

General Admission 95c
Ringside .... $1.50 and $2.00
Children ... . 50c (tax included)

SAN BERNARDINO ARENA
For Reservations Phone TU 9-6523
Sat. After 10 A. M. Phone TU 8-9169
137 South G St.

WRESTLING
Double Main Event
Brother Frank Jares   vs.   Jim Cofield
AND
Barbara Baker   vs.   Betty Hawkins
OPENER
Return Match For Last Fall Only
Angelo Martinelli   Doc "Madman" Galla
and   -vs-   and
Harry "Ga. Boy" Smith   Leo Warlick
SATURDAY, OCTOBER 29 — 8 P. M.
Spartanburg Memorial Auditorium Arena

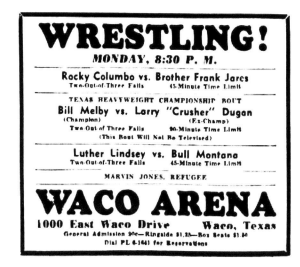

WRESTLING!

MONDAY, 8:30 P. M.

Rocky Columbo vs. Brother Frank Jares
Two-Out-of-Three Falls   45-Minute Time Limit

TEXAS HEAVYWEIGHT CHAMPIONSHIP BOUT

Bill Melby vs. Larry "Crusher" Dugan
(Champion)   (Ex-Champ)
Two-Out of Three Falls   90-Minute Time Limit
(This Bout Will Not Be Televised)

Luther Lindsey vs. Bull Montana
Two-Out-of-Three Falls   45-Minute Time Limit

MARVIN JONES, REFUGEE

WACO ARENA

1000 East Waco Drive   Waco, Texas
General Admission 90c— Ringside $1.25—Box Seats $1.50
Dial PL 6-1441 for Reservations

Enrique Romero and Zorro scored a tag team win over Brother Frank Jares and Matt Murphy in the San Bernardino Arena wrestling feature. Other results: Mr. Moto defeated Mike Mazurki, Hardy Kruskamp drew with Oni Wiki Wiki, and Bud Curtis stopped Dick Chaney.

Tag-Team At Hall Tuesday

A 6-man tag-team match heads the weekly wrestling show of promoter Bob Sanders at Memorial Hall Tuesday night.

The tag-team match, two out of three falls to a finish, will pit Ivan The Terrible, Joe Costello and Bob Clay against Lou Newman, Bad Boy Hines and Brother Frank Jares.

There will be three 15-minute matches preliminary to the tag-team match with these same matmen in action.

The matches start at 8 pm. The box office opens at 7.

(opposite page)
(top center) Blytheville, Arkansas: Feb. 6, 1956
(left center)
Knoxville, Tennessee arena program
Sept. 14, 1956

(bottom left) Spartanburg, SC: Oct. 27, 1955

(right) San Bernardino: May 11, 1957

(top) Waco, Texas: Dec. 16, 1957

(right) Salina, Kansas: April 14, 1959

(above) San Bernardino: May 23, 1959

Beginning in June 1955, Frank made a 16-month run in the Nashville, TN territory. During that time, he won the Southern junior heavyweight title In Birmingham, Alabama on July 25, 1955 from Sonny Myers. He held the title for ten months before dropping it to the Masked Bat (Bob O'Shocker) in Nashville on May 22, 1956, but regained it the following week. Two months later, on July 24, he lost the title to Jesse James, only to regain it once again two weeks later in Nashville. On Aug. 27, he lost the title to Herb Welch in Birmingham. After wrestling for a short time in the Carolinas and Texas, he returned to California and stayed there until May 1958, at which time he returned to Nashville for a five-week run. From there, he returned to the Carolinas to wrestle through August.

Frank spent the remainder of his career in California and made what seems to be his final road tour with a trip into Kansas in April 1959. The match in Salina (above) appears to be one of his last matches on the road. He wasn't booked on the May 23 San Bernardino card (above right), but teamed with Matt Murphy to take the place of Henry Lenz and Eric Pedersen.

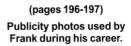

(pages 196-197)
Publicity photos used by
Frank during his career.

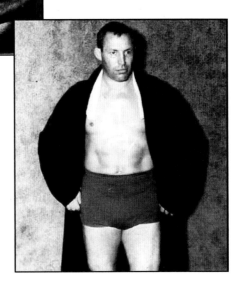

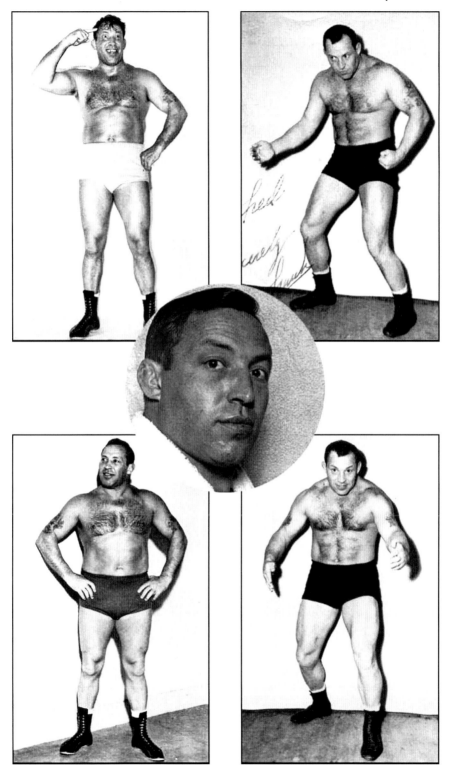

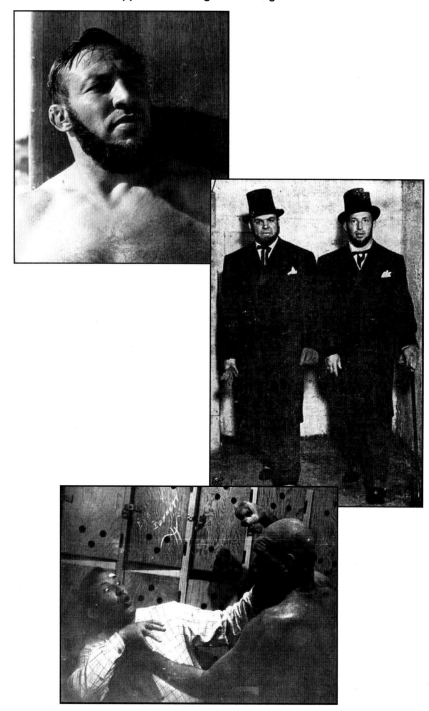

(top) A closeup of Brother Frank

(center) Brother Jonathan and Brother Frank

(bottom) Frank Jares clowns around with the Swedish Angel (Phil Olafsson)

Publicity photo of George and Bobby Becker with a miniature Frank Jares.

NEWSPAPER HEADLINES

Jares Will Wrestle Sepada Here Tonight.

Becker Brothers Tag Team
Takes on Jares, Davis Duo

Torres Flattens Jares at Arena

Newman to Fight Jares In Wrestling Main Go

Moto, Jares Out To Keep Record Clean

The Becker Brothers Conquer That Dreadful Frank Jares

Hans Schnabel, Frank Jares Defeat Foes

Could Be Natural . . . .

How's Rematch Between Brother Frank, Blassie?

Jares to Meet Thesz Here for Mat Title

Frank Jares' Los Angeles Times obituary, July 26, 1990

Frank Jares Sr.; Retired Professional Wrestler

Frank Jares Sr., a professional wrestler known as "Brother Frank" during early television's wrestling heyday, has died in Valencia. He was 77.

Jares, who started out as an amateur wrestler and weightlifter, played a villain in the professional wrestling ring from 1945 until his retirement in 1959.

He died Tuesday of complications related to pneumonia, said his son, Joe Jares, of Los Angeles.

Born Oct. 6, 1912, in Pittsburgh, Pa., Jares came to California as a teen-ager. At 14, his parents were killed in an auto accident and he dropped out of high school and started driving a truck for a living.

He began wrestling and lifting weights at the Los Angeles Athletic Club. He became the Pacific Coast amateur wrestling champion and, in 1932, was nearly placed on the U. S. Olympic weightlifting team as a lightweight-heavyweight. During the 1930s and '40s, he worked out at Santa Monica's legendary Muscle Beach.

Jares left weightlifting in 1941 and went into professional wrestling, appearing as Brother Frank, the Mormon Mauler from Provo, Utah, and the Thing, a villain with a bright orange beard and hair. (For this character, he toted a black box that emitted a hissing rattlesnake sound when he pushed a button.)

"One woman wrote to me that she got so mad watching me wrestle on TV that she threw a shoe at the set and broke the tube," Jares once said. "She said that if I was really a decent type, I would help her fix it."

Jares, who lost the sight in his right eye in an accidental finger-gouging during an amateur match, always said the greatest danger in the sport was not the opponents but the fans. One time, a ringsider gave him a swipe across the forehead, causing a cut that took 13 stitches to close.

"But it was good publicity. People jammed the place to see me fight with a bandage on my forehead," he said of the episode.

After he left the professional wrestling circuit, Jares went to work as a butcher for a packing-house in San Fernando. A knee injury a few years later forced him to quit.

In the mid-1980s, he moved to Valencia and was a regular at the Santa Clarita Valley Senior Center.

In addition to his son, he is survived by his wife of 53 years, Dorothy Jares of Valencia; son Frank Jares Jr. of Newhall; two sisters, Sophia Diehl of Eugene, Ore., and Helen Vetterly of Pittsburgh; six granddaughters and one great-grandson.

A funeral service is scheduled for 3 p.m. today at Eternal Valley Memorial Park, 23287 N. Sierra Highway, Newhall, which is handling the arrangements. Donations can 'e made in Jares' name to the Santa Clarita Valley Senior Center, 22900 Market St., Newhall 91321.

And the next generation ...

On May 16, 1014, USC inducted 16 alumnae into their Athletic Hall of Fame. Joe Jares was included with athletes like Jennifer Rosales (first female NCAA golf champion), Don Quarrie (five-time Olympic sprinter), Tim Rossovich (All-American defensive end), and Pete Carroll (head coach of Seattle Seahawks).

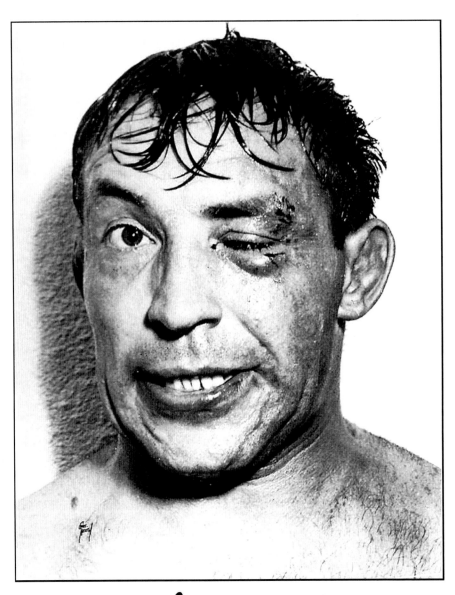

The End

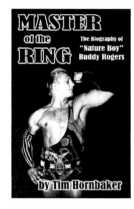
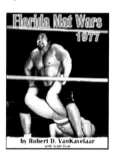

— RAISING CAIN: From Jimmy Ault to Kid McCoy —
by Frankie Cain & Scott Teal

"Antone Leone got John Swenski on the floor between the lockers and the bench and pounded on his head. Antone wasn't any kind of an outstanding wrestler, but he was on top, and Swenski couldn't move because he was wedged between the lockers and the bench. Of course, that's the way it always was. Anytime one of the wrestlers got into a scrap, it always wound up in a street-fight."

— Frankie Cain

If you ask any pro wrestler who plied their trade during the '50s and '60s who they consider to be the top minds in the wrestling business, invariably the name Frankie Cain will appear at the top of the list. Frankie has a keen recollection of things that took place in the wrestling business from the 1940s until wrestling evolved into what we know today as "sports entertainment."

But Frankie's story isn't only about his life as a wrestler. It's a fascinating journey that began when he was just plain Jimmy Ault, living on Depression-era streets of downtown Columbus, Ohio – learning hustles and cons from Gypsies, sleeping on rooftops, and selling anything he could – all simply to keep from starving. He came into his own and finally began to earn a decent living when prostitutes in Cherry Alley convinced him to work as their protector against the dangers they faced on the streets. Frankie, having fought on the streets almost every day of his young life, was born for the job.

Frankie tells about his discovery of pro wrestling and how he helped form the Toehold club, where young boys could mimic and learn the pro style. But it was his introduction to and training by tough shooter Frank Wolfe that set him on a path that would have him fighting in smoker clubs, athletic shows on carnivals, and eventually, pro wrestling. However, the majority of Frankie's early years were spent fighting on the road ... going into towns under assumed names and fighting ranked boxers. What his opponents didn't realize, though, was that he was there to "put them over," i.e. make them look good and give them a win to enhance their record. While they were trying to knock Frankie out, he was fighting back, but only enough to make it look like a real contest before he did what the promoters brought him there to do.

Frankie's story — presented in his voice just as he shared it with Scott Teal — will transport you back to a time of the true legends of both boxing and wrestling. Brutal, honest, and often hilarious, Raising Cain is an amazing look at the life and career of a self-made man who lived his life as none other.

— HOOKER —
by Lou Thesz, with Kit Bauman
Who was the greatest pro wrestler of the 20th century?

The debate is a real one among serious students of the sport. Like the arguments over any effort to crown "the greatest," "the best," or "the worst," that answer is unlikely to ever be resolved to everyone's satisfaction. One fact is indisputable, though. For those who watched wrestling before it became "sports entertainment," there is only one answer — Lou Thesz.

In the late 1940s and '50s, Lou Thesz was world heavyweight champion of the National Wrestling Alliance, and he carried those colors with dignity and class. "My gimmick was wrestling," he said, and it was evident to anyone who ever bought a ticket to see Lou Thesz that he was the real deal. Lou's book was one of the first published by a major wrestling star that discussed the business with candor from the inside.

This book contains pages and pages of new material — stories, anecdotes, and 215 classic photos — none of which has been published in any previous edition and all in the voice of one of the legendary figures of the game. Every sentence has been thoroughly combed over and vetted in order to answer any questions previously asked by readers, or to correct and/or re-order the "facts" as Lou recalled them, and each chapter now has detailed endnotes to supplement the text. Combined with all-new, spellbinding forewords by Charlie Thesz and Kit Bauman, an extensive 32-page "addendum" in Lou's own words, and a comprehensive name-and-subject index, and you have the definitive tome devoted to wrestling's golden era.

Also available from www.crowbarpress.com

This series, created by Scott Teal, features the most detailed books ever published on the history of specific wrestling cities and territories. Each volume contains a definite listing of every wrestling match we could find for each venue, illustrated with hundreds of images of program covers, advertisements, newspaper ads and headlines, and memorabilia. Also included, when available, are gate and attendance figures, match stipulations, and much more. These volumes represent an incredible amount of research that will be referred to over and over by both everyone.

v1 – Wrestling in the Garden, The Battle for New York
by Scott Teal & J Michael Kenyon

v2 – Nashville, Tennessee, volume 1: 1907-1960
by Scott Teal & Don Luce

v3 – Alabama: 1931-1935
by Jason Presley

v4 – Japan: The Rikidozan Years
by Haruo Yamaguchi, with Koji Miyamoto & Scott Teal

v5 – Knoxville, Tennessee, v1: 1905-1960
by Tim Dills & Scott Teal

6 – Amarillo, Texas, v1: 1911-1960
by Kriss Knights & Scott Teal

— Fall Guys: The Barnums of Bounce —
by Marcus Griffin, Annotated by Steve Yohe & Scott Teal

If you're like most people, who think professional wrestling was strictly "kayfabe" in the days before it morphed into "sports entertainment," then think again. In 1937, a book titled Falls Guys: The Barnums of Bounce was published. In the 215 pages written by sportwriter Marcus Griffin, the sport was exposed to the general public and the behind-the-scenes wheeling and dealing by promoters and wrestlers alike were brought to light. It was the first credible book ever published on the subject.

Fall Guys was, and still is, fascinating reading ... with one caveat. A great deal of the book was written by Griffin with an extreme bias for Toots Mondt ... his boss ... and against those whom Toots didn't like. It is filled with inconsistencies, contradiction, and ... yes, downright lies. Nevertheless, the book is the best resource of events that took place during that era, and wrestling scholars have used much of Griffin's writing as a launchpad for their own research.

That being the case, why would anyone want to read this book?

This is the annotated version, in which Yohe & Teal challenge Griffin's statements about events and correct errors that have been repeated through the years in other books and writings. They also add additional detail to the stories and the lives of the book's personalities.

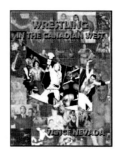

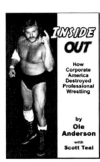
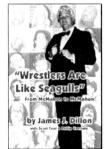

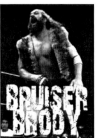

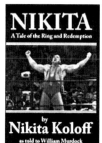
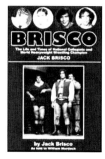

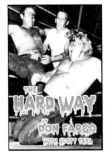

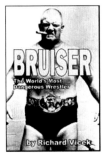

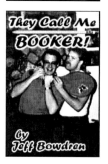

— When It Was Real —
by Nikita Breznikov

If you want to take a trip back to your childhood, your younger, less-stressful days, then journey with us back into the magical world of professional wrestling during the years 1970 to 1979 … a time "when it was real" … a time before Hulkamania took the world by storm. Author Nikita Breznikov tells the story from two perspectives — that of a starry-eyed fan, and as the manager and tag team partner of the legendary Nikolai Volkoff. Nikita details the matches and feuds that took place in the WWWF during the '70s and gives his insightful, often-hilarious perspective of the events that took place. Escape with Nikita as he transports you back to an era when wrestling was presented in an entertaining manner, but framed as legitimate competition.

— They Call Me Booker! —
by Jeff Bowdren

In the year 1990 in an alternate universe, Ted Turner hired an unknown and unproven booker to book World Championship Wrestling and save the company from what seemed to be impending disaster. Join author and wrestling history buff Jeff Bowdren as he rewrites and tweaks the storylines and matches he created when he penned a regular column — "Bowdren the Booker" — in the pages of the "Wrestling Observer Newsletter" in 1990 and 1991. "WHAT IF?" That's what we ask and resolve in "They Call Me Booker."

— Breaking Kayfabe —
by Jeff Bowdren

Since 2012, seven wrestling fans known as "The South Florida Marks," have been meeting with the wrestlers they idolized. One of the group members, Jeff Bowdren, took notes and recorded 24 interviews filled with anecdotes, tales of the road, and wrestling history. This book is the product of his efforts. Interviews include Arn Anderson, Barry Windham, Bob Backlund, Jerry Lawler, Kevin Sullivan, Larry Zbyszko, Masked Superstar, Paul Orndorff, Terry Funk, and more.

— It's Wrestling, Not Rasslin'! —
by Mark Fleming, with Scott Teal

Mark wasn't the type of wrestler who would showboat to catch the eye of the fans and promoters. He was a serious wrestler who believed pro wrestling should be conducted as a sport, and not as a show. His pure wrestling style caught the eye of Lou Thesz, who many consider to be one of the greatest pro wrestlers of all time. Mark's love for the wrestling game is evident as he tells the story of how he and Lou Thesz, together, attempted to change "rasslin'" back to what it had once been — WRESTLING!

— The Mat, the Mob & Music —
by Tom Hankins, with Scott Teal

Tom Hankins is not a recognizable name in the world of pro wrestling. As someone with a strong work ethic, and somewhat of a rebel against the establishment, he parlayed his talents into three careers: wrestling, music, and working for a mobster named Fat Eddie. In this narrative filled with personal anecdotes, Tom takes us behind the scenes to demonstrate just how much pro wrestling, rock 'n' roll, and the underworld have in common. He pulls no punches when writing about both friends and enemies.

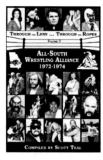